POLICIES, PROGRAMMES AND STRATEGIES FOR TRIBAL DEVELOPMENT

POLICIES, PROGRAMMES AND STRATEGIES FOR TRIBAL DEVELOPMENT

A Critical Appraisal

Dr. Nishakar Panda

Publications

KALPAZ PUBLICATIONS

DELHI-110 052

Policies, Programmes and Strategies for Tribal Development

Rs. 750

ISBN : 81-7835-491-8

Published in 2006 in India by
Kalpaz Publications,
C-30, Satyawati Nagar,
Delhi-110 052
E-mail : kalpaz@hotmail.com

Lasertype Setting by: Tact Computer Graphics, Delhi
Printed at: Salasar Imaging Systems, Delhi

For

Lord Jagannath

The Lord of the Universe

Contents

Preface

Tribes in India constitute a sizeable section of the population. In Orissa, it is more pronounced. There are as many as 62 tribal communities in the state. The different tribal groups differ widely in terms of number, social structure, cultural ethos and quality of life. They represent different levels of socio-economic development. They constitute an economically, politically and socially backward community. They suffer from various forms of economic exploitation, social stagnation and political isolation.

In the post-independence era, special efforts have been made to lift them out of the morass of poverty and stagnation. A host of specified programmes were launched to ensure welfare and development of the tribal people. But, it is disconcerting to note that only insignificant benefits have reached the tribal people. A lot has been said and done on tribal development. After 55 years of independence, the expected level of development has not reached them. There must be something wrong either with the development programmes or with the tribals themselves. This query propelled me to delve deeper into the genesis of the problem. I thought it worthwhile to evaluate how far the tribal programmes have been well conceived and implemented and to what extent they have mitigated the misery of the tribal people.

The suggestions of Late Dr. Bibekananda Das, Ex-Professor and Head of the Department of Economics, Berhampur University helped me to develop the line of approach. I greatly valued his suggestions. I express my heartfelt gratitude to him. The valuable suggestions and unique sense of dedication of Dr. L. N. Dash, D. Litt., Research Officer, W. S. R. C., Berhampur University at different stages helped me in shaping the work properly. His untiring assistance, unstinted cooperation and constant stimulation enabled me to complete the work successfully. I am grateful to him.

The library of the National Institute of Rural Development, Hyderabad, the Berhampur University Library, Secretariat Library of Government of Orissa, State Planning Board Library, Government of Orissa, Bhubaneswar, District Library of Kalahandi District, Bhawanipatna, etc. provided me scope to go through the relevant books, journals and periodicals. I am thankful to the staff of these libraries.

Required information and secondary data were collected from different central, state and quasi-government organisations/ agencies and institutions. I intend to make particular mention of the Office of the Census Commissioner, Orissa, Scheduled Caste and Scheduled Tribe Development Department, Panchayati Raj Department, Planning and Coordination Department and other departments of the Government of Orissa, Director of Economics and Statistics, Scheduled Castes, Scheduled Tribes Research and Training Institute, Government of Orissa, Bhubaneswar, Office of the Project Administrator, Thuamul-Rampur ITDA, Kalahandi District Welfare Officer, Project Officer, MADA, General Manager, the OSCSTDFCC, General Manager, TDCC, Kalahandi, District Revenue Officer, Collectorate, Kalahandi, Block Development Officer, Thuamul-Rampur Block, Branch Managers of Kalahandi Anchalika Gramya Bank in Thuamul-Rampur Block, etc. The officers and staff of these organisations helped me ungrudgingly in my endeavour in collecting required information. I am thankful to all of them for their cooperation and assistance.

I am also very much thankful to all the respondents and informants of the villages in Thuamul-Rampur Block in Kalahandi district where I undertook my field study. Their sense of affection, cooperation and hospitality was commendable.

My wife's contributions in my endeavour are many. She bore the family burden during the course of my work. She has encouraged me to complete the work in time. My children tolerated my negligence. I record my appreciation for them. I would, finally like to convey my thanks to the publisher for bringing out this book.

– Nishakar Panda

List of Abbreviations

NCAER	National Council of Applied Economic Research
NCERT	National Council of Education Research and Training
THRTI	Tribal Harijan Research-cum-Training Institute
TDB	Tribal Development Block
SMPTD	Special Multi Purpose Tribal Development
ITDP	Integrated Tribal Development Projects
ITDA	Integrated Tribal Development Agencies
MADA	Modified Area Development Approach
IRDP	Integrated Rural Development Programme
ERRP	Economic Rehabilitation of Rural Poor
NREP	National Rural Employment Programme
RLEGP	Rural Landless Employment Guarantee Programme
TSP	Tribal Sub-Plan
H and T. W: Deptt.	Harijan and Tribal Welfare Department
OSCSTDFCC	Orissa Scheduled Caste, Scheduled Tribe Development Finance Cooperative Corporation
DTDP	Dispersed Tribal Development Programme
DPEP	District Primary Education Programme
SCA	Special Central Assistance
SCSTRTI	Scheduled Caste and Scheduled Tribe Research-cum-Training Institute
MFP	Minor Forest Produce

SAP	:	Surplus Agricultural Produce
OAS	:	Orissa Administrative Service
OCS	:	Orissa Cooperative Service
TDA	:	Tribal Development Agency
BDP	:	Block Development Officer
PA	:	Project Administrator
ADM	:	Additional District Magistrate
Cr.P.C.	:	Criminal Procedure Code
TRW	:	Tribal and Rural Welfare
SDP	:	Sub-divisional Development Officer
MP	:	Member of Parliament
MLA	:	Member of Legislative Assembly
WEO	:	Welfare Extension Officer
MMLP	:	Margin Money Loan Programme
RDC	:	Revenue Divisional Commissioner
DRDA	:	District Rural Development Agency
PWD	:	Public Works Department
QPM	:	Quality Planting Materials
LIGH	:	Low Income Group Housing
KAGB	:	Kalahandi Anchalika Gramya Bank
Th. Rampur	:	Thuamul Rampur
G. P.	:	Gram Panchayat
K. Oil	:	Kerosene Oil
ASCO	:	Assistant Soil Conservation Officer
LAMPS	:	Large Sized Agricultural Multipurpose Societies
TDCC	:	Tribal Development Cooperative Corporation
PACS	:	Primary Agricultural Cooperative Societies
NAFED	:	National Agricultural Cooperative Marketing Federation of India Ltd.
TRIFED	:	Tribal Cooperative Marketing Development Federation of India Ltd.

List of Tables

Glossary

Odres: Believed to be a predominant tribe in ancient Orissa.

Tribus: A Latin word designating a particular kind of social and political organisations existed in traditional societies.

Adivasi: Refers to original settlers

Girijan: They are hill dwellers

Vanya Jati: It means forest castes

Adim Jati: It connotes primitive castes

Jan Jati: Folk communities

Anusuchit Jan Jati: Scheduled Tribes

Sagri: Designates bonded labour in Rajasthan

Gothi: Another name of bonded labour in Orissa

Vetti: Refers to bonded labour in Andhra Pradesh

Jeetha: Name of the bonded labour in Mysore

Naukarinama Mahidari: Local name of bonded labour

Jabali: A scheme for rehabilitation of prostitutes in tribal communities launched by Government of Madhya Pradesh.

Jagi: The settled Birhor tribal groups

Othul: The nomadic Birhor tribal groups

Sib: Refers to clan, which is the pivot of all socio-economic activities of tribals.

Totem: A social organisation of tribals, which is associated with a form of supernaturalism consisting of certain typical attitude towards species of animals or plants or classes of natural objects.

Majang and Darbar Dindaghar, Dhangar basa, Ingersin. Different names of youth dormitory called by Juangs, Khonds, Bhuniyas and Bondas respectively.

Podu:A primitive form of agricultural practice.

Kuden: Medicine man for tribals.

Buyya, Nagam, Buita, Pujari, Sisa, Jani, Dinwari:Different names of village priest called by tribals.

Gaur, Gotar, Push-Punei, Kedu, Karam, Chait Parab, Magha Parab: Different festivals observed by tribals of Orissa.

Raja, Laxmi, Puja, Dasahara, Gambha: Hindu festivals adopted by tribals of Orissa.

Ol Chiki: A Santali script

Soran Sompen: A Saora script

Sarana, Jahira: Place of worship

Sing Bonga:Sun God, which the tribals believe as Supreme God.

Bir Khumba:The shrine worshipped by Bhumiya tribes

Thakur, Dharma, Thakurani, Mahaprabhu, Jakari Basudha, Dharani Debta, Tari Pinnu, Sthanu, Sital Mata: Name of deities worshipped by tribals of Orissa.

Bijagudi: House of Gods

Sindhur: Centre of religious and social life in a Bonda village.

Meriah: Man or woman to be sacrificed

Jaris, Disaris, Bejus, Gunians: Tribal medicine men and magicians

Pedal: The head of a single village in Bagata tribe

Sanskar Kendras: A centre for educating tribals about their rights and preventing exploitation of tribals.

Noria tile: A small-sized clay tiles locally manufactured in Kalahandi district.

Bhumi: Land or soil.

Mulia/Halia:Tribals call day labourer as Mulia and those who work on annual contract basis as Halia.

Gurji: Name of a cereal produced by tribals.

Kolath, Gangei: Names of pulses produced by tribals.

Rasi:A kind of oilseed produced by tribals.

Kula:A winnowing fan

Duti:A round or square container for storing fish

Bisar Shalla and Kudarjal:Large vets for catching fish and entrapping rabbits respectively by tribals.

Changu: A musical instrument of tribals.

Dhemsha:A tribal dance

Voli, Sule:Bride price prevalent among some tribal communities.

1
Introduction

Tribes are one of the principal categories of the backward classes or the historically disadvantaged bottom groups of Indian society.[1] With very low rate of literacy combined with acute and abysmal poverty, they have remained outside the mainstream of national life. The benefits of planning and economic development have percolated to them scantily. Sustained and coordinated efforts have been made and special attention has been paid over the years to lift them out of poverty trap and stagnation.

Need and Importance of the Study

In Orissa tribal population constitutes 22.21 per cent of the total population of the State.[2] It is believed that the very name Orissa is derived from "Odres", a predominant tribe. With this demographic composition, they are an economically and socially backward and the most neglected community.

There has been piecemeal work on tribal problems in Orissa. It is necessary to evaluate how far the problems have been well conceived, how efficiently the programmes/projects and schemes have been executed and to what extent they have mitigated the misery of the tribal people.

The work has, therefore, considerable importance for the state and the country. Success and failures need to be identified and suggestions and alternative strategies recommended for all-round and balanced development of the area and the people.

Review of Literature

Accumulation of scientific knowledge is a slow and gradual process in which an investigator builds on the works of researchers. Findings and policy outlooks serve as a starting point for the future. The links that can be established between and among studies enrich knowledge and offer policy insights.[3] Anthropologists, sociologists, geographers and historians have made extensive studies in the fields of socio-cultural patterns of the tribes. Economists have studied their economic problems and evaluated the programmes and projects meant for the development of Scheduled Tribes.

In the context of the Indian tribes, Hudson (1922) has traced the complex historical evolution of various tribes of India.[4] Hulton (1941) has further analysed their conditions.[5] Fuchs (1973) has written a comprehensive account of the aboriginal tribes of the Indian subcontinent.[6] Dalton (1872) has provided an account of the tribal societies of north-eastern states.[7] Guha (1939-1951) has discussed the racial affinities of the Indian aborigines in different perspectives.[8] The major demographic structure of tribal India has been analysed by Mamoria.[9] Sengupta (1959) has studied the consumption and nutrition pattern of the aborigines.[10] Vidyarthi (1959-1978) has produced valuable studies on the socio-cultural-economic organisations of the Indian tribes.[11] Ghurye (1963) has depicted the historic development of the Indian tribes and made a chronicle of tribal development since independence.[12] Ambastha (1969) has studied the education system vis-à-vis the income and expenditure pattern of the tribes.[13] Bhowmick (1971) has dealt with the ethnographic structure and other characteristics of important tribes of India.[14] Bose has discussed the socio-cultural features of the Indian tribes.[15] Basu opines that development strategy of tribal communities has to be in tune with the development strategy of the nation.[16] Dube (1977) has examined the changing pattern of socio-cultural organisation of the tribes.[17] B.D. Sharma investigates into the impact of socio-cultural practices on the economic development of tribals.[18]

Besides, a good number of reports were published from time to time to highlight the tribal problems. These include (a)

Annual Reports on Commissioner of Scheduled Castes and Scheduled Tribes, (b) Report of the Backward Classes Commission, (c) Report of the Study Team on Social Welfare and Welfare of Backward Classes (1959), (d) Report of the Estimates Committee (1959), (e) Report of the Committee on Special Multipurpose Tribal Blocks (1960) headed by Dr. Verrier Elwin. Report of the Scheduled Areas and Scheduled Tribes (1960-61) headed by U. N. Dhebar, Report of the Study Group on Welfare of the Weaker Sections of the Village Community, Study Team on Tribal Development Programme (1966) headed by P. Shilu Ao, and Taskforce on Scheduled Tribes by Vidyarthi (1972) etc.[19]

Various seminars and workshops on Tribal Development have been organised from time to time in different academies and institutes. Two such seminars relevant in this context need be mentioned here. A seminar on '*Tribal Development Problems*' was organised at the H.C.M. State Institute of Public Administration, Jaipur in May 1975. The Centre for Tribal Development of the Manikya Lal Verma (MLV) Tribal Research and Training Institute in collaboration with the Tribal Area Development Department, Udaipur had convened a seminar on 'Tribal Development: Past Efforts and New Challenges' (December1987). The observations and findings of the seminars have been compiled in the form of a book entitled *Tribal Development: Past Efforts and New Challenges* by J. P. Singh and N.N. Vyas. The authors are of the opinion that not with standing the substantial benefits accrued to tribal people over Plan periods the results have not been commensurate with expectations.[20]

Having thus discussed the studies made on tribal development of India in general, it is pertinent to turn to tribal geography, tribal economy and tribal development of Orissa. Subsequently, studies on the tribes of Orissa were taken up by anthropologists of other Indian states. Studies of ethnographic nature were undertaken by Dalton and Hunter in 1872-73; the later British ethnographers published only a few notes and papers on the tribes of Orissa in the Journal of the Asiatic Society.[21] S. N. Roy is believed to be the first Indian scholar to write on the tribes of Orissa. He wrote on the Savara tribe of Orissa in a descriptive paper published in "Man in India" in1927 and later in1935 he wrote the first full-length monograph on the Hill Bhuinya. Verrier Elwin discussed about the 'Bondo' tribe in his book Bondo Highlands (1950).[22] Srivastav too discussed about 'the educational problems of Saora tribe in Orissa'.[23] The socio-cultural, religious and anthropological studies of Juang, Gadaba, Savara and Bhuinya tribes of Orissa have been conducted by Bose, Chatopadhyaya, Sitapati and Mohapatra.

N.C.A.E.R., New Delhi, made a study on the problems of Scheduled Tribes of the State and suggested specific recommendations for their development.[24] Sinha and Mishra (1976) have investigated into the spatial distribution and socio-economic-cultural organisations of Orissan tribes.[25] N. Patnaik (1972) analysed the impact of induced change in two tribal blocks.[26] P. C. Mohapatro (1987) has dealt with the tribals of Koraput district of Orissa and suggested spatial planning for their economic development.[27] S. Bose and N. Patnaik made a study (1976) on the tribals of Keonjhar district and recommended specific approaches for their development.[28] M. K. Mohanty has suggested spatial development strategy for the tribal regions of Keonjhar district.[29] The T. H. R. T. I. has conducted a few studies like survey of submersible tribal villages under Balimela Projects of Orissa (1964),[30] a study of shifting cultivation in Orissa (1974),[31] etc. The Evaluation Wing of the Planning and Coordination Department of the state carried out a study on the living conditions of the scheduled tribes of Orissa.[32] The programme evaluation organisation in the Planning Commission also made a few studies on specific tribal problems.

Extensive literature is not available on the appraisal of tribal development schemes and projects. No systematic attempt was, however, made to analyse the genesis of tribal development programmes of the state vis-à-vis the country. A few diagnostic studies conducted only concentrate on programmes of specific sectors rather than analysing the tribal development programmes in their entirety since its inception. It was, therefore, felt necessary to study this aspect to take stock of things so that lacuna at different stages can be identified and revision of policy can be suggested for facilitating effective planning, suitable policy formulation and efficient implementation of programmes.

Objectives

The objectives of the study broadly are as follows:

(i) Since the nature of the study is exploratory, it is intended, at the outset to get an idea about the history of tribal development strategy of the country against the background of their demographic composition and the need for their development.

(ii) To study the demography, social, economic, cultural and religious profiles of tribals of the state in general and of all the individual tribes of the state in particular.

(iii) To make an anatomical analysis of the development programmes at work in the light of the financial components and the mode of their execution.

(iv) To assess the impact of the programmes i.e., to examine to what extent the projects/schemes designed and implemented for the upliftment of the tribals so far have affected the tribal population in accruing benefits to them and raising their living standards.

(v) To suggest policy changes and to articulate appropriate development strategies based on the findings of the study and to lay emphasis on improvement of the programmes in the light of the shortcomings.

Problems Under Study

It is proposed to examine the following questions in the study:

(i) To what extent national policy was adopted and adapted and with what results?

(ii) What are the salient demographic features of tribes of India and Orissa distinguishing them from other sections of society?

(iii) What are the programmes/projects implemented for the development of scheduled tribes and the process of their execution?

(iv) What are the financial ramifications?

(v) Whether the programmes have a direct manifestation of the socio-economic characteristics of the tribals and how far proved effective in ameliorating and improving their living standards?

Hypotheses

The following hypotheses are put forward for corroboration and testing:

1. There is comprehensiveness in tribal development policy.
2. There is adequacy in flow of funds for tribal development. Corruption distorts people's and area development.
3. Impact of development programmes on tribal people is less than satisfactory.
4. Implementation of programmes is tardy and faulty.

Scope of the Study

Against this backdrop the nature of the tribal studies in Orissa can be discussed. Tribes are multiracial and multicultural. The background of each tribe is to be explored. Language, religion, culture and social background are to be noted. Each tribe's demographic features are to be narrated. The essence of socio-economic progress through government regulation and democratic intervention with aims and possibilities is to be mapped out. Backwash and spread effects in tribal areas are to be identified. Exploitative relation of tribal people with moneylenders, contractors, middlemen who engage them in work are to be revealed. Most of the tribes dwell in forest, hilltops and areas in which mineral deposits are found. Their survival mechanism is carved out of these factors.

Some of the nagging problems need emphasis. We are to examine tribal policies at the national and state levels. Do they suit or harm the tribes? Projects, programmes and programme elements are to be dissected and evaluated. Implementation processes need to be scrutinised. How are the tribals consulted and involved in the planning process are to be probed.

Approach and Methodology

A systematic approach and a scientific methodology to deal with the problems under study are required in order to arrive at valid conclusions. The methods employed and the approaches adopted in the present study are an inductive method based on secondary data and partly supplemented with primary data. The study is quantitative, descriptive and prescriptive. The descriptive statistics such as tables, diagrams and graphs are presented in order to support conclusions. The anecdote method is resorted to. The case studies are based on interviews, and questionnaires. It is also partly an assessment or evaluative study and the evaluation has been done on the basis of a set of criteria such as time dimension, goal attainment, objective fulfilment, implementation procedure, etc. In brief, the methodological approach adopted in this work involves the following:

(i) Various departments of the Government of Orissa and the offices of the Census of India have proved to be rich sources for the collection of secondary data.

(ii) A comprehensive schedule was administered for collecting primary data from the sample villages, Grampanchayats and banks. It was to assess the beneficiary-oriented income generating programmes. The questionnaire for the individual households covered a number of economic parameters. They include family composition, household particulars, landholding, employment, income, expenditure, consumption patterns, etc. (Appendix–I).

The field observation and on the spot data collection methods were adopted for assessing and evaluating the Area Development Infrastructure Programmes. It was mainly observational and informally guided conversations with as many people as possible.

An in-depth and careful interview method was adopted. The most important aspect of the fieldwork was that the author stayed in the villages and got himself acquainted with the place, people and their problems.

(iii) Library work supports the study with ideas and materials. Books, reports, research articles referred to in various libraries of the country helped the author to receive theoretical insights into the problem.

Structure of the Study

The chapterisation of the study is designed as follows:

The book contains eight chapters. The first chapter introduces the study with its objectives, problems, scope and methodology.

The second chapter gives a brief account of the evaluation of tribal development strategy and policy in the country.

The third chapter contains a bird's eye view of the profiles of each of the sixty-two tribes of the state of Orissa.

A thumbnail picture of various policies for tribal development is presented in the fourth chapter. This chapter also deals with an analysis of the projects and programmes for development of Scheduled Tribes implemented in the state.

The fifth chapter offers with a brief description on the financial aspects of the tribal development programmes.

The process of implementation of programmes at different stages are analysed in the sixth chapter.

The seventh chapter discusses the impact of the programmes. Apart from giving a brief description on the targets and achievements of different tribal development schemes under various sectors, it also presents a situational analysis of the sample block and case studies.

The last chapter provides the summary of findings and conclusions. Policy recommendations are projected for faster development of the tribes.

Notes and References

1. T. Prabhakar Reddy, *"Tribal Land Alienation in Andhra Pradesh"*, *Economic and Political Weekly*, Vol. XXIV, No. 28, July 15, 1989, p. 1571.
2. Government of Orissa, Directorate of Economics and Statistics, Bhubaneswar, Statistical Outline of Orissa, 1995, p. 27.

3. *Pawan K. Karma,* Cooperative Management, Practices, Problems and Prospects, New Delhi, Deep and Deep Publications, 1987, p. 12.

4. *T. C. Hudson,* The Primitive Culture of India, The Royal Asiatic Society, London, 1922.

5. *J. H. Hulton, "Primitive Tribes", in O'Malley, L. S. S. (Ed.),* Modern India and the West, Oxford University Press, London (First Edition, 1941 at Oxford), 1968, pp. 415-44.

6. *Stephen Fuchs,* The Aboriginal Tribes of India, *The Macmillan Co. of India, Delhi, 1973.*

7. *E. T. Dalton,* Descriptive Ethnology of Bengal, Government of Bengal, Calcutta, 1872.

8. *B. S. Guha, "The Aboriginal Races of India",* Science and Culture, *Vol. 4, No. 12, 1939, pp. 677-83; B. S. Guha, "The Indian Aborigines and Their Administration",* Journal of Asiatic Society, Vol. 17, No. 1, 1951, pp. 19-44.

9. *C. B. Mamoria,* Tribal Demography in India, *Kitab Mahal, Allahabad, 1957; C. B. Mamoria, "Tribes in India – Their Classification",* The Modern Review, *Vol. 150, No. 4, 1957, pp. 278-283.*

10. *P. N. Sengupta,* "The *Aborigines, Their Nutrition and Welfare",* Bulletin of the Bihar Tribal Research Institute, Vol. 1, No. 1, 1959, pp. 56-66.

11. *(a) L. P. Vidyarthi (Ed.),* Anthropology and Tribal Welfare in India, *Council of Social and Cultural Research,* Bihar, 1959.

    (b) L. P. Vidyarthi and B. K. Roy, The Tribal Culture of India, The Concept Publishing Co. , Delhi, 1976.

    (c) L. P. Vidyarthi, Rise of Anthropology in India *(two volumes),* Concept Publishing Co. , Delhi, 1978.

12. *G. S. Ghurye,* The Scheduled Tribes, *Popular Prakashan, Bombay,* 3rd Revised Edition, 1963.

13. *N. K. Ambastha,* A Critical Study of the Tribal Education, S. Chand, Delhi, 1969.

14. *K. L. Bhowmick,* Tribal India, A Profile in Indian Ethnology, *The World Press, Calcutta, 1971.*

15. *N. K. Bose,* Tribal Life in India, *National Book Trust, New Delhi, 1971; N. K. Bose,* Some Indian Tribes, National Book Trust, New Delhi, 1972.

16. *Ashok Ranjan* Basu, Tribal Development Programmes and Administration of India, National Book Organisation, The Mail, Shimla, 1985.

17. B. D. Sharma, *Tribal Development– Concept and the Frame*, Prachi Publications, New Delhi, 1978.

18. S. C. Dube, *Tribal Heritage of India* (in IV volumes), Vikash Publishing House, Pvt. Ltd., New Delhi, 1977.

19. P. K. Bhowmick, "Reports on Scheduled Tribes, An Appraisal", in L. P. Vidyarthi (ed.), *Tribal Development and Its Administration*, Concept Publishing Company, New Delhi, 1986, p. 49.

20. Harpreet Kaur, *Tribal Development Administration*, Shiva Publishers Distributors, Udaipr,1995, pp. 11-12.

21. Makhan Jha, *Readings in Tribal Culture*, Inter India Publications, 1982, p.1.

22. Elwin Verrier, *Bondo Highlands*, Oxford University Press, Bombay, 1950.

23. L. R. N. Srivastav, A. C. Pal and P. Pal, *Identification of Educational Problems of the Saoras of Orissa*, N. C. E. R. T., New Delhi, 1971.

24. N. C. A. E. R., *"Techno-Economic Survey of Orissa: Appraisal Report on Tribal Areas"*, September 1961 (MIMBO).

25. B. N. Sinha and B. K. Mishra, "Tribes of Orissa: A Geographical Analysis", *Geographical Review of India*, Vol. XXXVIII, No. 2, 1976, pp. 167-187.

26. N. Patnaik, *Tribes and Their Development*, NICD, Hyderabad, 1972.

27. PC. Mohapatra, *Economic Development of Tribal India*, Asish Publishing House, New Delhi, 1987.

28. N. Patnaik and S. Bose, *An Integrated Tribal Development Plan for Keonjhar District (Orissa)*, NICD, Hyderabad, 1976.

29. Tribal Research Bureau, Orissa, Adivasi, Vol. XIII, April-July 1971.

30. T. H. R. T. I., Orissa, Adivasi, Vol. XIV, January 1973.

31. Government of Orissa, Planning and Coordination (Evaluation) Department, Evaluation Study No.10, "Living Conditions of Scheduled Tribes, Scheduled Castes and Other Backward Classes in Orissa", 1963, Orissa Government Press, 1965.

32. M. K. Mohanty, "Tribal Society: Programme, Planning and Economic Change".

2

Tribal Development in India: Need, Strategy and Policy

This chapter takes a broad view of tribal development policy in the country. It consists of distinct elements. There are definitions of Scheduled Tribes and their demographic profiles, which are introduced as a necessary background. The compulsions of tribal development are examined; policy and strategy for tribal development is taken up next; finally certain concluding remarks are given.

What is a 'Tribe'?

Before discussing the demographic composition of Scheduled Tribes, need and compulsions for their development, it is relevant to highlight briefly what a 'tribe' is and what precisely the term 'tribe' connotes.

The English term 'Tribe' is derived from the Latin word 'tribus'[1] designating a particular kind of social and political organisation existing in all these societies. Originally, it was used to imply three divisions among the early Romans. Later on, it was used to mean the 'poor' or the 'masses'. In English language, the word appeared in the sixteenth century and denoted a community of persons claiming descent from a common ancestor. In India, the term 'tribe' has legal and administrative connotations. British census officials-cum-anthropologists first used the term 'tribe' for the purpose of enumerating social groups in India and the term was used from1881 to 1931 censuses. The Government of India Act, 1935 used the term 'backward tribe'.

The Indian Constitution has retained the terminology with slight modification using 'Scheduled' in place of 'Backward'.[2] But the Constitution does not contain a precise definition of the term.[3]

The dictionary of Anthropology mentions a tribe as a social group, usually with a definite area, dialect, cultural homogeneity and unifying social orgnisation.[4] The term 'tribe' in that sense refers to a type of society and designates a stage of evolution in human society. As a type of society, the term signifies a set of characteristic features and as a stage of evolution, it connotes a specific mode of social organisation.[5] Anthropologists define tribe as a collection of groups of people who share patterns of speech, basic cultural characteristics, and in the traditional sense, a common territory.[6] According to Ghurye, 'the common features possessed by all the tribal groups are as follows: (1) They live away from the civilised world in the inaccessible parts in the forests and hills. (2) They speak the same tribal dialect. (3) They belong either to one of the three stocks– Negritos, Austroloid or Mongoloids. (4) They profess primitive religion known as animism in which worship of ghosts and spirits is the most important element. (5) They follow primitive occupation such as gleaning, hunting and gathering of forest products. (6) They are largely carnivorous. (7) They live either naked or semi-naked. (8) They have nomadic habits and love for drink and dance.[7]

The assumptions of Lewis has been that ideally tribal societies are small in scale, are restricted in their spatial and temporal range of their social, legal and political relations and possess a morality of religion and world view of corresponding dimensions.[8] This definition, however, does not focus the essential characteristics of a 'tribe' and the scope of the definition is restricted to the ideas of tribal societies. Pathy was of the opinion that 'a tribe is a tribe which is included in the list of Scheduled Tribes'.[9] T. K. Naik, however, proposed seven criteria by which a 'tribe' can be recognised. They are: (i) functional interdependence within the community; (ii) economic backwardness; (iii) geographical isolation; (iv) common dialect; (v) politically a unit under a common tribal authority; (vi) own traditional laws and (vii) members are averse to change.[10] Vimal

Chandra was of the view that primitiveness and backwardness are the tests applied for specifying a 'scheduled tribe'. The main characteristics common to all the Scheduled Tribes are: (1) tribal origin, (2) primitive way of life, (3) habitat in remote and less accessible areas and (4) general backwardness in all respects.[11]

According to Stephen Fuchs, 'As far as Indian tribes go, the essentials seem to be only a comparatively simple and primitive economy combined with a certain degree of residential instability, a simple, though not always, classless social organisation.'[12] Tribe, as defined by Belleille is a collection of individuals sharing a common culture.[13]

Bailey, who has dealt with the tribal problem in his study of Kondhamal region of Orissa says that a tribal society consists in its (1) direct command over resources, (2) access to the products of economy by an independent status and (3) its population strength in total region.[14] Suresh Chandra Rajora has attempted to cite some basic features of a tribal society like (1) Tribal society is a whole society, (2) Tribal oral system is a normative binding force, (3) Culture of silence, (4) Tribals have their own specific economic system, (5) Polygamy is an institution of prestige and glory, (6) Clan solidarity and (7) Liquor economy.[15] Thus, the term itself bears an ideology of self identification.[16] High hills, deep valleys, evergreen forests, untouched natural resources, invaluable minerals, embedded in the earth, abode of simple people– happy, unconcern about the 'morrow', moving about freely like gentle breeze– unbound, unfettered by dictates of the modern world.[17] The most accepted definition in the Indian context is given by Prof. Majumdar. To him, "A tribe is a social group with territorial affiliation, endogamous with no specialisation of functions, ruled by tribal officers, hereditary or otherwise, united in language or dialect, recognising social distance from tribes or castes. But without any stigma attached in the case of a caste structure, following tribal traditions, beliefs and customs, illiberal of naturalisation of ideas from alien sources, above all, conscious of a homogeneity of ethnic and territorial integration".[18]

However, there is no particular definition, which is universally accepted. There are diversities of views of each anthropologist. Nevertheless, certain characteristic features as discussed above, have been put forward for determining a 'tribe' or a 'tribal community'. With the advent of modernity, large scale deforestation, penetration of Hinduism and Christianity into interior tribal pockets, large scale transformation of subsistence economy into a market economy, the historical specificity of tribal society and their structural features have become more or less extinct. They are, now-a-days, only attributional aspects. In India their comments designate are 'Adivasi' (original settlers), Girijan (hill dwellers), Vanyajati (forest caste), Adimjati (primitive castes), Jan Jati (folk communities), Anusuchit Jan Jati (Scheduled Tribes). In Orissa, however, the term 'Adivasi' is used commonly to designate the 'tribes'.

I
Demographic Profile of Tribes in India

The largest concentration of tribal communities in the world, next to Africa, is in India.[19] The tribal scene in India presents an extremely complex and intricate pattern. On the one extreme are the Gonds whose number is more than fifty lakhs. On the other extreme are the Onges numbering only about one hundred and twelve; the great Andamanese are barely nineteen strong.[20] There are 573 different tribal groups[21] most of which are divided into several subgroups. Among them are nine tribal groups namely, Bhil, Gond, Ho, Khond, Mina, Munda, Naga, Oraon and Santal, which are most numerous[22] and, therefore, are called major or large tribes. The Bhils and the Gonds, with their sub-tribes, together constitute more than one-fourth of the total tribal population. The Bhils are mostly inhabited in Rajasthan, Gujarat and South-Western Madhya Pradesh. On the other hand, the Gonds stay in South-Eastern Madhya Pradesh.

Next to these two tribal groups comes the Santal, which is the third largest tribe in the country. They are found in Santal Paraganas of Bihar, Birbhumi district of West Bengal and

Mayurbhanj district of Orissa. Among the other six tribal groups, Mina of Rajasthan, Munda of Bihar and Orissa, Oraon of Orissa had each a population of more than one million. The remaining tribes namely Ho, Khond and Naga are found largely in Bihar, Orissa and Nagaland. In contrast, there are as many as 109 tribal communities having each less than 1000 population and among them there are 43 tribes, which had a population of less than 25 persons. Most of these small tribes are found in Arunachal Pradesh, the Andaman and Nicobar Islands and the South India.

Demography

About seven per cent of India's population belongs to tribal communities, according to the1971 census.[23] Mizoram had the highest percentage of tribal population (94.28 per cent) followed by Lakshadweep (93.75 per cent), whereas Uttar Pradesh had the lowest percentage of tribal population (0.23 per cent) followed by Goa, Daman and Diu (0.82 per cent). The 1981 Census shows that the population of tribal communities was little less than 8 per cent.[24] The highest concentration of tribal population was seen at Lakshadweep (93.82 per cent) followed by Mizoram (93.55 per cent) and Nagaland (83.99 per cent).

The population of 573 different tribal communities constitute about 8 per cent of the total population of India as per 1991 Census. The Scheduled Tribes population of India is shown in Table 2.1.

Rural concentration of tribal population is, thus, more than the urban concentration. A little less than 8 per cent of total tribal population reside in urban areas. Further, male population is slightly higher than female population of Scheduled Tribes. State-wise total population and Scheduled Tribe population is shown in Appendix II depicts the total population and tribal population during three Census periods, 1971, 1981 and 1991.

Table 2.1
Tribal Population of India (1991 Census)*

Sl. No.	*Total Population / Tribal Population*	*Rural Urban Total*	*Persons*	*Male*	*Female*
1	2	3	4	5	6
1.	Total Population	R	622, 812, 376	321, 279, 405	301, 532, 971
		U	215, 771, 612	113, 936, 953	101, 834, 659
		T	838, 583, 988	435, 216, 358	403, 367, 630
2.	Tribal Population	R	62, 751, 026	31, 755, 930	30, 995, 096
		U	5, 007, 354	2, 607, 341	2, 400, 013
		T	67, 758, 380	34, 363, 271	33, 395, 109

* Excluding Jammu and Kashmir.
Source: Series– I, Paper–2 of 1991
Census of India–1991, Final Population,
Brief Analysis of Primary Census abstract.

Decadal Variation

Percentage variations of total population and tribal population during the last three decades i.e., between 1961 to 1991 are shown in Table 2.2.

There was a decreasing trend in percentage increase of total population between the three decades. In case of Scheduled Tribe population, there has been an upward trend in the percentage increase during 1971-81. Thereafter, percentage increase of population exhibited a downward trend.

Table 2.2
Percentage Decade Variation of Total Population and Tribal Population of India, 1961-71, 1971-81, 1981-91

Sl. No.	*Census Periods*	*Total Population*	*S. T. Population*
1	2	3	4
1.	1961-71	25. 5	25. 3
2.	1971-81	24. 3	30. 6
3.	1981-91	23. 79	25. 67

Source: Series– I, Paper–2 of 1991, Census of India–1991,

"Final Population, Brief Analysis of Primary Census abstract" and other Census Reports.

Sex Composition

The trend displays that the sex ratio of total population during census periods is declining whereas for that of tribal population it was increasing till 1981 and from 1981 to 1991 census it has declined from 983 to 972 (Table 2.3).

Table 2.3
Sex Ratio of Total and Tribal Population of India, 1961-91

Sl. No.	*Census Periods*	*Total Population*	*Tribal Population*
1	2	3	4
1.	1961	941	937
2.	1971	930	982
3.	1981*	935	983
4.	1991*	927	972

* Excludes Assam, Jammu and Kashmir.

Source: Series– I, Paper–2 of 1991, Census of India–1991.

"Final Population, Brief Analysis of Primary Census abstract" and other Census Reports.

Literacy

The level of literacy among tribals is extremely low as compared to non-Scheduled Caste/Tribe population (Table 2.4).

Table 2.4
Tribal Literacy in India, 1961-91

Population	*Year*	*Persons*	*Males*	*Females*
1	*2*	*3*	*4*	*5*
Total	1961	24. 0	34. 4	13. 0
	1971	29. 5	39. 5	13. 7
	1981*	36. 2	46. 9	24. 8
	1991*	52. 11	64. 13	39. 29
Tribal	1961	8. 5	13. 8	3. 2
	1971	11. 3	17. 6	4. 9
	1981*	16. 4	24. 5	8. 0
	1991	29. 60	40. 65	18. 19

* Excludes Assam.
Source: Collected and compiled from Census reports.

Tribal literacy has been increasing over the years. The picture among tribal women is dismal. It is abysmally low among them as compared to tribal men. There are large tracts where literacy among women is zero.[25] However, during 1991 Census, it has increased perceptively than the previous years.

State-wise literacy rates for Scheduled Tribe population by sex during 1991 Census is shown in Appendix III. It is highest in Mizoram (82.73 per cent) followed by Lakshadweep (80.58 per cent), it was lowest in case of Andhra Pradesh (17.16 per cent) followed by Rajasthan (19.44 per cent). In Orissa, the literacy rate of tribal population was 22.31.

Regional Distribution

The tribal communities are found in different parts of the country in varying concentration. The states like Mizoram, Nagaland, Meghalaya and Arunachal Pradesh and two Union Territories namely Dadra and Nagar Haveli comprise the tribal predominant zones in which the concentration of tribal communities varies from 70 per cent to 95 per cent. All the tribal groups of the country do not make a homogeneous tribal society. The Santals of Gujarat and the Bhils of Rajasthan do not come within the same tribal category. Each tribe has its historical specificity.[26]

Though the tribal communities are distributed in most of the states in India, there are a few concentration points of regional distribution. Broadly, the tribals are concentrated in the following regions of India.[27]

The Abor, Garo, Khasi, Kudi, Mismi, Naga, etc. tribes mostly belonging to the Mongolian racial stock are found in the North-eastern parts of the country. Tribes, like the Lepcha and Rebha belonging to the same racial groups live in the Himalayan region. The Central India covering the states of Bihar, Orissa, and West Bengal is inhabited by a number of tribal communities. They include the Bhumij, Gond, Ho, Oraon, Santal, Munda and so on.

In the Western India region covering the states like Rajasthan, Maharashtra, Gujarat, Goa, Dadra and Nagar Haveli live a number of tribal communities, the most important of them being the Bhil. They racially belong to the Proto-Australoid group.

The states of Karnataka, Andhra Pradesh, Tamil Nadu and Kerala, in the Nilgiri Hills and covering lines of the Ghats in South India like the Chenchu, Truli, Kadar, Kota, Kurumba, Toda, etc., having Nagristo, Caucasoid, Proto-Australoid or mixed physical features.

The Island region covering Andaman and Nicobar, Lakshadweep Islands has a number of small tribes, like the Andamanese, Onge, Sentinilese, etc.

II
Compulsions for Tribal Development in India

There are as many as 573 tribes and sub-tribes in India. They have been broadly classified into different classes, groups depending upon their present state of development and factors namely, mode of living in forest, shifting villages, forest villages, community villages and revenue villages.[28] They have got a heterogeneous cultural pattern with variegated economic condition and activities largely based on ecological settings and ethnic environment. The basic economic activities of the tribals may be classified under the following heads:[29]

(1) Food gathering, (2) Pastoral, (3) Shifting hill cultivation, (4) Handicrafts, (5) Cultivation, (6) Trade and Commerce, (7) Labour.

The need for tribal development in India hardly needs any justification. Their primitive way of life, economic and social backwardness, low level of literacy, hackneyed system of production, absence of value system, sparse physical infrastructure in backward tribal areas and demographic quality of tribal areas coupled together make it imperative for a systematic process of development of tribals and tribal areas. Below are explained some important factors for tribal development in India.

(I) Improvement in the quality of life

One of the long-term needs for tribal development is improvement in their quality of life. Certain basic services like drinking water, health, housing, nutrition, rural roads, etc. need to be provided to them.

The problem of drinking water in tribal areas is acute on account of the abinitio paucity of drinking water. Further, some villages suffer from contaminated water supply. Sanitation and hygiene are major casualties on account of these handicaps in tribal areas. Therefore, apart from the provision of food, provision of safe drinking water should be accorded highest priority.

Tribals suffer from poor health conditions.[30] The present state of health of tribals is the cumulative result of under-nourishment compounded by several other factors which include incidence of chronic endemic diseases such as malaria, filarial, tuberculosis, venereal diseases, yaws, leprosy, etc. The present health status of tribals is a contributory factor to their numerical decline. There is, therefore, an urgent need to bring such tribal communities within the fold of genetic, preventive and curative medical sciences concomitant with the attempt to improve their nutritional levels. However, the health treatment of tribal communities should be undertaken with a fine degree of perception without which the delicate natural balance in which they are set today may be upset.

A comfortable house, which the tribes used to construct with local available materials, is difficult to find in some areas now. Sometimes, local material is not available because of depleted forest resources. In some cases the relevant species have been replaced by commercial species and the tribe has no longer free access to forests. Housing condition has, as a result, deteriorated. Housing facilities, therefore, should be provided to tribals in tribal areas.

Nutrition programmes should have been implemented vigorously and should have universal coverage in tribal areas. On account of the prevalent low level of nourishment midday meals should be provided to all the children in the age group 6-11 and supplemental feeding programmes for all under-nourished in the age group of 0-6, pregnant women and nursing mothers.

(II) Reduction of the incidence of poverty

Reduction of the incidence of poverty of tribals through raising the levels of productivity and off-season employment is also an important factor for tribal development. Of late, tribals have been fast losing the areas traditionally under their possession and also the rights to exploit these areas. Poverty, indebtedness and the malafide mechanisms of the more advanced groups who have been extending their influence over the tribal areas are the reasons behind it. The tribals are gradually becoming tenants or working as labourers on the land owned by them earlier. This, no doubt, indicates gradual pauperisation of the tribals. The incidence of poverty is more acute in case of Scheduled Tribes. Old and outdated methods of production, chronic unemployment and serious underemployment contribute, to a great extent, to their poverty condition.

(III) Raising the levels of productivity

Raising their productivity in agriculture, horticulture, animal husbandry, forestry, cottage, village and small industries and provision of employment in all seasons will go a long way in reducing the incidence of poverty of Scheduled Tribes. However, creation of employment potential during the slack season is a prime need to ward off starvation for a few weeks in a year, which is a normal feature in some tribal areas. There should be provision of capital inputs, technology, marketing, training, etc. to augment production in tribal areas. Implementation of effective programmes may go a long way in removing poverty to a great extent.

There is, thus, a continued emphasis on raising the levels of productivity and creation of employment opportunities. This, in turn, will call for higher investment by way of special central assistance, flow from state plan, from financial institutions and central sector projects. This is inevitable as with increased price levels a much higher investment would be necessary for a family in order that the assistance can have a dent on poverty and enable the family to have a sustained but reasonable level of income to cross the poverty line.

(IV) To check extinction of lesser tribes

There is an urgent need for appropriate and effective development programmes to check extinction of lesser tribes. Presence of non-tribes in tribal areas results in net outflow of resources from the tribal areas leaving them impoverished. This is illustrated by instances of zones inhabited by the so-called primitive groups. One tends to presume that, on account of the small numbers comprised in each of such groups, the proportion between natural resources and human beings would be favourable. This is not borne out from experience of such small communities like the Juang in the district of Keonjhar, the Kutia Kondh of the district of Phulbani (both in Orissa), the Pahadia of the district of Santal Parganas (Bihar), the Saharia of Rajasthan. Such communities suffer from under-nourishment. The foremost requirement is to promote the production system of the tracts concerned and to provide off-season employment for means of sustenance of members of such communities for the entire year. The primitive tribal groups, nomadic groups, shifting cultivators, forest villagers, families displaced by development projects and migrant tribal labourers need special attention. Special and appropriate programmes for tribal women are called for. The disability, from which these vulnerable areas and groups suffer from, needs to be identified for remedial action.

(V) Removal of Illiteracy

Removal of illiteracy is an important component of tribal development. The educational level of tribals is very low.[31] (Table 2.4 and Appendix– III). Further, the insignificant literacy rate among tribal women is of great concern. Illiteracy gripping the tribal female-folk distorts the female role models. It perpetuates ignorance and superstition among them.[32] The socio-economic development of Scheduled Tribes depends on educational advancement. Education is more than a mere asset for some tribal communities;[33] investment in education is, in a way, crucial for their existence. Continued economic exploitation has brought them to a state of helplessness exemplified by migrant labour, debt bondage, etc. A medium of education will equip them to deal with middlemen, merchants and traders on a better footing. The adults need to undergo citizenship training to understand the process of law, revenue, police, forest and in fact, of the entire administration to remove their present disadvantage. On growing up, the educated tribal children can face the modern world better. Elementary and middle education has to be made more functional and relevant for them. The norm for establishment of a school should be subject to scrutiny by the state governments in the light of the scattered population in tribal areas and the low rate of literacy among the tribal communities.

Considering the basic objective of universalisation of education and removal of adult illiteracy (in the age group of 15-35) education both formal and nonformal has to be accorded high priority. The basis for vocationalisation and training, low literacy pockets and girls' education should receive special attention. The potentiality of education and vocational training in promoting self-reliance and self-employment should be recognised in the tribal context.

(VI) Elimination of exploitation

Elimination of exploitation and enforcement of protective and anti-exploitative measures are the basic needs of tribal development. Exploitation of tribals' forms a lait motife in the tribal canvas of today. Sometimes, the unscrupulous elements under one cover or another exploit the simple tribal situation.[34] Exploitation in tribal areas mainly occurs in the fields of liquor vending, land alienation,[35] money-lending, forestry, trade including collection and disposal of minor forest products and labour including forest labour. While generally the passing of lands from the ownership and control of the tribals is ascribed to the lacunae in the law, faulty implementation, rapacious exploitation by unscrupulous traders, moneylenders, etc., sometimes the tribals are overwhelmed by a sense of alienation from the socio-political system itself, which they think is responsible for their massive dispossession.[36]

There are numerous problems that the tribals are facing today of which economic crisis and poverty come to the forefront. It is through the traditional money-lending system that the tribals are greatly exploited. Indebtedness is, thus, the next pressing problem of these areas.[37] The tribal economy is characteristically a subsistence type of economy. Due to their traditional hedonistic type of world view, they have very little savings. Naturally, when they are in need of money, they are forced to depend on others particularly on the non-tribal moneylenders. Under this system, a person who takes a loan from a moneylender or landowner is required to serve him just like a slave according to the terms and conditions of the loan. Quite often, if he is unable to repay the loan, slavery descends to his son or even to the third generation.[38] This system is known by various names in different parts of the country– in Rajasthan it is called Sagri, in Orissa Gothi, in Andhra Vetti, in Mysore Jeetha, in Madhya Pradesh Naukarinama and Mahidari, etc.[39]

Countering exploitation through more vigorous enforcement of the various anti-exploitative measures and protection of the interests of the Scheduled Tribes through appropriate legal and administrative support is one of the basic needs. Article 46 of the Constitution specifically enjoins on the states the special responsibility of promotion with special care of the education and economic interests of weaker sections of the people and in particular of the Scheduled Castes and Scheduled Tribes and of protecting them from social injustice and exploitation. The Constitution provides adequate authority to a state for achieving these objectives. The Fifth Schedule to the Constitution provide, "the Governor may make regulations for the peace and good government in any area in a state which is for the time being a scheduled area".

(VII) Supportive Infrastructure in Tribal Areas

Another need for tribal development arise from the fact that the tribal areas have sparse physical infrastructure. Whatever exists might not be able to support beneficiary oriented programmes. These are poor in the matter of physical and mass communication. Adequate infrastructure is required for production, anti-poverty, education and anti-exploitative programmes. Supportive infrastructures have to be legislative, physical, institutional and administrative. Among items of physical infrastructure, special emphasis should be given on minor as well as lift irrigation, soil and water conservation, cooperation and land reforms, which support beneficiary oriented programmes. Capital intensive sectors like large and medium industries, roads and bridges, mining, power, road transport, may be given somewhat lower priority unless their spin off effects as such will have a great economic impact on the tribal economy.

(VIII) To Prevent Shifting Cultivation

To check and prevent the shifting cultivation[40] is another need for tribal development. Tribals were perhaps the original settlers of the Indian soil, hence called primitive or and aborigines. For a long period, dependence of the tribals on the forest for their sustenance was undisputed.[41] Forest is intimately connected with tribal life and economy. To a vast majority of the tribal people, the forest is their well loved home and their livelihood. Their very existence depends on it. It gives them food, fruits of all kinds, edible roots and leaves. Forests are a source of minor products, which are sold or exchanged. It provides them with materials to build their houses or to practice their arts, which are often financially gainful. By exploiting the natural products, they supplement their meagre income. It keeps them warm with its fuel and cool with its graceful shade.[42] They enjoy the rights of exploitation of the forest produce for their own benefit. The barriers and regulations imposed on them with the advent of Government control over forests resulted in a conflict in their lives in economic, physical and psychological terms.[43] The forest contractors exploited the tribal labourers in several ways and illegally collected fees from them for the use of flowers and fruits. Gradually, the dependence of the tribal economy on the forests decreased with a corresponding increase in agriculture. The agricultural situation in forest villages has become far from satisfactory. These forest villages are labour camps of the forest department, which are settled under the byelaws of forest manuals placing these labourers on the borderline of slavery.[44] Although, each family living in a forest village is allotted some land for cultivation, no tenancy rights are conferred on the tillers. Neither Patta is given to this effect nor can they enjoy any permanent right to cultivate the land.[45] Once the villagers migrate from the village, he lose their land, which is taken over by the forest department. During the decade from 1951-61, the promotional increase in the landless agricultural labourers belonging to Scheduled Tribes had been quite substantial.[46]

Land is not of much significance to the tribals as the symbol of social status but as a means of livelihood. An analysis of the tribal workers in various occupations shows that tribal economy revolves round farming. But it is primitive or rudimentary in nature adopting only a few known direct methods of production. Shifting cultivation is one such example.[47]

The age-old method of land use on the slopes of hills[48] necessitates the trees and bushes to be cut down and fired after drying. Seeds are then sown in little holes dug in the ground is known as 'shifting cultivation'. Such a field whose fertility is not replenished by manuring (except through ashes obtained from burn-out vegetative cover) yields a diminishing return and is practically exhausted in 2 or 3 years time.[49] The farmer then moves over to a new patch of forest area allowing the abandoned plot to recoup.

Jhum cycle depends upon the density of population of a particular area and availability of suitable hill slopes. As population increases, a vicious circle stands. The Jhumming cycle becomes shorter and soil fertility is not fully restored. Consequently, yields decline and further areas are brought under the Jhumming. The Jhum cycle is further shortened.[50] In Orissa, of late, with the increase in the pressure of population, the Jhum cycle which was about 10 to 22 years in Keonjhar district has reduced to 5 to 12 years now.[51] In Koraput district, it was 8 to 12 years. It came down to 4 to6 years in 1973. With further decrease of the period it stands at 2 to 5 years now.

Similar is the trend found in other parts of India. The Jhum cycle which was 30 to 40 years previously have shrunk to 1 to 17 years in Arunachal Pradesh, 4 to 5 years in Meghalaya, Mizoram and Tripura, 5 to 10 years in Assam hills, 6 to 8 years in Manipur and 6 to 15 years in Nagaland.[52] The immediate consequences of rapid rise in population are extension of areas of Jhum cycle resulting in low productivity, out migration to some rich villages in search of jobs as hired labourers at low wage and indebtedness.[53] There are 109 tribes in India alone who practise shifting cultivation.[54] Excepting in extreme climatic regions like Polar or Tundra or deserts where conditions are unfavourable for quick growth of plants, this practice is prevalent with minor variations even now throughout the world.[55]

In Orissa, this method is practised by the tribes of 'Bonda', 'Didayi', 'Koya', 'Gadaba' and 'Paraja' of Koraput, the 'Kutia Kondha' and 'Dangria Kondh' of Koraput and Phulbani, the 'Langia Saora' of Ganjam and Koraput, the 'Kondh' and 'Pengo Kondh' of Kalahandi and Sambalpur, 'Juang' and 'Pauri Bhuyan' of Keonjhar District.[56]

It has been estimated by the Taskforce on Shifting Cultivation set up by the Ministry of Agriculture that approximately 9.95 million hectares in the tribal and hilly areas of the country are under shifting cultivation. About 223 development blocks in 62 districts in 16 states are affected by this practice. Shifting cultivation is a dominant production activity for approximately 12 per cent of the tribal population of the country. The shifting cultivators lived in below subsistence level. The period of rotation has dangerously come down from around 7 years a few decades back to about 3-4 years in several forests and hilly areas in the country.

Shifting cultivation is a wasteful activity from environmental and forest wealth point of view. It has deleterious effects on soil and water regime. The effects of prolonged shifting cultivation are starkly in evidence in certain areas like Koraput district of Orissa where the barren rounded reddish brown hills are unable to grow a blade of grass and the soil has been reduced to ferruginous laterite due to continual erosion and leaching. Ecologists and environmentalists have expressed their concern and demanded its discontinuation. A number of control measures have been undertaken by the Government during the Five Year Plans.[57] Emphasis has been laid on their settlement and resettlement. A comprehensive development package has been framed and undertaken for this.

(IX) Exploitation of Vast Natural Resources in Tribal Areas

Another factor, which necessitates tribal development is that there are vast natural resources waiting to be tapped in shape of water, soil, forest, minerals in contradiction to some developed areas of the country. Where they have already been tapped or where such natural opulence is hardly seen, these abundant natural resources should be tapped for all round development of tribal areas.

(X) Demographic Quality and Gender Dimension

Besides, the demographic quality of tribal areas is unique in as much as there is ethnic diversity, economic backwardness and low level of technological development. They do not generally seek economic prosperity. Their source of happiness lies elsewhere. They are essentially satisfied if their bare necessities of life are fulfilled. Their institutions are mostly informal socio-cultural and unquestioned traditional loyalty and obedience.[58]

Gender dimension of tribal communities of India also has a bearing on the need for tribal development. In some tribal communities, female members are the chief bread earners for the family in addition to their household works. In some other communities, tribals take pride in having more than one wife. More number of women a tribal man marries, more economic support he gets from them. Here the earning capacity and support to the family determines her position and status in the family.

Among the Banchhara and Bedia tribes of Madhya Pradesh, there is widespread prevalence of caste-based prostitution.[59] It is even ritually sanctioned. In their social system, a married girl is not engaged in prostitution but her sister and mother could practise this. Among the Bedias, the father may marry off some of his daughters but others are introduced into this profession. Among the Banchharas, at least one daughter is pushed into prostitution and others could be married off. The prevalence of this practice prevents them from getting into the national mainstream. The Madhya Pradesh government has started a scheme called "JABALI' for rehabilitation of these tribes.

The levels of socio-economic development vary considerably between non-tribal and tribal population, between one tribe and another tribe and even among different sub-groups of a tribal group. The disparities and diversities make tribal development and micro-level planning for tribals at grassroots level imperative.

These are the basic needs for any developmental effort in the tribal areas. Unless, the forces of destabilisation are checked and corrective measures applied, the provision of social and economic services will not have any significance. Our concern for the development of tribals is not new. Since the promulgation of the Constitution and the implementation of the Five Year Plans, we have been making efforts for the development of these scheduled masses of people. Our evaluation of the progress made so far strikes a sordid note. It appears that our package of development programmes is not compatible with the realities of the tribal society.[60]

III
Policy and Strategy

Policy is a general prescription whereas translating policy into action is strategy. Conceptualising directions of any area of development is the policy for development while systematic approaches meant for their attainment within a time frame is the strategy for development. Whereas the policy is a general framework, strategy is the specific programming directed to achieve the spelt-out objectives. Different policies for economic development are necessary for providing specific strategies of development to specific areas. Strategy is thus, a device for meeting various aims and targets. The extent of success of any policy depends on how best the strategies are evolved. In the present context, for example, terminology of tribal development presupposes a proper and realistic appreciation of the functional basis, which breeds their socio-economic backwardness. It should, then, be followed by a proper identification of target groups, which will again be followed by bringing them under specific programming directed to change the functional basis of their deprivation and economic backwardness. Here, the specific programming may be considered as components of strategy under the general policy of tribal development.

Tribal Development Policies and Strategies in India

The tribal communities generally, live mostly in the inaccessible hilly and forest regions. Their economy is largely self-sufficient. Their social system is simple. This situation has, however, changed with the process of new development. Industrial and mining complexes have been established in some tribal regions. Intensive development programmes have been taken up in some other areas. The level of tribal economy is quite uneven. On the one extreme there are tribal communities who are at the food gathering and hunting stage and at the other extreme, they have become indistinguishable from the modern agricultural and industrial societies. Differences have appeared in their educational status. Some of these communities, particularly in the northeast, are far ahead of the general educational level in the country. On the contrary, there are communities, which are at a preliterate stage. The level of literacy amongst the tribals in 1991 was only 29.60 per cent compared to 52.11 per cent for the entire country.

The administrative system in the tribal areas has undergone sea change in the last 30 years. There was no specific systematic strategy for tribal development during the pre-independence era. Some major changes occurred in our country with the integration of states after independence. During this period the foundations for evolving a new system were laid with the adoption of our Constitution. The era of planned development was inaugurated with the launching of the First Plan in the early Fifties. The community development movement gave a new direction to the evolution of our administrative system and basic strategies. The tribal areas moved with the main current. In the Five Year Plans a new direction has been sought to be given to the developmental process in the tribal areas, which has resulted in restructuring of the policy and strategy for tribal development.

Tribal Development Policy

Tribal Policy in Ancient India

For thousands of years, the primitive tribes of India remained in oblivion, secluded in the dense forests and attracting less attention. For the ancient Hindu states the tribal people never existed as a problem and as such there was no need of a "tribal policy". It is true that during their military and hunting expeditions, some civilised people especially the kings and princess came in contact with groups of tribal people. Stories about such contacts are to be found in the Puranas, especially the epics of Ramayana and Mahabharata. These contacts were casual. Sometimes, these resulted in brief subjugation of some tribal people. They, however, never broke their isolation from civilisation. There are also stray instances of tribal groups being assimilated into the Hindu society. But such cases did not attract any attention and presented no problem for administration.

Lord Rama's acceptance of the hospitality of a Sabara woman and also his friendship with Guhaka Sabara are such instances from Ramayana. The stories from Mahabharata, which are mostly allegorical in nature, describe innumerable contacts of the Pandavas with forest dwellers and even some matrimonial alliances with them. Apart from these mythical evidences, there is also recorded evidence of great historical importance. This is to be found in the rock-edicts of Asoka.

It may, therefore, be summed up that due to sparse population, contact with the tribals was seldom seen. The attitude of the State was almost apathetic. A policy based on liberalism and piety was not found.

It appears that the Aryans evolved stable regional economic and social units. The relatively isolated and backward ethnic groups (tribes) found place in terms of corporate social status and economic and political functions. It may safely be assumed that such a situation existed at least at the time of Buddha. Bose has described this process as "Hindu method of social absorption".[61] This process assured cultural autonomy to the newly-integrated tribes. Ultimately, it released a cultural process by which the subordinated and low-ranked tribes gradually emulated the cultural pattern of the dominant Hindu upper castes. This process of integration has brought about regional capsules under the superstructure of small states. They were sometimes headed by tribal derived Rajput Chiefs.[62]

Tribal Policy in the Medieval Period

The medieval period in Indian history roughly covers the period from Mohammedan conquest up to the beginning of the British rule. This period is characterised by two contradictory trends of isolation and assimilation. These trends were possible due to the process of history and not of conscious innovation. As a matter of fact, no medieval state had a definite policy towards the tribals. The policy of each state was determined in the context of specific situations. The period saw the growth of certain tribal people as martial races who ultimately came to rule over territories inhabited by them and their neighbours. The chief among these are the Rajput and the Gond kingdoms. The Rajput and Gond rulers were gradually accepted as warrior castes and came to occupy a high position in the caste hierarchy of Hindu society.

The policy of the Mohammedan and Moghal rulers and later on the Marahathas entertained a patronising attitude towards these chieftains. They recognised their courage and valour and were willing to offer high offices and vast areas to them. They were, however, not willing to recognise them as independent rulers or as peers. The result was that many Rajput and Gond chiefs came to occupy high positions in the civil and military ranks in the administration of the Mohammedans, Moghals and Marahathas.

The other trend during the medieval period was the drift of some groups of tribal people into the forests and inaccessible areas. These people were driven away by their more advanced Hindu neighbours, the latter acquiring their land. This trend was due to the growth of population, which made the marginal people to seek new territories. This process is responsible for keeping some tribes in extreme primitive condition up to the present day.

British Rule

After the medieval period the tribal people remained isolated in remote hills and forests for more than a century. When the missionaries made their entry into these areas, the British administration became aware of them. The contact thus established was only superficial. The influence of British rule on the tribals has been aptly described by Dr. J. H. Hutton in the following words:

"Far from being of immediate benefit to the primitive tribes the establishment of British rule in India did most of them much more harm than good. It may be said that the early days of British administration did very great detriment to the economic position of tribes through ignorance and neglect of their rights and customs, many changes have been caused incidentally by the penetration of the tribal country, the opening up of communication, the protection of forest and the establishment of schools, to say nothing of the opening given in this way to Christian Missions. Many of the results of these changes have caused acute discomfort to the tribes". Professor G. S. Ghurye, another distinguished anthropologist, has also observed as follows: "Acuteness of discomfort was very often so great that it led to apathy, indifference, moral deterioration, and even a decline in population".[63] The British policy led to the exploitation of tribal people by their non-tribal neighbours and government officers. It was a policy of total neglect and a mage of exploitation. The British assumed that these tribals were primitive and backward in all respects.[64] The rules passed for the conservation and preservation of forests encroached on the age-old rights of the tribal people over the forest. With the restriction imposed on the rights of the tribal people, unrestricted rights were enjoyed by the Zamindars, moneylenders, contractors and unscrupulous traders. The whole basis of British administration in India was to support its supporters.[65] However, the unrestricted exploitation of the tribals, which pushed them to a state of abject poverty and misery resulted in a series of rebellions.[66]

Pre-independence Policy

The tribal areas were the last to come under the British power because of their difficult terrain and inaccessibility. The tribals continued to rise in rebellion for a long period for asserting their right to self-governance particularly in relation to their rights over land and forest.

The British declared some of the tribal areas as 'excluded'[67] and some as 'partially excluded'.[68] They adopted the policy of lightly administering these areas. The normal administration of the provinces, in which the tribal areas were located, was not extended to them. In many regions, single line administration was established where all authority was vested in one individual who was the chief representative of the Government in that area. The local custom was honoured and there was judicious intervention only when it was considered inevitable.

Thus, mainly two approaches to tribal problems were followed during the British time. The earliest one was that of complete isolation followed by the policy of exclusion or partial exclusion of the tribal areas.[69]

The British rulers who had this approach to leave them alone[70] towards the tribal communities held the view that the task of administration in the tribal areas, especially the thickly wooded border areas, was difficult and rather unrewarding. Moreover, they were inclined to quarantine the tribes from possible political infection.[71] A number of officers believed that the tribal people were better and happier in their own society. They believed that there was no need for extending British rule to these areas and interference in their life-style was considered to be unnecessary.

Though the policy of isolation could not eliminate all cultural contact, economic competition between the tribals and non-tribals, but it certainly reduced the possibilities of intervention between them to a great extent. As a result, the tribes could pursue their distinctive life-ways and preserve their dialectical marks undisturbed by the external forces of change.

The system of tribal areas was in conformity with the normal pattern of general administration in British India which gave considerable discretion and authority to field administration. The basic objective of the administration was to maintain law and order and an effective control of the Raj. The special socio-political situation in the tribal areas made vesting of discretion in the local administration even more necessary. The simple tribal communities had to be protected from the more articulate groups who moved into these areas with their opening up and establishment of the new administration. As the local administration considered itself responsible for good administration in these areas, it acquired a paternalistic attitude.

Bringing about transformation of tribal people had been the special concern of the administration right from the days of Warren Hastings. The Nineteenth century saw the utilitarians like Munro, Elphinstone and Metcalfe. They devised a method of administration to bring about a change in tribal areas.[72]

In sharp contrast to the policy of isolation is that of detribalisation and assimilation. Christian missionaries[73] and social reformers who were supporters of this approach took a poor view of tribal life. They were actuated by an obligation to convert our erring brethren to the faith of Christ.[74] They looked askance at some of the tribal customs and practices. The followers of this policy were of the view that tribalism was a mark of inferiority in all respects. It should be replaced by civilised life ways. According to them no progress can be achieved in the tribal society without a break with its tradition and culture.

In fact, assimilation creates many problems. It involves a total loss of cultural identity for the tribes who are assimilated. In some cases, it tends to make the tribes ashamed of their own culture and religion and creates an inferiority complex leading to a political and social crisis.[75]

A sudden deviation from the traditional values sets the tribals adrift in an unfamiliar world. The arts and crafts of the tribal people, self reliance and independence, corporate discipline and reciprocity tend to disintegrate and disappear.

Post-Independence Strategy

A new policy between the preceding two extremes of doing too little and doing too much was evolved in the post-Independence era. This approach essentially lays emphasis on their life and culture. It is known as the strategy of emotional integration.

The foundations for a secular democratic society were laid as soon as India won freedom. Steps were undertaken to frame a Constitution for the country. The Constituent Assembly accepted the tribal problem as an integral part of the development of Indian people as a whole. The Constituent Assembly incorporated some of the provisions like Article-46, which embodied the 'message of hope' for millions of our citizens hitherto neglected. Out of Article-46 flows all safeguards for members of the Scheduled Tribes.[76] The constitutional obligation to make the tribals equal with the non-tribals was a kernel of planned action in the different Five Year plans.[77] In the new federal structure, a special place was carved out for the tribal areas. The founding fathers of the nation appreciated their unique socio-economic situation. Tribal development or administration of tribal areas was not formally assigned to any one of the three lists in the Constitution. These areas were brought under two Schedules (fifth and sixth) for which special provisions were made.[78] When we read the Indian Constitution, we come across the word special when there is a reference to the Scheduled Castes or the Scheduled Tribes. These special provisions are incorporated in Part-III on Fundamental Rights, Part-IV on Directive Principles of State Policy, Part-X on the Scheduled and Tribal Areas, Part-XII on Finance, Property, etc., Part-XVI on special provisions relating to certain classes.[79] The excluded areas were covered under the sixth schedule. The partially excluded areas and some of the tribal areas in the erstwhile Indian states were included in the fifth schedule.

Besides enjoying the rights; which all citizens and minorities have, the members of the scheduled tribe have been provided with special safeguards[80] as enshrined in various articles of the Constitution. They are: (i) Protective safeguards: like educational safeguard[81]– Art. 15(4) and Art. 29, safeguards for employment– Art.16(4),320(4) and333, economic safeguards– Art.19, protection from all forms of exploitation–Art.46; (ii) Political safeguards: like reservation of seats for Scheduled Tribes in the Lok Sabha and Vidhan Sabha[82]– Art.330, Art.332 and Art.334, special provisions in respect of Nagaland, Assam and Manipur– Art.371(A),371(B) and371(C); (iii) Developmental safeguards such as promotion of educational and economic interests of the Scheduled Tribes under Art. 46, Grants from Central Government to the states for welfare of Scheduled Tribes and raising the level of administration of Scheduled Areas– Art. 75 and provisions of free legal aid.[83]

The Constitution also provides for establishment of a 'tribes advisory council' under the fifth schedule, which is constituted by the Governor in relation to his regulation making power. Thus, the need to consult the state legislature was itself dispensed within the case of these areas. The provisions for the Sixth schedule areas are more stringent. The Constitution recognises the traditional council and their right to self-governance. No law about certain specified subjects can be extended to these areas without consulting the District Councils.

It was also appreciated that equality of rights in an unequal situation may really mean emergence of vested interests in these areas. The Constitution, therefore, envisages that even the Fundamental Rights could be comprised for protecting the members of the Scheduled Tribes and for achieving the faster pace of development. Thus, the Constitution, as a legal frame, provides an ideal setting for effectiveness of administration and its adaptability and responsiveness to the local situation, keeping the interests of the tribal communities always the upper most.

The Constitution also made special financial provisions for the tribal areas under the first provision to Article 275(I) raising the level of administration. Any scheme prepared for this purpose and approved by the Central Government presumes automatic financial sanction. The Constitution under Art. 164 provided that in the states of Bihar, Madhya Pradesh and Orissa there shall be a minister in charge of tribal welfare.[84]

In this way, the Constitution provides for all contingencies in relation to the administration and development of the tribal areas and tribal communities. The central point in this scheme is its flexibility. The intention is that, on no account, the task of tribal development should suffer. To cap all this effort, the Constitution envisaged setting up of a commission after10 years of the commencement of the Constitution to review the development of these areas and made suitable recommendations for future action.

From 1952–1974

The early Fifties witnessed some important structural changes in the administrative system in our country. For the first time, a clearly defined plan of development was initiated. The administration was equipped for undertaking the new development responsibilities. In the beginning, the general administration was assigned this task. Gradually, separate developmental administration machinery got established in some states.

The tribal areas received special attention during this period. After the inauguration of the community development movement in the country, special programmes of Tribal Development Block (TDB)[85] in tribal areas and Special Multipurpose Tribal Development Blocks (SMPT) in the most underdeveloped areas of tribal concentration were taken up.[86] These special schemes were jointly undertaken by the Ministry of Home Affairs and the Ministry of Community Development and Cooperation.

Thus, with emphasis on understanding of "tribal life and culture" it was proposed to promote economic development facilities of communication and provisions of social services in tribal areas, intimately paving paths for a good and prosperous life for the tribals.[87] Nehru envisaged a keen interest in the integration of Scheduled Tribes. Accordingly, he advocated five fundamental principles.[88] The Panchasila are as follows:

1. The most important principle was to impose nothing and allow the people to develop along the lines of their own genius and tradition. It was everywhere applauded but little followed. In day-to-day work, the block officials in their natural enthusiasm forced the tribals to do things, which were not a natural growth from within and unsuited to their economy, habitat and society. The result has been total loss of self-reliance and other adverse effects of imposition.
2. The second principle of this approach was to safeguard by special measures the interest of the tribals in land and forest and protect them from all forms of exploitation. Unless the tribals are made free from the clutches of moneylenders, sycophants and liquor vendors, their problem would basically remain unsolved about the quality of community life.
3. The third principle of the new policy was not to crowd the tribal areas with undesirable elements and unwilling personnel. These officials without having any knowledge of tribal life would impose their points of view, their programmes and push some of their known contractors into the tribal areas to carry on business at the cost of the tribal people. Through such agencies, many unscrupulous people would find way into the tribal areas. This would create a pressure on the indigenous inhabitants by various dishonest practices. They would not only alienate lands of the tribals but also interfere with their life.

4. The fourth principle of tribal development was to avoid over administration and overloading of schemes on the tribal people.
5. The last principle of the tribal Panchasila was to judge results not by statistics or the amount of money spent but by the quality of human character that was evolved.

Changes are taking place in the tribal communities as a result of the impact of developmental programmes and political modernisation. The development of road communication, commercial transactions and industrial and mining activities have given rise to the crowding of tribal areas by the migrant non-tribals from the plains. Consequently, some political reactions are now manifesting certain tribal pockets. Moreover, the process of land alienation[89] has been accentuated and the exploitation[90] by the merchants and moneylenders has been intensified. Various obnoxious systems such as serfdom or bonded labour still continue in many tribal areas, in spite of law prohibiting such practices. As a result of the social consequences, land alienation and other forms of exploitation have been very serious in many tribal pockets.

However, it was being realised that the tribal development blocks were not touching even the fringe of the problem and that greater effort was needed. Therefore, in some case, the tribal welfare departments looked beyond these narrow schemes and assumed additional responsibility.

From 1974 onwards

The next phase in strategy for tribal development begins with a review in depth of the tribals' scene in the country on the eve of the Fifth Plan. In the First Plan, the main emphasis was on health, housing and communication. The Second Plan shifted emphasis to "economic development" (agriculture, cottage industries, forest, cooperative societies and setting up of multipurpose tribal blocks). The Third Plan renamed these blocks as tribal development blocks with the priorities for economic uplift, education, health, housing and communications.[91] These schemes continued during Fourth Plan.

Experience shows that most of the programmes in the backward classes sector in the absence of adequate financial backing and organisational support had little impact on the poverty, educational backwardness and social disability of backward classes.[92] Even in case of area-based programmes such as tribal development blocks (taken up since the Second Five-Year Plan), the impact has not been satisfactory. The factors ascribed to are limited areas covered and absence of substantial investment called for on such programmes as minor irrigation, development of communication and electrification, etc.[93]

The principal deficiencies of the earlier plans were: (a) lack of special attention to tribal and scheduled areas in spite of constitutional provisions; (b) inadequate allotment of funds in both general and special sectors to cover all aspects of development of the tribal areas; (c) inadequate administrative machinery to integrate all the sectoral programmes. Coupled with it is the lack of coordination and integration of inter and intra-departmental levels within the state as well as at the sectoral levels of the state and centre; (d) lack of effective personal policy of the government, etc.[94] In1969, the Shilu Ao Committee examined the working of the tribal development programmes of the Planning Commission and did not feel enthusiastic about giving a clear verdict about the progress. It was very clear to the team that, "if progress is to be judged by what remains to be done to bring the tribals on par with the rest of the population, the lee way to be made up is still considerable and that the delay in the implementation of considered recommendations made by the scheduled areas and scheduled tribes commission and other high level bodies in the past to project the rights of the tribals has worsened the position which these recommendations were intended to correct, while the failure to pay attention to and profit by their advice on matters pertaining to the formulation and implementation of tribal development programmes has resulted in failure of ambitious schemes and consequent waste of valuable resources".[95] According to them, the tribal development block was too small an area-unit for comprehensive planning and effective implementation. The programmes were not compatible with local needs.

Fifth Plan Approach

The Fifth Five Year Plan marks a new phase in tribal development in India. The first step in this regard was a clear policy frame by the Government.[96] A special chapter was devoted on tribal development in the Plan documents. In the Fifth Five-Year Plan, it was considered that utmost priority was to be accorded to drawing upon integrated area plan after identifying specific tribal areas.[97]

The tribal scene was comprehensively reviewed. The Planning Commission appointed a Task Force on Development of Backward Classes. It considered the problem in its numerous facets. The Task Force appointed a number of working groups. It suggested a three-tier developmental structure of micro, meso and macro levels. The meso unit was suggested to be the main building block of this strategy.

The Central Coordination Committee[98] for Welfare of Backward classes was set up in the wake of the new strategy for development of tribal areas in the Fifth Plan for ensuring the flow of sectoral funds for tribal development for watching the progress of schemes in tribal areas and for suggesting measures for effective implementation of the programmes. This Committee decided to constitute a working group under the Chairmanship of Sri B. R. Patel to work out the details of integration of various sectoral programmes in the tribal development projects.

These working groups and committee evolved a new strategy for tribal development at the beginning of the Fifth Plan.[99] The strategy is called the sub-plan approach. The sub-plan is not a scheme; it represents a new approach.[100] The sub-plan for tribal regions is the smaller plan within the state plan. The distinctive features of the sub-plan are: (a) it caters to the special needs of the tribal areas, (b) it employs the integrated area approach of developmental strategy, (c) its resources are the sum total of the resources of the state plan for the sub-plan areas, the central sector outlays, special central assistance and institutional finance, (d) substantial supplementation of state efforts by the union government, (e) major thrust of development to be provided by the general sector, (f) evolving a suitable frame for development of these areas and restructuring/reconstructing the administrative and institutional frame.[101] The long term objectives of the sub-plan area are: (i) to narrow the gap between the levels of development of tribal and other areas, (ii) to improve the quality of life of the tribal communities. The immediate objectives will be to eliminate exploitation in all forms, speed up the process for social and economic development and improve the organisational capabilities.[102] It was agreed that a general strategy for achieving these objectives has to be evolved, reviewing the entire local, administrative and institutional frame, as also the inter-sectoral and intra-sectoral priorities, keeping the primary focus on the welfare and development of the people.

The scope of the sub-plans, thus, is much wider than that of the state plans. In this case, a "problem solving" approach has been accepted for the first time not only in principle but with adequate provision for policy review in all important matters in financial support for any action necessary.[103] The guidelines for preparation of sub-plans have set this frame in very clear terms.

As the development of the people has to be the central point of attention of the sub-plan in many cases, it may be necessary to look at the problem unfettered by the existing formal, procedural or legal frame.[104]

The concerned state governments have sufficient freedom of framing the sub-plans for the tribal areas within their respective states. The first exercise in this regard is to demarcate the tribal areas based on the tribal population. Three zones[105] are thus envisaged:

1. Zone of tribal concentration of 50 per cent and above.
2. Zone of dispersed tribal population below 50 per cent.[106]
3. Zone of extremely backward and isolated little communities.

All districts, tehsils, and blocks having 50 per cent or more tribal population are being included in the sub-plan area. They are taken up first for the purpose of project formulation and for delineating within each project area sub-regions, if any, which requires special attention. Isolated small tribal niches, zones of influence of mining and industrial complex and hinterland of urban and big marketing centres constitute such special sub-regions in the project areas. Similarly, the areas under shifting cultivation within the project area or any other problems peculiar to it would need special attention. In other words, the sub-plan in each state would comprise of a number of viable project areas. For each project area, an integrated area development programme focussing attention on the specific problems of the tribes in that region is to be formulated. Likewise, for each sub-region, problem oriented strategy will have to be evolved and suitable action programmes initiated for its development.

Integrated Tribal Development Project/ Integrated Tribal Development Agency (ITDP/ITDA):

The entire tribal sub-plan area has been divided into a number of viable integrated tribal development projects (ITDP) subsequently renamed as integrated tribal development agencies (ITDA). Since the tribal development block was too small a unit for planning and coordination, it was decided to constitute a project comprising a group of development blocks for administrative reasons, a project was not expected to intersect the existing administrative boundaries. Since the situation varied from one state to another, the project size was decided keeping in view the specific situation in a particular case.

Integrated tribal development approach envisages multilevel planning at macro, meso and micro levels. First, it is necessary to identify areas with more than 50 per cent tribal concentration. Secondly, from these, viable project areas will have to be carved out at various levels for the purpose of planning. These should be delineated keeping in view various considerations such as natural resources, physical features, level of development of the tribal communities inhabiting the region and other socio-economic considerations to suit the planning functions at these levels. To the extent possible the existing administrative boundaries should be taken into consideration for the purpose of delineating planning units at various levels. Micro areas could be coterminous with blocks which may be divided into clusters on the basis of space preference of people. For certain developmental programmes the clusters may be split into sub-centres depending upon the terrain and the need for grouping the functions at the lowest level. The meso areas could normally coincide with districts/subdivisions/tahasils and the macro areas could conveniently fall into separate revenue divisions.

The salient features of the approach of Integrated Tribal Development Planning are to establish functional inter-linkages between the multi-level planning units. This enables the dependent villages to be linked with service centres. Similarly, the service centres will be linked with higher centres at the divisional and state levels.

The ITDP has characteristics of both an area programme as also a target group programme. It is an area programme for the development of the tribal region and it is a group or family based programme addressed to the development of the tribal communities living in that area. It has been designed as a form of an "umbrella organisation"[107] which must accommodate whatever is considered desirable for the given area of the people. Ideally the programmes for the project area should evolve their own scheme and priorities in specific response to the problems and socio-economic conditions of the area.[108]

In this way, a clear-cut strategy for tribal development has been adopted for the tribal areas after a long period of time. The plan formulations for these areas have been initiated with the "problem-solving" approach, identifying the problems of each area and evolving a total programme for solving the same. The total state effort is gradually being unified under the ITDPs/ITDAs.

Micro-Projects for Primitive Tribes

The primitive tribes are numerically minor tribe and have not been able to attend the attention of policy makers and the administrative machinery so far owing to their isolation and lack of preparedness to face the challenge of backwardness.[109] The problems of these less developed tribal communities of India was considered to be taken up on an urgent and priority basis. Therefore, during the Fifth Five Year Plan, micro projects strategy was adopted for the development of primitive tribal communities. Primitive tribes were taken as a special category for whom specific programmes have been initiated for their all-round development. Suitable measures were taken up for their development and for helping them in adjusting themselves to the new socio-economic forces of change. As a first step, the primitive tribes were identified on the basis of their pre-agricultural economy, low level of literacy, low growth rate and inhospitable and isolated habitat. Most of these tribal communities are "closed groups" with a high degree of tradition orientation. The impact of modernisation in terms of acceptance of education, technology and peculiar style of living is almost non-existent. As illustrated in the study of the Maler Hill Tribe,[110] their lifestyle may be well conceptualised in terms of the nature-man-spirit complex. To ensure special attention for their development as well as to bring about their all round uplift, micro projects were formed and started functioning. These micro projects are made to refine and improve upon the traditional vocation of primitive tribes residing in the micro project areas while planning for their social and economic development.

Modified Area Development Approach (MADA)

During the Fifth Five Year Plan, MADA was adopted as a special strategy for all-round development of dispersed tribals living outside the tribal sub-plan area. MADA pockets, each having a total population of 10,000 or more, of whom 50 per cent and above are tribals, were identified and started. Different development programmes have been implemented for the socio-economic benefit of the scheduled tribes residing in these MADA pockets.

Sixth Plan Period

In order to handle the multifaceted problems of the tribal population coming within the new sub-plan strategy in a coordinated manner, integrated tribal development agencies for substantial tribal areas and special (micro) projects for primitive tribes were conceived and adopted. For dispersed tribals living in pockets of tribal concentration outside the sub-plan area, the modified area development approach (MADA) was adopted.

While the sub-plan approach as initially conceived was continued during the 6th Plan period, increasing emphasis was attached to poverty amelioration programmes amongst the scheduled tribes with a view to ensure a sustained and reasonable level of income for these families. The tribal development strategy during the Sixth Plan period was area development with focus on development of tribal communities. The tasks as defined by the working group on tribal development during 6th Plan were 'elimination of exploitation in all forms, speeding up the process of socio-economic development, building inner strength of the people and improving their organisational capabilities.[111] The tribal sub-plan strategy was slightly reoriented during the Sixth Plan period laying greater emphasis on specific objectives, namely,

1. Raising the productivity level of different fields of tribal economic activities like agriculture, horticulture, animal husbandry, forestry, industry, etc. with a view to enable 50 per cent of scheduled tribe families to cross the poverty line.
2. Development of human resources and upgradation of education.
3. Elimination of exploitation of tribals in the fields of land tenure, money lending, debt bondage, trade, excise, forest, labour, etc.
4. Development of critical infrastructure in tribal areas and strengthening of delivery system in tribal areas through streamlining of LAMPS.
5. Accordingly, positive attention was focused during the Sixth Plan period on family approach for development. The process of planning was built up, funnelling upwards from block through ITDP, district, state to national levels. Interweaving of sectoral programmes was taken place at the block, ITDP as well as state levels. However, some ground works on development of Scheduled Tribes were laid during the Sixth Plan. This was also observed by the working group on development of Scheduled Tribes during the Sixth Plan, "It may suffice here to say that good ground

has been covered in the tribal development sphere in the country up to the end of the Sixth Plan".[112]

Seventh Plan

The objectives and strategy of the tribal development had been spelt out in the report of the working group on tribal development during Seventh Plan. They are:

1. Raising the levels of productivity[113] as a means for alleviation of poverty. Efforts were, therefore, concentrated in these fields in which the tribals were by and large engaged as in agriculture; horticulture, animal husbandry, forestry, cottage, village and small industry. This was affected through provision of capital inputs, technology, education, marketing, training, etc. Specific anti-poverty programmes had been taken up on a scale, which enabled 50 per cent of Scheduled Tribe families (including those that spill over from the Sixth Plan target) to cross the poverty line. These programmes with their sustenance from those of IRDP, NREP, RLEGP, as well as others were undertaken with different sources of funds, all of them brought under the broad TSP umbrella. Since raising a family above the poverty line required a package of schemes drawn from different sectors, there was close coordination and inter-linkages. Serious attention hence, was paid to this aspect at all levels commencing from the village through block, district and state levels to the national level.
2. Emphasis was laid in the national plans in the past to progress in education but, by and large, the sector had not received its due. The basic objective of universalisation of education and removal of adult illiteracy (in the age group 15-35) was set to be achieved by 1990, education, both formal and informal, had been accorded high priority. In the Sixth Plan Working Group Report on Tribal Development, it had been stressed that education should become a key sector during the Sixth Plan period. There is no evidence to indicate that this has happened. The percentage of literacy of Scheduled Tribe population, as per 1971 census, was 11.3 and this was increased to 16.35 during the 1981 census.

Even for bridging the gap between the tribal literacy percentage of 16.35 and the national literacy percentage of 36, an effort was mounted which had hitherto not been in sight. The bias for vocationalisation received special attention. The potentiality of education and vocational training in promoting self-reliance and self-employment was recognised in the tribal context.

3. As mentioned earlier, the one area that can yield immediate dividends to the tribals is that of anti-exploitative measures. The fifth schedule of the Constitution provides that framework for legislation. Several State Governments have adopted legislative provisions against land alienation, for regulation of money-lending, adoption of policies against sale of liquor by liquor vendors in tribal areas and administrative measures like creation of cooperatives aimed at regulation of exchange transactions, etc. It was realised that the situation did not improve markedly not with standing such provisions. Land continued to be moving out of tribal's possession. Much more vigorous enforcement of the various measures was, therefore, felt necessary considering the present situation.

4. The foregoing objectives would require adequately strong infrastructure for production, anti-poverty, education, and anti-exploitative programmes. The supportive infrastructure had to be legislative, physical, institutional and administrative. Among the items of physical infrastructure, particular emphasis was paid to minor irrigation, soil and water conservation, cooperation and land reforms, which support beneficiary-oriented programmes. Capital-intensive centres like large and medium industries, roads and bridges, mining, power, road transport were to be given lower priority than hitherto. Drinking water supply received special attention.

5. Vulnerable areas and groups had also received special attention, e.g. primitive tribal groups, nomadic groups, shifting cultivators, forest villagers, families displaced by development projects, migrant tribal labourers. Special and appropriate programmes for tribal women were called for.

Problem areas like the areas of influence of industrial and other major projects also needed special attention. The disability from which these vulnerable areas and groups suffer were identified for remedial action.

6. The degrading environment of tribal areas had been posing problem not only of precarious resources availability in the form of soil, forest, fuel, grass, fodder, etc., but also of ecological insecurity in the form of proneness to natural disasters like drought, floods, etc. Determined efforts were initiated to scientifically survey, plan and implement programmes for the improvement of the quality of tribal environment and upgrade resources.

Eighth Five-Year Plan

A review of the patterns of tribal development adopted by the non-official and official agencies from the second quarter of the current century to the late seventies is convincing of the fact that some weaknesses in one form or other were identified at various levels.[114]

However, there has been no fundamental change in the tribal development strategy during Eighth Plan period. The objective and strategy during the Eighth Plan period[115] are as follows:

1. While implementing the Tribal Sub-plan strategy during the Eighth Plan, steps were taken to make it more result oriented and purposeful so that not only adequate flow of funds was ensured but also the benefits of the investments under Tribal Sub-Plan go towards improving the socio-economic condition of Scheduled Tribes. This was backed up further by decentralised planning.
2. The quantification techniques are being refined so that it becomes more realistic and only such schemes and programmes, which are directly relevant and beneficial to the tribals, are reflected as flow of funds to tribal sub-plan.
3. Adequate emphasis was laid on the development of irrigation, horticulture, crop diversification and improvement in the quality of the education of the tribals.

4. Special schemes were formulated for all-round development of primitive groups and nomadic and semi-nomadic and other vulnerable tribes.
5. Greater efforts were needed during the Eighth Plan period for the educational development of Scheduled Tribes particularly in the field of women's education and reducing the dropout rate among the Scheduled Tribe students at primary level.
6. The Seventh Plan programmes were primarily aimed at providing economic assistance to the tribals to raise the productivity level, to take them above the poverty line and to develop the economic and educational infrastructure. The said programme was continued during the Eighth Plan period.
7. Review Committees were constituted under the Chairmanship of Chief Minister/Minister of Harijan and Tribal Welfare/Chief Secretary at the state level for coordinating the implementation of tribal development programmes and for reviewing the policies on a regular basis.

Ninth Five-Year Plan

The Ninth Plan commits to empower the Scheduled Tribes as the agents of socio-economic change and development. Therefore, a major shift is visualised in the approach as it envisages advancement of those socially disadvantaged groups through a process of 'empowerment'.[116] The empowerment of these Groups, as envisaged, will be a long-drawn process, with support policies and programmes directed towards empowering the Socially Disadvantaged Groups to be the active partners and partakers of the country's development rather than continuing as passive recipients of various developmental benefits.

The approach towards empowering these Groups in the Ninth Plan is holistic in nature so as to accomplish all-round development of these weaker sections with an inter-sectoral approach and inputs from both the governmental and non-governmental agencies.

The strategy to be adopted during the Ninth Five Year Plan was to:

1. Create an environment that is conducive for the Scheduled Castes, Scheduled Tribes, OBCs and Minorities to exercise their rights freely, enjoy their privileges and be able to lead a life with confidence and dignity.
2. Adopt a three-pronged strategy of Social Empowerment; Economic Empowerment and Social Justice in empowering these disadvantaged groups.
3. Ensure removal of disparities, eliminate exploitation and suppression and provide protection to the disadvantaged groups.
4. Ensure the developmental benefits to 'Reach the Unreached' through equitable distribution and with social justice.
5. Ensure participation of the Socially Disadvantaged Groups in the process of planning not merely as the beneficiaries but to take part effectively in the formulation of the need-based programmes/ projects, their implementation, supervision and monitoring.
6. Accelerate the on-going process of improving the socio-economic status of the disadvantaged groups through effective implementation of various policies and programmes and thus bring them on par with the rest of the society.

So far, 194 ITDAs, 252 MADA pockets, 78 clusters, and 75 micro projects for primitive tribal groups have been identified in States and Union Territories of the country.[117] They are shown in Table 2.5.

Table 2.5
State-wise Integrated Tribal Development Projects/ Integrated Tribal Development Agencies (ITDPs/ ITDAs), Modified Area Development Approach (MADA) Pockets, Clusters and Micro Projects

Sl. No.	*State / Union Territory*	*Number of*			
		ITDPs / ITDAs	*MADA Pockets*	*Clusters*	*Micro Projects*
1.	Andhra Pradesh	8	41	17	12
2.	Assam	19	-	-	-
3.	Bihar	14	41	7	9
4.	Gujarat	9	1	-	5
5.	Himachal Pradesh	5	2	-	-
6.	Karnataka	5	-	-	2
7.	Kerala	7	-	-	5
8.	Madhya Pradesh	49	39	8	7
9.	Maharashtra	16	37	21	3
10.	Manipur	5	-	-	1
11.	Orissa	21	46	13	13
12.	Rajasthan	5	44	11	1
13.	Sikkim	4	-	-	-
14.	Tamil Nadu	9	-	-	6
15.	Tripura	3	-	-	1
16.	Uttar Pradesh	1	1	-	1
17.	West Bengal	12	-	1	3
18.	A and N Islands	1	-	-	5
19.	Daman and Diu	1	-	-	-
20.	Jammu and Kashmir	-	-	-	-
	Total:	194	252	78	75

Source: Evaluation Report on Integrated Tribal Development Projects by Programme Evaluation Organisation, Planning Commission, Government of India, New Delhi, July, 1997.

Conclusion

The economic position of Scheduled Tribes is determined from their income and the scale of employment. The programmes have generated opportunities for the Scheduled Tribes. The Scheduled Tribes are coming to the forefront and are trying to be assimilated in the main process of development. They have been gainfully employed and their income has been increased. Their political participation is being taken care of through the introduction of Panchayati Raj system. They are gradually participating in the political process of the country. In general, their dignity and self-image are not properly articulated. Review of this chapter leads us to think that the development process is not being properly framed to take care of the social status of the Scheduled Tribes in India.

Notes and References

1. G. C. Biswal, Tribal Development and Education, Some Issues, VANYAJATI, January1985, Vol. XXXII, No.1, p.14.
2. Ibid.
3. C. Parvathamma, Scheduled Castes and Tribes: A Socio-Economic Survey, Asish Publishing House, New Delhi, 1984, pp.4-5.
4. K. L. Bhowmick, Tribal India, A Profile of Indian Ethnology, The World Press Pvt. Ltd., Calcutta, 1971, p.1.
5. *N. K. Behura, "Tribal Societies in Orissa", in* Tribes of Orissa *(Ed.), H and T. W.* Department, *Government of Orissa, p. 1990.*
6. *Morris Desmond and Peter Marsh,* Tribes, *Pyramid Books, London, 1988, p.6.*
7. *Dr. Ghurye, "The Scheduled Tribes".*
8. *I. M. Lewis, "Tribal* Society", *in* International Encyclopaedia of Social Sciences, *The Macmillan Co. and the Free Press, 1968, Vol.16, p.147.*
9. *Pathy,* et al., *"Tribal Studies in India: An Appraisal"*, The Eastern Anthropologists, *1976.*
10. *T. B. Naik, "What is Tribe" Conflicting Definitions", in L. P. Vidyarthi (Ed.),* Applied Anthropology, *Allahabad, 1968, pp. 84-97.*
11. *Vimal Chandra,* Handbook on Scheduled Castes and Scheduled Tribes, *Office of the Commissioner for Scheduled Castes and Scheduled Tribes, Government of India, New Delhi, 1968, pp.27-28.*

12. *Stephen Fuchs,* The Aboriginal Tribes in India, *The Macmillan Company of India* Ltd.,*1973, p.25.*

13. *Beleille Andre,* The Definition of Tribe: Tribe, Caste and Religion, *Macmillan, India, p.10.*

14. *F. G. Bailey,* Tribe, Caste and Nation, *Oxford University Press, Bombay,1960, pp.263-266.*

15. *Suresh Chandra* Rajora, *"Tribal Society and Its Differential Profile",* VANYAJATI, *Jan.1986, Vol. XXXIV, No.1, pp.7-10.*

16. *Gail Om Vedt, "*Are *Adivasis Subaltern",* Economic and Political Weekly, *Sept.24,1988, Vol. XXIII, No.39, p.2001.*

17. *BD. Sharma,* Planning for Tribal Development, *Prachi Prakashan, New* Delhi,*1984,* p. V.

18. *D. N. Majumdar* and *T. N. Madan,* An Introduction to Social Anthropology, *Asia Publishing House,1980, p. 241.*

19. *Verrier Elwin,* New Deal for Tribal India, *Government of India, New Delhi,1963, p.5.*

20. *B. D. Sharma,* op. cit., *p.1.*

21. Final Population Totals: Brief Analysis of Primary Census Abstract, *Census of India,1991, Series-I, Paper-2 of 1992, p.38.*

22. *B. K. Roy Burman, "A Preliminary Appraisal of Scheduled Tribes of India", Office of the Registrar General, Government of India, New Delhi,1969, p. 2.*

23. *C. Von Furer-*Haimendorf, Recent Developments in the Position of Indian Tribal Population, *p.1.*

24. *Buddhadeb Choudhury (Ed.),* Tribal Development in India, Problems and Prospects, Inter *India Publications, Delhi,1982, p. XVII.*

25. *B. D. Sharma,* op. cit., *p. 24.*

26. *Suresh Chandra* Rajora, *"Tribal Society and Its Differential Profile",* VANYAJATI, *Vol. XXXIV, No.1, p.7.*

27. *Buddhadeb Choudhury (Ed.),* 'Introduction' Tribal Development in India, Problems and Prospects, *Inter India Publications, Delhi,1982, p. XIX-XX; P. K. Bhowmick, "Reports on Scheduled Tribes: An Appraisal" in L. P. Vidyarthi (Ed.),* Tribal Development and Its Administration, *Concept Publishing House, New Delhi,1986, p. 47.*

28. *M. L. Patel, "Directions of Tribal Development",* VANYAJATI, *Vol. XI, No.2, April 1992, p.31.*

29. *Buddhadeb Choudhury and Sumita Choudhury, "On Some Tribal Problems" in Buddhadeb Choudhury (Ed.),* Tribal Development

in India, Problems and Prospects, *Inter-India Publications, Delhi,1982, p.83-84.*

30. NCAER, "Report on Socio-Economic Conditions of Primitive Tribes in Madhya Pradesh", New Delhi,1963, p. IX.

31. *M. L. Patel, "Some Aspects of Educational Development of Tribes",* Bulletin of Cultural Research Institute, *Calcutta, Vol. X, No.3 and 4; G. P. Reddy, "Introductory Agriculture in Tribal Community: The Case of Chenchus" M. K. Raha and P. C. Coomar (Eds.),* Tribal India: Problems, Development Prospect, *Vol. II, Gian Publishing House, New Delhi,1989, p.90.*

32. *S. N. Rath and D. K. Behera,* A Glance at the Problems of Education among the Tribal Child in India: A Socio-Economic Profile, *Anmol Publications, New Delhi,1991, pp.206-207.*

33. *M. Chakravarti and C. S. Singhrole, "Problems of Tribal Education– A Key to Development",* Man in India, *Vol.14, Nos.1 and 2, pp.91-96.*

34. *Om Mehta,* Tribal Development: The New Strategy, *Government of India, New Delhi,1976, p. 2.*

35. *The Problem of Unwanted Transfer of Land Ownership from the tribal to non-tribal* is, *in short, described as Land Alienation. For further details, see M. L. Patel, "Agro-Economic Problems of Tribal India",* op. cit., *p.63.*

36. *B. K. Roy Burman, "Transfer and Alienation of Tribal Land" in Buddhadeb Choudhury (Ed.), Tribal Development in India,* Problems and Prospects, Inter India Publications, Delhi,1982, *p. 69.*

37. *Government of India, New Delhi, Tribal Development: The New Perspective, p. 2.*

38. *Buddhadeb Choudhury* and *Sumita Choudhury, "On Some Tribal Problems",* op. cit., pp. 89-90.

39. Ibid.

40. *Report of the* Commissioner *for Scheduled Castes and Scheduled Tribes (Twenty Fifth Report),1977-78, Part-I, pp.96-97; For further details, see, M. L. Patel,* Agro-Economic Problems of Tribal India, *Progress Publications, Bhopal,1972.*

41. *M. L. Patel, "Agro-*Economic *Problems of Tribals in India" in Buddhadeb Choudhury (Ed.),* Tribal Development in India, Problems and Prospects, *Inter India Publications, Delhi,1982, p. 51.*

42. *Buddhadeb Choudhury and Sumita Choudhury,* op. cit., *p. 87.*

43. *Report of the Committee* on *tribal Economy in Forest Areas,1967, New Delhi, p. 11.*

44. M. L. Patel, *"Agro*-Economic *Problems of Tribals in India"*, op. cit., *pp. 53-54.*

45. Report of the Scheduled Area and Scheduled Tribes Commission, Government of India, New Delhi, p. 513. This Commission recommended that shelters in Forest villages should be granted security of land tenure.

46. B. K. Roy Burman, "Various *Dimensions of Land Problems among the Tribes of India"*, VANYAJATI, *Vol. XIX, No.2, p.70.*

47. *M. L. Patel,* Agro-Economic Problems of Tribals in India, op. cit., *p. 59.*

48. N. K. Jaiseal, "Barriers of Diffusion of Farm Innovations among Tribal People", A paper discussed in Workshop (April18-20,1974), N. I. C. D., Hyderabad, pp.4-5.

49. *B. W. Hoddev,* Economic Development in the Tropics, *Methuen and Co. Ltd., London,1973, pp.44-45.*

50. *Trinath Gupta and Shreekant Sombarni, "Control of Shifting Cultivation: The Need for a Systematic Approach and Systematic Appraisal"*, IJAE, *Vol. XXXIII, No.4, Oct-Dec.,1978, p. 2.*

51. *N. K. Banerjee, "An Appraisal of Shifting Cultivation in India", in M. L. Patel,* Agro-Economic Problems of Tribals in India, op. cit., *pp.113-114.*

52. *F. K. Wadia, "Control of Shifting Cultivation in North Eastern Region"*, Prajna, *Vol.3, July-*Sept.*1976, p. 315.*

53. *Saradindu Bose, "Carrying Capacity of Land Under Shifting Cultivation"*, Asiatic Society,*1967, pp. 131-135.*

54. In India Shifting Cultivation is widely practised in North Eastern Region of the country comprising of Assam, Manipur, Meghalaya, Nagaland and Tripura and Union Territories of Arunachal Pradesh and Mizoram, Kerala, Madhya Pradesh, Andhra Pradesh and Orissa. This practice is known as 'Jhum' in Assam, Pendo, Bewar and Dahi in Madhya Pradesh, Tekunglu in Nagaland, Hookismong in Tripura, Adiabik in N. E. F. A. and Biringa, Podu and Dahi in Orissa.

55. The Yoraba of Cargo basin, the Bemba of Northern Rhodesia, the Yao of Southern Nyasaland, the Malasion of Solomon Islands, the Boro of Western Amazon Forest, the Bakairi Indians of Upper Xingu Region of South America, Hill Tribes of British, North Bornes and Veddah of Ceylon are still practising this shifting cultivation. The primitive cultivators of West Africa call it 'farming' and it is known as 'Sartage' in French. The Veda of Ceylon call it 'Chena' and the Burmese hill tribe as 'Taungia'. For further details see: Nag, D. S., Tribal Economy (An Economic Study of the

Baija), Bharatiya Adimjati Seva Sangha, New Delhi,1958, pp.410-418.

56. *P. C. Mohapatra,* Economic Development of Tribal India, *Asish Publishing House, New Delhi,1987, p. 130.*

57. *M. L. Patel, "Some Aspects of Shifting Cultivation"*, The Newsletter, *July 1972, Government of India, Department of Social Welfare, New Delhi, pp.23-29.*

58. R. K. Mishra, "Some Problems of Developmental Administration of Tribal Areas in India", Paper presented in Workshop on "Perspective on Tribal Development and Administration", April18-20,1974, N. I. C. D., Hyderabad.

59. *"Caste Based* Prostitution *Prevalence in M. P. "*, Times of India, *12 August1997.*

60. *Suresh Chandra Rajora, "Tribal Society and Its Differential Profile (A Case* for *Development Programmes)*, VANYAJATI, *Vol. XXXIV, No.1, p.7.*

61. *N. K. Bose, "The Hindu Method of Tribal Absorption"*, Science and Culture, *1941, Vol.7, pp.188-194.*

62. *Surjit Sinha,* "State *Formation and Jajput Myth in Tribal Central India"*, Man in India, *1962, Vol.42, No.1, pp.35-80.*

63. *G. S. Ghurye,* The Scheduled Tribes, *2nd Edition,1958.*

64. *D. R. Methe, "Legal* Protection *to Tribals and Tribal Development– A New Deal for Tribals and Tribal Development" in S. G. Deogaonkar (Ed.),* Problems of Development of Tribal Areas, *1980, pp.23-24.*

65. *Verrer Elwin,* A New Deal for Tribal India, *1963, p.10.*

66. *Gopinath Mohanty,* "Evaluation *of Tribal Policy"*, Adibasi, *1962-63.*

67. *Verrier Elwin,* A Philosophy of NEFA, *Shillong,1964, pp.45-46.*

68. *S. C. Dube,* "Approaches *to Tribal Problems in India" in L. P. Vidyarthi (Ed.),* Applied Anthropology in India, *Kitab Mahal, Allahabad,1968.*

69. *G. T. Trewartha,* Tribal Development: Retrospect and Prospect, *New Delhi,1975.*

70. *M. K. Rath and S. C. Das, "Constitutional Safeguards for Scheduled Tribes", in* Buddhadeb *Choudhury (Ed.),* Tribal development in India: Problems and Prospects, op. cit., *p.310.*

71. *N. Patnaik and S. Bose,* An Integrated Tribal Development Plan for Keonjhar District, Orissa, *National Institute of Community Development, Hyderabad,1976, p.1.*

72. *Haridwar Rai, "Politico-Administrative Basis of India, Field Administration"*, The Indian Journal of Public Administration, *Vol. XVI, No.4, p. 474.*

73. *K. N. Sahay, "Christianity as an Agency of Tribal Welfare in India", in L. P.* Vidyarthi *(Ed.)*, Applied Anthropology in India, op. cit.; *M. N. Srinivas*, Caste in Modern India and Other Essays, *Asia Publishing House, Bombay,1962.*

74. *Rev.* Alexander *Duff,* India and Indian Missions, *London,1840 (Second Edition), p. 308.*

75. *R. Metcalfe Thomas,* The Aftermath of Revolt, India1832-1870, Princeton, *Princeton University Press, 1965, pp. 250-252.*

76. *S. P. Sinha, "Tribal Development Administration", in L. P. Vidyarthi (Ed.),* Tribal Development and Its Administration, *Concept Publishing Company, New Delhi,1986, p.70.*

77. *S. P. Sinha, "Tribal Development Administration–A Historical Overview", in L. P. Vidyarthi (Ed.),* Tribal Development and Its Administration, op. cit., *p.65.*

78. C. Parvathamma, Scheduled Castes and Tribes: A Socio-Economic Survey, op. cit., *pp.4-23.*

79. *K. K. Lenva, "Impact of the Constitutional Safeguards on the Scheduled Tribes"*, Journal of Social Research, *September 1964; K. V. Rao,* Parliamentary Democracy in India, *The World Press, Calcutta,1965, p. 205.*

80. *M. K. Raha and J. C. Das, "Constitutional Safeguards for Scheduled Tribes" in Buddhadeb* Choudhury *(Ed.),* Tribal Development in India: Problems and Prospects, op. cit., *p. 312.*

81. *A. C. Banerjee,* The Constitution of the Indian Republic, *Calcutta, A. K. Mukherjee Company,1950; H. N. Banerjee, "Statutory Safeguards for Scheduled Tribes, Scheduled Castes"*, Bulletin of the Cultural Research Institute, *Vol. I,1962.*

82. *P. K. Bhowmick, "Report of* Scheduled *Areas, An Appraisal", in L. P. Vidyarthi (Ed.),* Tribal Development and Its Administration, op. cit., *p. 51.*

83. *E.* Chandran, Economic and Social Problems of India,*1990, p. 91.*

84. *K. V. Rao,* Parliamentary Democracy in India, *World Press, Calcutta, 1965, p. 215.*

85. *D. R.* Pratap, *"Approach to Tribal Development", in Buddhadeb Choudhury (Ed.),* Tribal Development in India: Problems and Prospects, op. cit., *p. 287.*

86. *Ibid.*

87. *B. M.* Pandey, *"Development Schemes as Factors of Change in Rural Areas"*, Journal of Social Research, *September1968, p. 49.*

88. *V. C. Kumaran, "Development of Tribal Areas", in S. G. Deogaonkar,* Problems of Development of Tribal Areas, *p. 40.*

89. Report of the Commissioner for Scheduled Castes and Scheduled Tribes (Twenty-fifth report),1977-78, Part-I, pp. 96-97.

90. Ibid., *pp. 1-2.*

91. *S. P. Sinha, "Tribal Development Administration– A Historical Overview", in L. P. Vidyarthi (Ed.),* Tribal Development and Its Administration, op. cit., *p.73.*

92. Approach to the Fifth Plan (1974-79), *Planning Commission,1973, p. 57.*

93. *Report of the Steering Group on Development of Backward Classes and Social Welfare for the Fifth Five Year Plan (Planning Commission),1973, p.10.*

94. *L. P. Vidyarthi, "Problems and Prospects of Tribal Development in India" in Buddhadeb Choudhury (Ed.),* Tribal Development in India: Problems and Prospects, op. cit., *p. 376-377.*

95. *Shilo Ao Committee Report, New* Delhi,*1969 (Mimeographed), p. 25.*

96. *B. D. Sharma,* Planning for Tribal Development, *Prachi Prakashan, New Delhi,1984, p. VII.*

97. *S. P. Sinha,* Tribal development Administration– A Historical Overview, op. cit., *p.75.*

98. The Planning Commission set up Taskforce on Development of Tribal Areas in1972; Working Group on Identification of Tribal Development Area and Less Developed Tribal Communities (Chairman Dr. L. P. Vidyarthi); Working Group on Legislative and Administrative Set up (Chairman Dr. B. K. Roy Burman); Working Group on General Problems and Area-wise Programmes on Infrastructure and Social services in Tribal Areas (Chairman Sri K. V. Natarajan); Personnel Policy in Tribal Areas (Chairman Sri R. N. Haldipur).

99. Report of the Commissioner for Scheduled Castes, Scheduled Tribes (Twenty-fifth report),1977-78, Part-I, p. 124.

100. *L. M. Prasad, "A Survey of Administration in Tribal Areas with Special Reference to Bihar", in L. P. Vidyarthi (Ed.),* Tribal Development and Its Administration, op. cit., *p. 229.*

101. Ibid., *p. 231.*

102. *K. Shanmuga Velayuthan, "A Sub-plan Approach to Tribal Development"*, The Indian Journal of Social Work, *Vol. XI, No.2, July 1979.*

103. *B. D. Sharma*, "Administration *for Tribal Development*", The Indian Journal of Public Administration, *Vol. XXIII, No.2, July-September 1977.*
104. "Preparation of Sub-Plans for Tribal Regions" (Guidelines Issued by the Planning Commission), Government of India, New Delhi,1975, pp.9-10.
105. *N. Patnaik and S. Bose*, op. cit., *p.7; L. M. Prasad*, op. cit., *p. 230.*
106. *Report of the* Commissioner *for Scheduled Castes and Scheduled Tribes (Twenty-fifth Report),1977-78, Part-I, p.124.*
107. *B. D. Sharma*, op. cit., *p. 229.*
108. Government of India, New Delhi, "Tentative Outline and Checkpoints for Examination of IIDPS", p. 53.
109. L. P. Vidyarthi, "Problems and Prospects of Tribal Development in India", in Buddhadeb Choudhury (Ed.), Tribal Development in India: Problems and Prospects, op. cit., p.380.
110. S. Sinha, "The Problem of Land Alienation of Tribals in and around Ranchi" (1955-56), Bihar Tribal Welfare Research Institute, Ranchi.
111. Government of India, New Delhi, "Report of the Working Group on Tribal Development During Sixth Plan",1980, pp.13-14 and 99-103.
112. Government of India, New Delhi, "Report of the Working Group on Development of Scheduled Tribes During Seventh Plan",1985-90, p.6.
113. Ibid., *pp.14-18.*
114. R. S. Mann, "Tribal Development–An Alternative Strategy", M. K. Raha and P. C. Coomar (Eds.), Tribal India, Problems and Development Prospect, Gian Publishing House, New Delhi,1989, p. 51.
115. Government of India, "Report of the Working Group on Development of Scheduled Tribes During Eighth Plan", 1992-97.
116. *Government of India, New Delhi,* Ninth Five Year Plan1997-2002, *Vol. II, pp. 366-376.*
117. Programme Evaluation Organisation, Planning Commission, Government of India, New Delhi, July1997, "Evaluation Report on Integrated Tribal Development Projects", p. 3.

3

PROFILE OF INDIVIDUAL TRIBES

In order to probe tribal problems thoroughly and deeply, it is necessary to take a broad view of the tribes, stressing their commonalities and even to go into the socio-economic background of each tribe. This chapter is intended to build up profiles of all individual tribes of the state of Orissa. There are also flashes of demographic profile and regional distribution of Scheduled Tribes of Orissa. This would help us to capture the various aspects of tribal problems in the state. The tribal communities of the state are concentrated in all the 30 districts of the state in different proportions.

Demographic Profile

Orissa is one of the fascinating ethnographic states of India. It has been the epitome of as many as 62 different tribal communities. 1. Next to Madhya Pradesh, the State has the largest tribal population in the country. It is said that, "Orissa can be proud of her wealth in the form of tribal people because she stands first among all the states in India by the size of the Scheduled Tribes population". 2. Barring the tribal states of north-eastern hill areas, it ranks first in terms of percentage of tribal population among the other states in the country.

According to the 1991 census, the total population of the state was 31,659,736, out of which the Scheduled Tribe population was 7,032,214 (Table 3.1)

Table 3.1
Tribal Population of Orissa (1991 Census)

Sl. No.	*Total Population / Tribal Population*	*Rural Urban Total*	*Persons*	*Male*	*Female*
1	*2*	*3*	*4*	*5*	*6*
1.	Total Population	R	27, 424, 753	13, 794, 955	13, 629, 798
		U	4, 234, 983	2, 269, 191	1, 965, 792
		T	31, 659, 736	16, 064, 146	15, 595, 590
2.	Tribal Population	R	6, 670, 506	3, 325, 42	3, 345, 064
		U	361, 708	187, 449	174, 259
		T	7, 032, 214	3, 512, 891	3, 519, 323

Source: Series– I, Paper–2 of 1992

Census of India–1991, Final Population,

Brief Analysis of Primary Census abstract.

Whereas the male and female population of Scheduled Tribes are equally distributed, there is slight difference between male and female population of the total population. It is also revealed from Table 3.1 that the concentration of Scheduled Tribe population in rural areas is more than in urban areas. The Scheduled Tribe population constitutes 22.21 per cent of the State's population. It was 22.43 per cent during 1981 census.

The Scheduled Tribe population of the State constitutes 10.84 per cent of India's tribal population. On the contrary, the total population of the State is 3.88 per cent of the total population of India. The figure was higher in 1981 census (Table 3.2).

Table 3.2
Percentage Distribution of India's Total, SC, ST and Non-SC/ST Population in Orissa

Sl. No.	*Population Category*	*1981 Census*		*1991 Census*	
		*India**	*Orissa*	*India**	*Orissa*
1	*2*	*3*	*4*	*5*	*6*
1.	Total	100	4. 00	100	3. 88
2.	Scheduled Castes	100	3. 71	100	3. 76
3.	Scheduled Tribes	100	11. 46	100	10. 84
4.	Non-SC/ST	100	3. 30	100	3. 17

* Excludes Assam and Jammu and Kashmir.

Source: Series– I, Paper–2 of 1992

Census of India–1991, Final Population,

Brief Analysis of Primary Census abstract.

The percentage distribution of India's Scheduled Tribe population in Orissa was 11.46 per cent during 1981, which declined to 10.84 per cent during 1991. The distribution of Scheduled Tribe population in different districts of the State shows an uneven picture. It is not in consonance with the general population of the State.

A district-wise divide of tribal population in the State gives us an insight into the distribution pattern. All the census figures show that highest concentration of the tribals are noticed in the districts of Mayurbhanj, Koraput, Sundargarh, Malkangiri, Rayagada, etc. On the other hand, the districts of Puri, Cuttack, Kendrapara and Jagatsinghpur show low concentration of tribal population (Table 3.3).

Table 3.3
District-wise Percentage of Scheduled Tribe Population: 1971, 1981 and 1991 Census

Sl. No.	*District*	*Percentage of Scheduled Tribes to total population*		
		1971	*1981*	*1991*
1.	Balasore	7. 06	6. 84	10. 57
2.	Bolangir	19. 72	19. 12	22. 06
3.	Cuttack	2. 89	3. 13	3. 49
4.	Dhenkanal	12. 91	12. 96	12. 68
5.	Ganjam	9. 98	9. 48	2. 93
6.	Kalahandi	29. 26	31. 28	28. 88
7.	Keonjhar	46. 96	44. 82	44. 52
8.	Koraput	56. 34	55. 22	50. 67
9.	Mayurbhanj	58. 56	57. 67	57. 87
10.	Phulbani	40. 31	38. 94	51. 51
11.	Puri	3. 70	3. 45	0. 27
12.	Sambalpur	28. 13	27. 21	35. 08
13.	Sundargarh	53. 40	51. 26	50. 74
14.	Angul			11. 68
15.	Baragarh			19. 56
16.	Bhadrak			1. 69
17.	Boudh			12. 92
18.	Deogarh			33. 31
19.	Gajapati			47. 88
20.	Jagatsinghpur			0. 61
21.	Jajpur			7. 40
22.	Jharsuguda			31. 88
23.	Kendrapara			0. 40
24.	Khurda			5. 14
25.	Malkangiri			58. 36
26.	Nawapara			35. 95
27.	Nayagarh			5. 96
28.	Nowrangpur			55. 27
29.	Rayagada			56. 04
30.	Sonepur			9. 50
		23. 11	22. 43	22. 21

Source: Census of India, 1971, 1981 and 1991.

Note: The reorganisation of districts of Orissa increased the number from 13 to 30 during 1991 Census. Therefore, the decreasing figures of 1991 census are not due to a decreasing trend, but because of the smaller size of the districts.

During the decade 1981-91, when the total population increased by 20.06 per cent, the Scheduled Tribe population registered an increase of only 18.89 per cent. The sex ratio of total population during 1981 census was 981, while it was 1012 in case of Scheduled Tribe people. During the 1991 Census the figures were 971 and 1002 respectively.

The density of total population of Orissa during 1991 Census is 203 persons per square kilometre and for Scheduled Tribes it is four persons per square kilometre. The density of total population and Scheduled Tribe population per square kilometre during 1991 Census is indicted in Appendix– IV.

Functional Distribution and Occupational Structure

The occupational structure of any region denotes the economically active population involved in various economic activities. The classification of working population among the Scheduled Tribes shows that more than half of their strength is non-workers. During 1981 Census, the percentage of non-workers among them is 50.57 as compared to 61.99 per cent for the whole state. The main workers who were engaged in some economic activity over a period of six months or more in a year constitute 39.78 per cent as against the State figure of 32.75 per cent. The marginal workers, who were engaged less than six months in a year, constitute 9.64 per cent as compared to 5.26 per cent for the whole state. Among the Scheduled Tribes, out of the total main workers, cultivators and agricultural labourers together constitute 88.36 per cent in comparison to 74.69 per cent for the whole state. Scheduled Tribe workers engaged in household industry, manufacturing, processing, servicing and repairing, etc. constitute 1.42 per cent and the rest 10.12 per cent are other workers.

Regional Distribution of Tribes

Broadly, there are four distinct geophysical zones in which the tribes of Orissa have been distributed in uneven proportions.

The Northern Plateau

Sundargarh, Mayurbhanj, Keonjhar, Bamra and Kuchinda area of Sambalpur, the interior plains of Balasore and Pallahara region of Dhenkanal districts come under the Northern Plateau. As many as 58 tribal groups totalling about 2 million people inhabit in this zone. The ITDAs, which are included in this zone, are Sundargarh, Panposh and Bonai, Baripada, Karanjia, Udala and Rairangpur, Keonjhar and Champua and Kuchinda. The Pallahara Paudi Bhuinya Development Project is also included in this zone.

The Central Tribal Land

This zone covers the whole of the Brahmani and the Mundari basins. There are as many as 45 tribal groups in this region. The population of two major tribes in this zone– the Gond and the Saora–constitute about one lakh each.

The Eastern Ghat Region

The Peninsular Plateaus are bordered on the east by the Eastern Ghats, a tectonic range out by many rivers into discontinuous blocks of mountains. Broadly, it is divided into five sections.

The Northern Section starts from Nilgiri and stretches up to Boud border rising to a height of 2239 feet. The number of tribes inhabiting this zone comes to about 39. The Khond and the Sabar are most numerous. This zone includes the Nilgiri ITDA. The Central Section of the Eastern Ghats cover Boud, Baliguda, G. Udayagiri areas and the hills of this section are very high ranging in height from 1000 feet to 4000 feet. There are 29 tribal groups inhabiting this section. The Khond population constitutes a majority of the population. This zone can be called the Khond zone. It includes Phulbani and Baliguda ITDAs. The Rayagada Section comprises Parlakhemundi and Rayagada hill areas with an elevation of 1000 feet. These hill areas have been inhabited by as many as 43 tribal communities. The Khond and the Saora are the most numerous. This section includes Parlekhemundi, Rayagada and Gunupur ITDAs. The South-Eastern Section covers the areas of Koraput, Pottangi, Jeypore, Nowrangpur and Malkangiri. Many important and primitive tribes are found in this area. The Koya and the Bhuinya with relatively higher population live in the Malkangiri districts. The extinctive and primitive Bonda Paraja inhabit in this region. The Koraput, Nowrangpur and Malkangiri ITDAs come under this section. The South-Western Section comprises the Plain and the Dongar of Kalahandi district. The Dongar portion includes Lanjigarh and Thuamul-Rampur areas inhabited mostly by the Khonds who are very primitive.46 tribal communities live in this section. This section includes Thuamul-Rampur ITDA.

Coastal Region

This region inhabits a total of 51 tribes. The Saora, Sabar, Santal, Khond, Bhumij, Kolha and the Munda are the numerous tribes.

Socio-Economic Lives of Tribal Communities

The description that follows gives a detailed account of socio-economic lives of all 62 different tribal communities.

1. Bagata

The Bagatas are primarily a fishing community. Some of them are hill cultivators in the agency tracts of Vizagapatam. They are considered as an offshoot of Kapus caste. The head of a single village is called a Padal, the Padal being the name of an exogamous sept of the Kapus. Census Report 1871 states, "In the low country, the Bhaktas consider themselves to take the rank of soldiery and rather disdain the occupation of ryots (cultivators)". In a note to the Bagatas, Mr. C. Hayavadana Rao writes, "the Bagatas are divided into a number of exogamous septs or *intiperulu*". Girls are married either before or after attaining puberty. Cross-cousin marriage is almost obligatory.[1] The system is called 'menarikam'. Bride price is known as "Voli". The bride is in the form of jewellery by the groom's parents as substitute for the bride price.

2. Baiga

The total population of this tribe is 188. They are very small in number compared to other tribes of Orissa. Shifting cultivation is practised by them. They live on wild fruits, roots and animal meat. They are darkish in complexion. They have no permanent homes as they move from place to place looking for fresh cultivable lands. The Baigas of the plains work as labourers. They are great magicians.[2]

3. Banjar

The total population of this tribe is 10925. Banjaris are a small tribe mainly found in the districts of Kalahandi, Koraput and Sambalpur.[3] Russel and Hiralal describe the tribe as having migrated from Rajputana and its surrounding places. They also deduce from the word Bangara, which is a derivation from the Sanskrit word, Banijya Kara, a merchant. Formerly, they were migratory in their habit and sold commodities in various places moving in large groups. History supports the fact that the Banjari were employed by the Hindu as well as Muslim kings to carry necessities for the soldiers to the war front. In course of time, they have migrated to different places in Orissa. As described by Hiralal and Russel, the two parties of a marriage meet at a particular place where bride price is fixed. The groom goes to the bride's house to stay for few days after the negotiation. Widow marriage is prevalent. When a man dies, the widow is taken either by the elder or younger brother of the deceased. The deities worshipped by the Banjaris are Banjaridevi, Mithu, Bhukia, and Siva Bhaia. Cattle worshipping is prevalent among the Banjari as they provide the means of transportation.

4. Bathudi

Bathudis are said to be a branch of Bhuiyan tribe. According to Russel, the 'Bathurias' form an inferior subsection of the Bhuiyans and are looked down upon because of having taken food from other low caste. Oriya is the mother tongue of the Bathudis. Most of the families possess more than one living room, built around a rectangular courtyard. Houses are built either in a linear or in a scattered fashion. Most of them own Kachha houses with mud walls and straw thatched or local tile thatched roof. Sometimes, walls are made of wooden planks planted up right and plastered with mud.

Marriage among the Bathudi is an expensive affair when compared with their economic condition. Previously, there were marriages by capture and marriages by service. But now these are rarely practised. Widow remarriage is allowed. Divorce with the approval of the village council is prevalent. The religious beliefs and practices of Bathudis are similar to the Hindus of the neighbouring villages. The main occupation of the Bathudis is settled agriculture. Amount of land owned by most of the families is not sufficient to meet their requirements. There are landless Bathudis who solely depend on wage earning or petty business. Consequently, most of them work as part time labourers and do petty rice business. They grow paddy and other cash crops such as pulses, sugar, potato, groundnuts, etc. Hunting and fishing are no more practised as gainful economic pursuits.[4]

Rice is their staple food. Some green leaves or vegetables constitute side items. They prepare cakes from rice flour. Alcoholic drinks such as Mohua liquor and rice beer are generally avoided. At present, they have a status of a clean caste in the caste hierarchy of the Hindu society.

5. Bhottara

The Bhottaras are one of the efficient agricultural communities of Orissa. It is believed that they are immigrants from Bastar district in Madhya Pradesh. They speak a corrupt form of Oriya language. Nuclear families are more in number than the extended ones among them. They live in heterogeneous villages along with other neighbours like Omanatya, Dom, Rona, etc. The village is a unit from socio-political point of view. The most significant and elaborate event in the life of the Bhottaras is their marriage ceremony. They follow both adult and infant marriage systems. Widow remarriage is permitted. Marriage by arrangement and by capture are recognised in the society. The former seems to be honoured and widely prevalent. Polygyny is adopted if the wife is found to be barren. Bhottaras have a great belief in spirits, gods and goddesses. Budhi Thakurani, Bharabi, Budhi Pardesi, Basumata, Bana Durga and Sun are a few of their deities. They are propitiated during the festivals of Chaitro Parb, Akhitrutiya, Srabana Ambasya, Nuakhia, Dasahara, Diwali, Punia and Suriya Jatra. The Bhottaras are good agriculturists.[5] They know wet cultivation and do not practise shifting cultivation as a mode of their occupation. They work as wage earners when there is no work in the fields. A few of them also serve in firm and Government institutions. They produce all sorts of vegetables in their land. Paddy, sugarcane, pulses, tobacco are the main crops which they harvest.

6. Bhuiyan

The term Bhuiyan is derived from the Sanskrit word 'Bhumi', meaning land. They consider themselves as the children and the owners of the land and hence are known as Bhuiyans. The Bhuiyans of Orissa speak Oriya and they have no other tribal language of their own. The Bhuiyans adopt both child and adult marriage. Marriage among them is endogamous so far as the main divisions are concerned, but exogamous so far as Kutumbs are concerned. Widow marriage is prevalent in their society. The Bhuiyans perform public feasts and festivals all the year round so as to ensure safety and prosperity in their seasonal occupations. They are very fond of dance and music. The sources of living of the Pauris are food gathering, hunting and shifting cultivation.[6] They collect edible roots, fruits and worms (Kai) from the nearby streams. As agriculturists, they practise shifting cultivation. Wet cultivation of rice and terracing the field are gradually adopted. The plain Bhuiyans are mostly settled agriculturists. Rice is their staple food and are considered superior to all other types.

7. Bhumia

The Bhumias are mostly concentrated in Nowrangpur district. They are divided into totemistic units or clans. In their community the clan organisation is a simple one. In every village Naik is the accepted leader. He is ordinarily the richest man possessing land and cattle in opulence. Bhat Naik is second in the hierarchy. Both these offices are ordinarily hereditary.

The houses in a Bhumia village are arranged in two rows flanking the principal village road. In large villages like Batia, houses are scattered about in all directions. Arranged and forced marriages are the practices among the Bhumias. Arranged marriages are fixed by the parents of the boy and girl. When the boy is incapable of paying any bride price, he forcibly takes the girl to his house. Bride price in the shape of a fowl and rice is paid. In addition to agriculture work, the Bhumiyas prepare implements like Kula and Duti. From various kinds of fibres like jute, sabai and siali, they weave a large net for catching fish and Kudarjal for entrapping rabbit. From Siali leaves they prepare Talari, which is a country umbrella. They prepare other agricultural implements. Since, the Bhumias are mainly agriculturists, they do not practise Podu (upland) cultivation. They grow grams, oilseeds, etc.

8. Bhumij

The Bhumij, writes Risley, are nothing more than a branch of the Mundas who have spread to eastward and migrated with the Hindus and thus for the most part severed their connections with the parent tribe. In Mayurbhanj, Munda is another name for Bhumij. The tribe has got its aboriginal tongue but they now speak both Oriya and Bhumij at home and outside. They practice both child and adult marriage and thus, there is no fixed age for marriage. The most common type of acquiring a bride is through negotiation and by payment of bride price. Divorce is allowed and divorced women can remarry.

A Bhumij house is rectangular in size. Ordinarily, verandahs are built in the front. The houses with mud walls have generally straw or wild grass thatched root. Most of them own more than one room with opening to the courtyard. As regards, dress and ornament, they follow their Hindu neighbours.

The Bhumijs are agriculturists. Their main occupation is settled cultivation supplemented by wage earning, collection of jungle products and hunting. After harvest when they do not have openings for wage earning, the Bhumij men go to work in the mining quarries and in tea gardens of Assam. They stay there for a period of three to four months and come back when the agricultural operation is started for the next crop. They grow only one crop of paddy in a year. In addition to this, they grow *rabi* crops such as oilseeds, pulses in their uplands and vegetables in the kitchen garden. As land holding is not sufficient for livelihood for most of the families, they work as part time labourer for the neighbouring cultivators when agricultural operation is in swing. Hunting as a gainful economic pursuit has been given up due to depletion of forest and restrictions imposed by the government. Rice is their staple food and is taken throughout the year. They take rice beer and Mohua liquor like the neighbouring tribes.

9. Bhunjia

Bhunjias are a small tribe. According to R. V. Russel and R. B. Hiralal, "the term *Bhunjia* may perhaps signifies one who lives on the soil, from Bhum the earth and Jia, 'depended on'. The word *Binjia*, a synonym for Bhinjhwar, is similarly a corruption of Bewar Jia, and means one who is dependent on dahia or patch of cultivation.

The Bhunjias eat pork, but abstain from beef and the flesh of the monkeys. Rice is their staple food. In spite of their strict observance of many rites for virtual parity, they rank lower in status than the Gonds. They have their own method of curing and they hardly go to Government dispensary for medicine. The most popular method of curing disease is by branding the skin with a hot iron. The exogamous division of the Bhunjias are derived from those of the Gonds. The Choukathias marry off their daughters before puberty. The marriage takes place in the bridegroom's village. The function is conducted by a priest known as Dinwari. Widow marriage and divorce are permitted; but a husband would often try to avoid it.

Mata, the deity for cholera and small pox is worshipped every year in the month of *Chaitra* (March) and is offered a goat and coconut, liquidation of debt is considered to be a primary obligation by the Bhunjias and they worship the Sun for gratitude by offering coconut. The Bhunjias are cultivators.[7] They are not an advanced community in the sense that majority of them are illiterate.

10. Binjhal

The Binjhals or Binjhwars, a Dravidian tribe, are advanced and resemble to the local non-tribals. They live amidst non-tribals. R. V. Russell and Rai Bahadur Hiralal have described them as "a comparatively civilised Dravidian tribe" who are "an offshoot of the primitive Baiga tribe". Etymologically Binjhal (Bin and Jhal) means without sweating. Among the Binjhals exogamy is the general rule. Marriage is allowed between a boy and a girl having blood relationship. The girls marry after they attain puberty. Child marriage is not followed.

The Binjhals worship the God and Goddess of Hindus, besides, their own deities. *Bindhy Basini* is their principal Goddess. Rice is the staple food of the Binjhals. Generally, they take food twice a day. Their meal consists of rice, vegetables and occasionally meat or fish. Rice beer is the important drink of the Binjhals.

The economy of Binjhals is based on agriculture. Majority of them are agriculturists. The landless Binjhals are labourers. Day labour is called *mulia* and those who work on annual contract basis are called *Halia* or *Goti*. Paddy is the major crop of Binjhals. They also grow pulses, summer and winter vegetables. The economic condition of the Binjhals is not as poor as that of the jungle tribes whose economy is based on hunting or crude type of agriculture. The Binjhals have adopted advanced type of agriculture. They are one of the advanced and assimilated tribes of Orissa.

11. Binjhia

The Binjhias migrated from Nagpur region many generations ago. They came in search of cultivable land and finally settled in this region. The concentration of the Binjhias are found in the villages lying in the northern region of Sundargarh district. They inhabit the areas of Bolangir and Keonjhar districts. The language they speak is known as Jaspuri, a crude type of Hindi. They have, in course of time, incorporated many Oriya words into their language. They too speak Oriya and Hindi.

The festivals observed by them are Hindu festivals. They are *Rath Jatra, Gamha Purnima, Dashara, Holi* and *Dipavali*. Agriculture constitutes to be the basic economy of the Binjhias. They are settled cultivators.[8] The Binjhias depend on the cultivation of Gurji, Paddy, Maize and Ragi, pulses like Kolath, Rahad and Mung, Biri, Gangei, and oilseeds like Til and Rasi. They also grow vegetables like brinjal, tomato and chillies.

12. Birhor

The Birhors are one of the earliest nomadic tribes in India. As the very name implies, they are the people belonging to the forests. They not only belong to the forests but are in close association with the basic features of the forests and the connected environments from time immemorial.[9] The Birhors fall to the category of hunting and gathering group. Instead of being settled up in a particular place permanently, the Birhors wander from place to place within a circumscribed area and, therefore, known as a nomadic tribe.[10]

It may be noted that the local people used to call the Birhors in different ways. In the district of Kalahandi and Sundargarh they are named as Mankidi whereas in Mayurbhanj and Sambalpur districts they go by the name of Mankirdia. In fact, both the Mankirdia and Mankidi are one and the same and both types are none but the Birhors. The reason for calling the Birhors as Mankidi or Mankirdia is that they are experts and skilled in catching monkeys. Birhor means people (Hor) of the forest (Bir). They are dark skinned, short-statured, longheaded, wavy-haired and broad-nosed people.

There are two types of Birhors, the Uthals i. e., nomadic and the Jagi i.e., settled Birhors. These nomadic or mobile Birhors move from one place to another in different groups in a specified area within the state.

The calanderical year of the Birhor centres round three seasons i.e., rainy season, winter season and summer season. Their movement from place to place is more frequent in summer than in other seasons.[12] The frequent change of settlements is primarily responsible for search of livelihood. Some groups of Birhors change their place of abode frequently, that indicates the extent of availability of forest products in different areas. Moreover, the destruction of the forest by some other tribal communities who practice shifting cultivation and by non-tribal people who gather fuel wood from the forest make it difficult for the Birhors to earn their livelihood.

The primary occupation of the Birhors is preparing ropes from the bark of siali creepers. In addition to this, the Birhors make small baskets (Tupa) out of the siali barks. On an average a Birhor turns out finished products of bark worth Rs.10/- to Rs.12/- per day.

The Birhors are skilled monkey catchers. They use nets made of siali creepers for catching monkeys and consume the flesh of the monkeys. The skin is sold to the local scheduled caste people. Although the Birhors tap different sources for their livelihood, they run deficit in their food supply many a times. During scarce period they eat mango kernels, which are preserved at home for use in difficult times. The staple food of the Birhors is rice. With the sale proceeds of ropes and forest produce, they buy their weekly requirements of rice and other things from the market. They also buy corn and minor millets in addition to cooked rice. They collect various types of green leaves and mushrooms, fruits such as 'Kendu', palm and mango from the forest for their consumption. While collecting barks from the forest, they dig out roots, fibres and collect honey, which supplements their principal cereal diet.[13]

13. Bonda

In the district of Koraput, on the high hills to the northwest of the river Machkund lives the wildest, rudest and possibly the most interesting tribe known as 'Bonda' or naked people. The scanty dress of Bonda women and homicide tendency of Bonda males have made them most fascinating and thus, they stand in sharp contrast from other tribes of Orissa. They concentrate on or near the high hills, named after the tribe as Bonda hills. Though few in number, the tribe has successfully retained the distinctive features of its culture, chiefly on account of its geographical isolation and more perhaps due to its stubborn and independent spirit. The Bondas call themselves 'Remo' and speak a very difficult Austro-Asiatic language belonging to Mundari group. The Bonda houses are individual huts with some enclosure either in its front or around it. The walls are of mud mixed with straw or these are plast ed bamboo. The roof is supported by a number of wooden pillars and is thatched with grass. The selection of spouses is left completely to the individual choices. Once such selection is made, the consent of parents are subsequently obtained and marriage rite is performed. Widow marriage is permitted in the Bonda society. The Bonda domestic life is affected by two usual factors. The first is that the wife is often older than the husband. Older girls prefer to marry younger boys who would earn for them when they grow old. Secondly, the husbands are found at times intriguity with younger brother's wife. They are extremely aggressive. Age-old isolation, poverty, intoxication and fear of sorcery are the chief reasons of their aggressiveness.

Bondas are mainly agriculturists. Gruel of ragi and rice are the chief food of the tribe. They collect wild vegetables, bamboo shoot, mushrooms, etc. They keep cattle, goats, pig and poultry. They drink enormous quantity of wine called salap, the juice of Sago palms. The Bondas are expert cultivators. The irrigated and terraced paddy fields on the high hills prove their skill in rice cultivation. They have their own hill cleanings where they practise Podu. According to customary practices, these clearings become individual property and each household owns a number of sites on the hillsides, which are cultivated in rotation. In spite of their primitiveness and poverty, the Bondas enjoy a high degree of economic self-sufficiency. The geographic isolation has been a blessing in disguise as the Bondas are less exposed to exploitation by outsiders. Very rarely they borrow money from outsiders. The modern civilisation has not changed them very much. They maintain their primitive custom and tradition.[14]

14. Chenchu

This is an important South Indian tribe. Their population in Orissa is only 39 as per 1981 census. They are semi-nomadic food gathering tribe of Orissa. They live exclusively under tree in small conical or oblong huts. Their huts are haphazardly scattered and reconnected by a network of footpaths.

15. Dal

The Dal constitute a small tribe and are mostly found in the Southern and Western region of Bolangir district.[15] Arranged marriage is the most commonly prevalent form of marriage among the Dals. In choosing a bride, father's sister's daughter and mother's brother's daughter are preferred to. A person can marry the 'Kanya' or wife of a person belonging to his own clan if the person dies.

Dals cultivate ragi and Kodua more than paddy and Gurji. Among the pulses they grow are Kolath, Munga, Biri and oilseeds like Rasi and Til. Maize and Khed Jandre (millet type) are also grown. Vegetables like brinjal, tomato and chillies are grown in the kitchen gardens. Tobacco is cultivated by almost all. Apart from these each Dal owns a number of Mahul trees. Mahul is collected and stored by each family on which they depend for their food. Mostly Mahul is exchanged for Ragi and Kondu with the contractors who bread liquor in the neighbourhood. The Kultas, Bhuitiyas and Marwaries also exploit by advancing loans before harvest. The Dals sell their products at a nominal rate as a precondition of getting loan. They have separate sacred houses for the Gods and Goddesses. They follow the Hindus in worship.

16. Desua Bhumij

The Desi or Desua Bhumij are also known as Sing Bhumia. Bhumij constitute a section of the Bhumij tribe of Munda origin. They have totally forgotten their aboriginal language and have adopted Oriya as their mother tongue. Arranged marriage is the general rule. But there are also marriages by capture and marriage by intrusion prevalent among them. They celebrate every festival and the marriage ceremonies with dance and music. Girls in a row dance while the boys play on changu.

The Bhumij have taken to wage earning as the main source of income. Most of them are landless and only a few families have got land which is not sufficient to meet their requirements. Almost all of them work as labourers for the neighbouring cultivators. Children are employed to tend cattle. The depleted forest in the neighbouring area does not provide much scope for collecting green leaves, roots and fruits as in the past. With much difficulty, they can bring fuel and Sal leaves, for sale. In leisure time, they manufacture bricks. During summer, a few Bhumij men go to work in the tea gardens of Assam or in Calcutta or in the Mining Quarries in Keonjhar. Although rice is their staple food, they hardly get full meals throughout the year. They eat beef, pork, fowl, white ant, mouse, termites and other unclean food. Rice-beer and Mohua liquor are taken too.

17. Dharua

Dharuas or *Dharua* Gonds are one of the oldest tribes of Orissa. According to Risley, "They are one of the several steps of the Gonds and are otherwise known as Naiks".[16] He is of the opinion that the Dharus are the ordinary Gonds, who in most of the district form an endogamous group. According to Russel, the word Dharua may be derived from "*Dhur*" (dust); that is the common people and they are inferior to Raj Gonda.

Marriage is an important social obligation. There is no prescribed age for the marriage for both the sexes except that they should marry as early as possible. However, the practice of both child and adult marriages are found among the Dharuas. The widows and widowers are allowed to marry again without any function. The Dharuas worship the Gods associated with their clans. Their supreme Gods are known as *Bar Deo* and *Dhulla Deo*. In olden days the Dharuas were mostly agriculturists, though some of them were employed in military service maintained by the native Rajas. In course of time, a great change has taken place in their economic life. Now, besides being agriculturists, they are found in different wage-earning jobs.

18. Didayi

The Didayi are a primitive hill tribe of the district of Koraput inhabiting the 4,000 feet plateau of the Eastern Ghat range. They are described as a wild tribe by V. Elwin (1950) and as the stratum of primitive semi-nomadic shifting cultivators by C. Harmendor (1995). They are divided into two groups i.e., the hill and the plain Didayi. The people living the hilltops have social ties with the plains people who, to a considerable extent, have been influenced by the Telugu-speaking people living close to them.

The houses in hill as well as plain villages lie scattered all over and no regular street is found. The houses are built in an individualistic manner and the villagers do not share a common roof like the Kandhas.

Generally, three forms of marriages are prevalent in the Didayi society. They are *Bihay* or marriage by negotiation, *Gube* or marriage by capture and *Posiamundi* in which the girl forcibly enters the groom's house and enters into sexual relationship with him. Marriage by negotiation is very elaborate and expensive and is generally avoided. Preference is given to cross cousin marriage. The Hill Didayi practice shifting cultivation whereas the plain people have adopted settled agriculture. Both the groups cultivate ragi and susan extensively, which is their staple food. The Didayis of the plains do not have sufficient virgin forest for practising shifting cultivation. They depend on paddy and ragi. The hill and plain Didayis collect a variety of roots and fruits during the entire year to supplement their food. The Didayis are voraciously addicted to juice or salap tree which is available in abundance in the forests. Thus, the hill Didayis live on subsistence level whereas the plain Didayis are economically better off having scope for wet cultivation as well as for raising various types of cash crops like oilseeds and pulses.

19. Gadaba

The Gadabas are one of the early settlers of this country and trace their origin to the time of Ramayan. It is said that their original home was Godavari from where they have derived their name Gadaba. They have their own language known as Gutab or Gadaba language. A few of them living near the towns and working as labourers in firms can speak Oriya. The Gadabas are not a migratory folk. They live permanently in villages situated on inaccessible mountain areas.[17]

Marriage takes place after the attainment of puberty. The usual age of marriage is 19–21 years for boys and 15–18 years for girls. The cross-cousin marriage is usually preferred to. The marriage of a widow is permitted. Polygyny is also in vogue. The main source of their livelihood is cultivation. Since cultivation provides food and work to the members of his family, an Ollar Gadaba considers it more stable, dependable and regular than any other occupation.[18] The Gadabas practise both shifting and wet cultivation. Those who live in plain adopt some amount of shifting cultivation in a localised area. Each family divides its holding for shifting cultivation in two parts and cultivates a part, when the other remains barren. The places are alternated once in every three years. The chief agricultural products are paddy, ragi, suan, maize, several types of grams, etc. Their staple food is ragi. Rice is only a supplementary food. Since their production is insufficient they resort to food collection in the jungles. Mango Kernel, edible roots, etc. support them for two months in a year.

20. Gandia

This tribe has a total population of 2263 according to the 1981 census. They form a section of the Koya tribe.

21. Ghara

Their total population in the state is only 616 according to 1981 census. They are regarded as a part of the Gond tribe.

22. Gond

The Gonda of Kalahandi, Koraput and Phulbani may be taken to belong to the primitive section whereas the rest can be taken to belong to the acculturated section. The acculturated Gonds live in villages inhabited by other castes and tribes. They especially live along with Kondh, Bhuyan and Gour. The primitive Gonds live in homogeneous villages. Marriage is strictly forbidden within the same clan and brother-clans. Cross-cousin marriage, marriage by service and regular marriages arranged by the parents are commonly practised. Gonds are tillers of the soil. Their main occupation is agriculture supplemented by the collection of jungle products, hunting and shifting cultivation (only among the primitive Gonds of Koraput). They grow rice, millet, maize, mustard and a few varieties of pulses. They also grow tobacco and vegetables. The Hindu Gonds have developed a commercial sense and do petty business in the local markets. Their staple food is rice, gruel of millet and maize. The Hindu Gonds abstain from eating beef, pork and other unclean foods and drinking of rice-beer or wine. But among the primitive Gonds every householder breeds a large number of goats, pigs, and poultry for meat. They drink rice beer and alcoholic drinks. The Hinduised Gonds who claim themselves to be Kshatriya, have styled themselves as Hindus by copying many Hindu customs and practices.[19] The Gonds are honest and trustworthy people. If a Gond dies without clearing his debt, his son would not rest till he repays his father's debt.

23. Ho

The Hos form a major group among the Orissan tribes. The word 'Ho' has probably been derived from the word Horo, which in their language means man. Among the Hos, there are various ways of acquiring a mate. The principal among them are Andi, Diku Andi, Oportipi, Rajikhusi and Anadar. In the first two types of marriages, ceremony plays an important role. Andi is their traditional form whereas Diku Andi is borrowed from the Hindus. Marriage by capture is known as Oportipi. The Rajikhusi type of marriage is done by mutual consent without any ceremony or bride price whereas Anadar is marriage by intrusion. Both the joint and nuclear types of families are found in the Ho society. The Hos are purely agricultural people. The people of this community are engaged in agricultural operations during rainy season. The womenfolk take part in all agricultural pursuits except ploughing. The Hos use cows and oxen as drawing animals. They do not take the milk of the cows. Buffalos are also preferred to plough land. Paddy, maize, and ragi are the main crops they cultivate in the hill slopes. Besides these, they grow vegetables like brinjals, gourds, etc. in their kitchen gardens. Hunting and collection of edible roots and tubers are a part and parcel of their economy. Rice is their staple food. The females collect the roots, tubers, green leaves, mushrooms from the jungle. The Hos go for wage earning to earn their livelihood.

They prefer to wage in terms of kind rather than wage in money terms. Every Ho village is a social as well as a political unit. The headman is the supreme controller of the village. They are gradually developing in all aspects of life and are coming forward to associate themselves with the national endeavour for progress and prosperity.

24. Holva

The Holvas of Orissa are an agricultural community. They trace their caste name from the term 'holo' means a plough.[20] They claim Bastar district in Madhya Pradesh to be their original home from where they have migrated to Orissa. They speak Oriya with outsiders but their own dialect is peculiar to them. Family is nuclear. Extended and joint families are seen to a certain extent. The village acts as a socio-political unit for all practical purposes. Girls are usually married off at the age of 10 or 12 before they attain puberty. In case they fail to arrange a bridegroom, they perform the pseudo marriage with a Mahua tree. They adopt two forms of wedding known as 'Small and Large'. The former being held at the bridegroom's place with less expenditure and is much cheaper than the latter which is held at bride's place. Marriage is arranged through a mediator called Mahalia. The small wedding is more popular among the Holvas. The widow and divorced woman can remarry by the simple procedure of marking vermilion on her head. Their main occupation is agriculture. They cultivate the land as owner and on share basis. Many of them remain as labourers with the people who own land. Shifting cultivation is almost given up. The main produces are paddy, suan, ragi, maize, pulses and different types of gram. Sugarcane and tobacco are also cultivated. They collect jungle products. They take resort to hunting as leisure activity. Fishing is also practised occasionally. A few have accepted jobs in Government and under different firms. They have started sending their boys and girls to the schools for education. They are economically, educationally and socially better off than other tribals.

25. Jatapu

The name Jatapu is popularly believed to be an abbreviated form of Kondajatapu Doralu or Lords of the Kond caste. They appear to be a recent offshoot of Khonds. Marriages are performed generally after the marrying partners become adults; but child marriage is not completely absent. Various forms of marriage like marriage by arrangement, by capture, by service, by mutual consent, and by selection and negotiation from 'Dhangda Bass' are prevalent among the Jatapus. Remarriages are approved by the society. Divorce is permitted and divorcees are allowed to remarry. The Jatapus are mainly agriculturists but the poorer sections earn their bread by wage earning or being employed as labourers. Rice and gruel constitute the staple food of the Jatapus.

26. Juang

Among the aboriginal tribes found in the state of Orissa, the Juangs form a major group in the district of Keonjhar and Dhenkanal. The Juangs were considered 'most developed' by the Scheduled Areas and Scheduled Tribes Commission of 1961 and were specified as 'backward' by the study team on tribal development programme of 1969. The family, which is the basic unit of the social organisation, is mostly of nuclear type. There are few joint families in the Juang society. The Juangs principally observe festivals like Amba Nuakhia, Dhana Nuakhia and Magha Parab. They give high priority to music and dancing.[21] Primarily the Juangs are agricultural people. They practise two types of cultivation: Jhum or shifting cultivation and wetland cultivation.[22] In most areas of the district of Dhenkanal, the Juangs have switched over to Toila land cultivation in the highlands and wetland cultivation in low lands. The studies in Dhenkanal show that the Juangs have given up shifting cultivation long ago and in its place has been taken up by permanent cultivation. In addition to agriculture, food gathering occupies a prominent place in Juang economy. They collect roots and tubers, green leaves, mushrooms from the jungles to supplement their diet. Moreover, they collect minor forest products like honey, wood leaves and sell them in the villages and towns and earn money for their subsistence. Very few people among the Juangs possess good cultivable land. The rest of the population are landless and earn their livelihood by earning daily wages and selling fuel and other minor forest products in the market. The point, however, remains that when fast changes are taking place in the Juang community, their old network of relationship in economic activities and marital and religious ceremonies remains and is being strengthened wherever it is being weakened.[23] The ethnic unity is strengthened by social solidarity movement which is being launched by the progressive section of this community and it is this unity which gives the Juangs an assurance of security.

27. Kandha Gouda

Their number in Orissa is 15,190 as per the 1981 census and they are known to be the crossbreed of Kandha tribe.

28. Kawar

In Orissa the Kawars are found in all the districts, but found in large numbers in Sundargarh, Sambalpur and Kalahandi. Marriage within the same sept is not allowed. The Kawaras practise adult marriage. A man can marry his wife's younger sister but marriage with wife's elder sister is prohibited. Marriage by negotiation is common among Kawars. The proposal for a match always comes from the boy's father. The boy's party have to pay the bride price known as 'Sule'. Widow remarriage is permitted except in the Tanwar sub-caste. The younger brother of the deceased has the right to keep her. If the widow intends to marry, she looses her right to property. Neither it involves any ceremony nor does any bride price is paid. Polygamy is permitted, but is not common. Divorce is permitted for serious disagreements or bad conduct on the part of the wife.

Kawars have given up their traditional occupation of military service and they are now cultivators and labourers.[24] Routias weave ropes and make sleeping cots, but the other Kawars consider such work to be degrading. Hunting in the forest is carried out at times. Collection of edible roots and forest product supplement their food and economy.

29. Kharia

The tribe is broadly divided into three divisions, viz.- the Pahari or hill Kharia or Erenga Kharia, the Dhelki Kharia and Dudh Kharia. Besides, there are a few more divisions such as Munda Kharia, Oraon Kharia, Berga Kharia and Setera Kharia; but these are minor sections. The three divisions represent the three grades of primitive culture. The hill Kharia depends mainly on food gathering.[25] They collect honey, skin, cotton, lac, the edible herbs and tubers and other minor forest products. The Dhelki Kharias have adopted settled plough cultivation. The traditional occupation of Kharias was to carry Dholis or Palanquin. At present, they are mostly agriculturists. Besides agriculture, they depend greatly on daily wages. A large number of Kharias used to go to tea gardens of Assam in the past. But now most of the Kharias are employed as farm servants. Some educated Kharias have been employed in different types of government services. But hill Kharias still remain backward.

30. Kharwar

Their total population in Orissa is 1435 as per the 1981 census. They are considered as a part of Kharia tribe.

31. Kondha

The Kondhas are the largest tribal group in Orissa.[26] The Kondhas of Orissa are the seventh largest tribal group in India and they are twice the size of the better-known Naga people of Assam.[27] The tribe is divided into different subdivisions according to different localities. It has separate names in separate regions. Mainly the Kondhas are divided into three subdivisions: (1) Desia Kondhas who live in plain area along with other non-tribals. (2) Dangaria Kondha live on highland hills. The name of Dangar means highland. (3) Kutia Kondhas are found in Phulbani district.[28]

The Kandha life and culture are based on the forest economy. The self-sufficiency that they enjoy is mainly due to their living in the midst of forests. Their life revolves round the forest from where they produce food and shelter.[29] The chief occupation of the Kondha people is agriculture. The hill Kondhas practise shifting cultivation or Podu and Desia Kondhas have learnt ploughing from non-tribals. They depend upon nature. The most important crop they raise is turmeric. But due to primitive method of cultivation, it is less profitable. The Kondhas on the hills practise shifting cultivation. In the summer months, before the outbreak of monsoon, the Kondhas who live on the hills cut woods and set fire on them. When woods are turned into ashes they leave it till the onset of rain. The site is ploughed and maize or paddy seeds are sown. They harvest paddy or maize in the months of October/November. The particular piece of land is cultivated continuously for one or two years.

Nowadays, the Kondhas are experiencing change and transformation. The Kondhas formerly possessed little property. A red cloth or a brass plate was rare. Today in most of the houses one can see brass utensils. They have acquired considerable wealth in terms of silver and brass ornaments. They have now abundance of food and a liberal supply of raiment. Cultivation is extended and they grow large quantity of cotton, oilseeds and turmeric for export. Barter economy widely prevalent among the Kondha society is now replaced by money economy.[30] This inevitable replacement of the barter economy by money economy was a great economic change, which facilitated easier communication between the tribals and the people of the plains. Indebtedness is one of the occurrences in the life of Kondhas. The Panos (non-tribal Harijans) who live nearby and other rapacious and unscrupulous traders exploit them through money lending. Paternal debts are repaid by their successors. Another type of exploitation is selling them ornaments, agricultural implements, clothes at high rates by the non-tribals.

32. Kisan

The little known tribe, Kisan, remained obscured on account of its Hindi appellation, which means cultivator. The tribe seems to be an offshoot of the great Oraon tribe, which belongs to the Dravidian groups. But at present, they take pride in declaring themselves as a separate tribe and calling themselves as Kisan. The Kisans are both industrious and intelligent. Most of them possess land. They work hard in their fields. Even the wealthy

Kisans do not hesitate to work in the fields along with the labourers.[31] The Kisans are efficient earth workers. Some of them have acquired the skill of carpentry and bricklaying. Most of the poor cultivators and all the landless people depend greatly on daily wages or serve as Goti or Halia under rich cultivators. Besides, they also supplement their resources by way of food gathering and collect Mahulchar, Kendu and other green leaves and tubers. Educationally, they are still backward. After independence, the situation has improved and a good number of Kisan youths are now entering into schools and colleges. A few educated Kisans now serve in different government jobs and in factories.

The Kisans do not reside in any compact area of their own, but live in multi-caste and multi-tribal villages. They have their own Tola or ward at the end of the village.

33. Kol

Their population in Orissa is 4235 as per 1981 census and they form a section of Kolha tribe.

34. Kollohara

Their total population in Orissa is 7562 and they also constitute a part of Kolha tribe.

35. Kolha

During the pre and post-independence periods various writers like Col. E. T. Dalton and Sir H. Risley have described socio-cultural life and values of the Ho, Kol-Lohara, Kolha and Larka-Kol. Most often, these terms have been used to denote a single group of people inhabiting different areas. The name Munda seems to have been given to these people by their ancient Hindu neighbours. The Munda called themselves Horoko (men) and their tribe Horo (mankind). The appellation 'Kol' generally used for Munda, Mundari, and other Kelarian tribes is now strongly resented by them simply because it is regarded as derogatory. The term Munda is liked by them as in their own language it signifies the well-to-do secular village headman.

This tribe inhabit the mining and industrial belt of Bihar-Orissa border and is exposed to the force of industrialisation right from the beginning of the century. In Orissa, the Kolhas constitute 5.05 per cent of the total tribal population and scattered throughout the state. They live along with their Kolarian tribes like Santal, Munda, Ho, etc.

The Kolhas were subsisting on hunting and gleaning in the past. Their gradual contact with the Hindus led them to practice cultivation and to adopt plain-land wet agriculture. Their long contact with the Mahato community enabled them to learn the techniques of agriculture in a more sophisticated way. Most of them depend on agriculture either as cultivators or as agricultural labourers. But the main source does not prove adequate to sustain them throughout the year and they are, therefore, allured by the remunerative daily wages. They prefer to be engaged as daily labourers in industrial areas. This sort of employment opportunity and eventual cash earning exposed them to the evils of an urban industrial culture. Agriculture has become an occupation of the old and disabled. Whatever landed property is possessed goes into the clutches of moneylenders. Paddy is produced in the lowland. During summer 'Dhipa' land are used for growing vegetables, blackgram, redgram, and many other local varieties.

The Kolhas have the specialisation in crafts too. Some families in the village have the reputation of being competent brewers and they are approached to brew liquor at the time of feasts and festivals. Basket-making and rope-making from Bobai grass is a skill possessed by everybody.

36. Koli, Malhar

Kolis and Malhars have been identified as one and the same tribe in Orissa and jointly enumerated by the census organisation. According to 1981 census their population was 4700 of which 2388 were males and 2312 were females. The sex ratio is 968 females per thousand males. Their literacy rate is 28.5 per cent. Malhars are a nomadic tribe whose main occupation is collection of honey. The Kolis are a class of weavers. They are two separate tribes who bear apparently no regional or ethnic affinity.

affinity. However, under what circumstances both these tribes have been clubbed together is a matter for more detailed enquiry.

Madras Census Report of 1901 mentions Kolis as a fisherman and boatman caste of Bombay who were found in South Canara. It is also stated that a low class Bengal weavers called Koli migrated to Orissa and were found in Ganjam district. Some Kolis, however, claim that the members of the tribe were once in numerical preponderance near and around Ichhapuram of Andhra Pradesh and were living in close association with the Telugu-speaking people. They were in primitive state. Some were weavers and some of them were rearing goats and poultry. Subsequently, they migrated to different regions of Orissa. The Kolis are spread over different parts of Orissa; but mainly concentrated in the district of Ganjam. The social status of the Kolis is higher than the other tribal communities of Orissa. They speak Oriya with Telugu accent. Weaving is the main occupation of the Kolis. They do not prefer agriculture as an occupation. The tribe is very much acculturated. Many of them are highly educated and some of them have become doctors and engineers. In the social status hierarchy they occupy a higher status among the scheduled communities.

The Malhars are a semi-nomadic community. They are mainly found in Dhenkanal district. The traditional occupation of the Malhars is collection of forest products. In the absence of land and plough, they do not practise cultivation. They also work as daily labourers to supplement their income from forest collection. After the denudation of forest, their economic condition has gone down. Due to their poor economic condition and traditional occupation of forest collection, the Malhars have not developed like the Kolis. They have remained backward as before.

37. Kondadora

The Khonds are a well-known tribe found in different parts of Orissa and the Konda-Doras are a section of this major tribe and are found in different parts of the state. The major concentration of this tribe is in the district of Koraput. Means of livelihood between both the groups are different. The Pedda-

Kondalu depends mainly on agriculture, both shifting and wetland cultivation. Some of the Chinna-Kondalu people hold low-rung government jobs. A few of them work as labourers in the nearby villages. The Konda-Doras are not only consumers but also are producers. The Pedda-Kondalu grow and harvest paddy, millets and other crops. Majority of this group own acres of paddy land and are very rich. They sell their surpluses to the nearby villagers. With the impact of industrialisation and establishment of new townships around the areas inhabited by the Konda-Doras, they have changed a lot. Changes in the economic, religious, political and social aspects are noteworthy. Due to the establishment of Dandakaranya Project, D. B. K. Railways and Mig-Aero-Engine Factory, many Konda-Doras have established shops and have got employment in the new towns and factories around Koraput, their original home.

38. Kora

According to Risley, Kora is a Dravidian caste. Probably they are an offshoot of the Munda tribe. They are good earth workers and cultivators. It is said that they owe their name 'Khaira' from their occupation of making catchu (Khair). They speak Oriya. They adopt both infant and adult marriage. The Hindu marriage ritual has been developed. Polygamy is permitted. The widow is allowed to marry again. The husband can divorce the wife but not vice-versa. The Koras claim to be Hindus, worship Hindu gods and call themselves Saktas or Vishnavas.

Digging tanks, making road and earthwork is their traditional profession. In course of time, they had adopted the making of catchu as their profession. Having cut down a tree, they strip off the bark. The inner wood is cut into pieces and the pieces are boiled with sufficient water for 4 days. A black paste is obtained. The water is let out and the residue is dried under the sun in the form of cakes. It is consumed with betel leaves. The adoption of this profession depends on the availability of catchu plants. Most of them have now given up this profession and have taken up agriculture. Today, they are the first-rate agriculturists and labourers.[32] They produce paddy, pulses and different kinds of oil seeds from their field. Hunting in the forest is carried out at times. Fishing is rarely practised. Collection of edible roots and forest products supplement their food and economy.

39. Korua

The total population of this tribe is 986. They are a section of Kera tribe.

40. Kotia

Kotia, also known as Katia, Khatia or Kutia are a little known and numerically small tribe found mostly in Koraput, Kalahandi and Phulbani districts of Orissa. They are mainly concentrated in Mathili Police Station area of Koraput district. The Kotias are an agricultural tribe. Most of the people who have landed property are settled agriculturists. Those who do not have land take to agricultural labour and wage earning. Catching of fish is one of their subsidiary occupations as they like fish very much. Fish trap and nets of various types are found in their houses. Dried fish is preserved for use in future. The most important deity of the tribe is 'Mauli Debta' whose shrine lies under 'Kendu' tree. 'Nisaniguda' is their goddess who protects them from small pox. Both the deities are worshipped in the month of Chaitra (March-April). Besides, they are adopted Hinduism to a certain extent. Many Hindu Gods and Goddesses are worshipped by them.

41. Koya

The Koyas constitute the principal tribe of Malkangiri. The Koya villages are situated on patches of clearings in the midst of forests. Approach to the villages are by narrow footpaths diverging from the kachha road. The language spoken by the Koyas belong to the Gondi dialect of the Dravidian group with mixed Oriya and Telugu words. This dialect also differs among the two groups of the north and the south. The Koyas have incorporated a number of Hindu Gods and Goddesses into their pantheon and the local Hindu Gods and Goddesses are worshipped by the Koyas. The Koyas were primarily shifting cultivators. But nowadays, they have taken up settled cultivation. As the yield of paddy does not suffice for a family to pull on for the whole year, the Koyas resort to other types of food quest i.e., collection of roots and fruits from jungle and growing of minor crops like Suan, Maize and Pulse. The Mahul trees abound in the Koya areas. During the months of March and April large quantities of Mahul are collected, dried and stored for future use. The Koyas own large herds of cows and bullocks. Towards, the interior regions one will be surprised to see a family possessing three or four hundred heads of cattle. The Koyas seldom milk their cows. The calves will die if the cows are milked, they believe.

42. Kuli

It is said that the name 'Kuli' has been derived from the word 'Kula', a dumb bell of the cow used for the process of carding. The Kulis are like Kuli weavers by occupation. They are known by their title as Mehar. The sole occupation of the Kulis is weaving. Both the sexes participate in this. A couple can weave 20 to 25 pieces of clothes per month ably under ideal conditions. The limit does not exceed twelve pieces as they face problems of capital and market. Agriculture is a subsidiary occupation for a small fraction of people. Less than one per cent of the Kulis own lands and in no case the holding is more than two acres.

Girls are generally married between the age of 5 and 12 years and if a girl is unmarried till puberty, she is married to a bow and arrow tied to a post made up 'Mohua' wood. Divorce is allowed in case of incompatibility of temper or if the wife is unfaithful or is barren. The religion of the Kulis presents no special features. They worship all Hindu Gods and especially Goddesses Mahalakshmi. It is said that they care more for money than moral virtues.

43. Lodha

The Lodhas are an ex-criminal scheduled tribe of Orissa. They are famous for their aggressiveness and criminal activities. Their neighbours have always held them in contempt. The jungle-card hilly terrains of Chhotnagpur Plateau running across Bengal-Orissa-Bihar border covering Mayurbhanj district of Orissa is the homeland of the Lodhas. In Orissa Lodha population is small and mostly confined to two blocks, i.e., Morada and Suliapada of the Sadar Subdivision of Mayurbhanj district. The Lodhas are economically backward.[33] Most of them are in a pre-agricultural stage of economy. Their occupational pattern varies according to local environment. The Lodhas living in the forest area stick to their age-old pursuits like hunting, food gathering, collection of minor forest produces, tassar cultivation, etc. They also work under forest department and forest contractors in plantation programmes and timber operations. Apart from collection of edible fruits, roots and tubers for their own consumption, they collect Kendu leaves to roll bidi, sal and siali leaves to make leaf cups and plates, sabai grass to make ropes, tassar cocoons, honey, lac, resin, sal seeds, mohua, firewood, etc. They sell the forest products to earn their livelihood. They hunt with bow and arrow and use different kinds of traps and snares to catch animals. With rapid deforestation and prohibitory forest laws, they have been deprived of their forest-based subsistence. The Lodhas living in plains mainly thrive on wage earning as agricultural labourers and construction workers. They also earn and supplement their livelihood from a variety of occupations like petty trades, rearing of livestock, carpentry, weaving, mat-making and rope-making. They also earn by selling the hide of the reptiles which are in great demand for making musical instruments, shoes and fashionable articles.

Instances of organised highway robbery, murder, theft, burglary, committed by the Lodha gangs mostly in West Bengal-Orissa border areas have made terror. The problem of Lodha criminality is of psycho-emotional nature. Attempts have been made to socio-economically rehabilitate them in rehabilitation colonies. A micro project named Lodha Development Agency started in 1986 has implemented various welfare schemes for socio-economic upliftment of the Lodhas in Mayurbhanj district. All these efforts to wean the Lodhas away from their criminal activities are yet to produce satisfactory result.

44. Madia

This tribe forms a part of the Koya tribe with a total population of 1064. In 1908, the Imperial Gazetteer of India wrote, "The Mania Gods are almost a separate race"[34] and by this it fulfils the significant separation between the Maria and the Gonds. Grigson coined the name Hill-Maria and Bison-Horn-Maria and he stressed himself "whatever the derivation of the word Maria and the Muria, they are not Gondi words. It has been suggested that Muria is formed from a word meaning root the term meaning 'aboriginal' and that Maria means merely "Man of Woods".[35]

45. Mahali

Mahali tribe constitutes a negligible percentage. They speak their own language, which is very akin to Santali. They are rapidly adopting Oriya. Marriage is arranged by the parents in most cases. Marriage by service and marriage by capture are not uncommon. Widow remarriage is allowed and the younger brothers can marry the deceased brother's wife. Divorce is permitted. Mahali religious festivals are mostly communal in nature. Every festival is marked by communal dancing and music. They have separate dance and song for separate occasions. Both males and females dance. Their priest is called Naga. The primary occupation of the Mahalis is basket-making. A few who have sufficient land have got agriculture as their main economic pursuit,[36] but for the rest it is a subsidiary source of income. All families know basket making. They do not grow bamboo, but purchase it from the locality. They exchange their baskets to the neighbouring population for cash or food grains. Boys above eight or nine years of age are required to earn by tending cattle. Girls of this age group are trained in the craft of basket-making, collection of jungle products such as fruits, green leaves, roots and tubers to supplement their diet.

46. Mankidi

They are the synonyms of Birhor. According to the 1981 census the population of this tribe is only 202.

47. Mankidia

The Mankidia is a nomadic tribe scattered in the forests in the districts of Mayurbhanj, Sundargarh and Sambalpur. Their language is composed of a mixture of Mundari and Santali words. The study of the Similipal hills of Mayurbhanj district reveals that the Mankidia or the Mankirdia belong to the same ethnic group, some racial and cultural stock of the Birhor.[37] They had migrated from Chhotanagpur of Bihar long ago. The Mankidis carry on rope-making from the fibres of Siali creepers. They catch monkeys and birds and gather roots and tubers from the forest. They visit weekly market places to sell their ropes.

They have formed into several bands called Tandia. Each band consists of 10-12 families belonging to different lineage groups. Each household of a Tanda sets up its hut called Kumbha made of twigs and sal leaves. Each Tanda has a bachelor's dormitory called 'Dangua-Kumbha' and spinster's dormitory called 'Gitishikumbha' where young boys and girls above 10 years of age spend nights. Each Tanda has a headman called 'Dehuri' who is supposed to be elected by divine power and assisted by a messenger called 'Naya'. Dehuri serves as a religious headman. The band-life, continuous migration from place to place within the district, hunting, monkey catching and food gathering are the cultural landmark of the Mankidia society.

48. Matya

They owe their name from their association with soil and land. They use sacred-thread. They are mostly found in Koraput and Dhenkanal districts. The family is nuclear and is the main social unit. The sons get separated as soon as they are married and live in separate hamlet. Village is the next larger unit. The secular headman is known as Nack, the religious head is Pujari, the village attendant is Barik and the attendant of the visitors is Challan. The villagers join together in hunting and festivals of the village. Cross-cousin marriage is the rule. In case of refusal, the male is entitled for compensation from the boy who marries her. Bride price is paid. The four forms of marriage such as Jhiamaga (arranged), marriage by elopement, captured marriage and marriage by service are adopted. The widow and divorced women are allowed to remarry.

The main occupation of the community is settled agriculture. Most of them cultivate their own land. They produce maize, paddy, suan, pulses and tobacco. They cultivate various types of vegetables. Forest products are collected and fishing is resorted to at times. Some of them have taken up jobs. They are expert in each work and are employed in it by the contractors. They take paddy for a part of the year. They manage with edible roots of the forest, mango kernel, maize flour and suan, etc. for 4 to 6 months in a year. Liquor of various types like rice beer, salapa, mohua liquor, date palm juice are their favourite drinks.

49. Mirdha

The Mirdha is a small Dravidian tribe which is commonly referred to as Koda in the district of Sambalpur and Bolangir. The traditional occupation of the tribe is earthwork. They are, therefore, known as Koda. The term Mirdha means head coolie. Previously, they used to serve as earth workers not individually on the basis of daily wages but worked in groups on contract basis. The headman of such groups is called Mirdha. Thus, the so called Kodas have adopted the honourable terms Mirdha instead of derogatory term Koda, which means earth working labourers. Marriage is of great importance in the life cycle of a Mirdha. Marriage by negotiation is the common occurrence. Divorce is socially approved and divorced women can remarry.

50. Munda, Munda Lahara

Their total population in Orissa is 3,38,937. They are considered to be the crossbreed of Ho and Kollohara tribes.

51. Mundari

They belonged to the same group as Ho and their total population is 24,667.

52. Omanatya

The Omanatyas or the Amanatyas are one of the agricultural communities of Orissa. It is said that their ancestor was a minister

(Amatyan) of Sri Ram. After Ram had gone to heaven there was no one to take care of them and hence they took to agriculture. They have the different titles given by the king such as Pradhani, Pujari, etc. They speak Oriya and have no other tribal language of their own.

The Omanatyas live in heterogeneous villages with other communities like Bhottada, Rana Dom, Paik, etc. Nuclear families are the chief social units. There are extended and joint families but the number is very few. Cross-cousin marriage is the general rule. At times, the Omanatyas take recourse to marriage by elopement and marriage by service as is the case with Bhottaras. The instances are very rare. Polygamy is allowed. The younger brother marries the wife of the decreased elder brother. Widow and divorced women can marry again.

They are good agriculturists and practise wet cultivation. Shifting cultivation is not practised. Sugarcane, paddy, tobacco, ragi, several varieties of pulses, oilseeds are their major crops. Vegetables like brinjal, onion, potato, etc. are cultivated. Fishing is usually carried out. Hunting is practised as a leisure time activity. A few of them have joined government service. Most of them own some amount of land. In the social scale, they enjoy higher status. They do not touch the untouchables like Dom, etc. They do not take food from Bhottaras, Bhumias. They are gradually taking interest in education.

53. Oraon

The Oraons constitute one of the major tribes of Orissa. They concentrate mainly in the Sundargarh and Sambalpur districts of Orissa. They have their own language, which has been classed as a Dravidian language. But they know Oriya and to some extent Hindi. The Oraon tribe is emphatically the rigidly endogamous. A person marrying from any lower or higher caste would be outcasted and at no cost he or she would be readmitted into the tribe. A bride belonging to one's mother's totemic group is given the first preference in marriage. Marriage among them is monogamous though polygamy is practised in certain cases.

The Oraon religion represents a combination of indigenous beliefs and practices of Hinduism. Christianity as a new religion has received the favour from Oraons. Other neighbouring tribes such as Kisan, Kharia, Munda and Ho have also been converted in large number.

Agriculture continues to be the main source of livelihood. Many of them have acquired proficiency in several rural crafts such as carpentry, tile, brick and rope-making. Women still weave mats of wild date palm and make broomsticks from wild grass. Whenever there is leisure and opportunity, they work for wages. It is not uncommon to find educated Oraons serving in offices, schools and factories. Their principal crop is paddy, which is grown once in a year. They also grow millets, maize and several varieties of pulses in their uplands. Hunting, fishing and collection of jungle products have ceased to be profitable sources of livelihood. Depletion of forests and pre-occupation with the expanded settled cultivation have forced them to give up hunting.

54. Parenga

Thurston has treated the Parenga as a sub-division of Gadaba. They have some similarities with Gadabas. Bell has dealt it as a distinct principal tribe of Munda group. It is ascertained from the areas near Padwa in Koraput district that there are certain similarities among the Parengas and the Gadabas. The village is a socio-economic unit. The festivals are observed in the village communally, they go to hunt together. All the births and deaths are communal affairs where all the villagers participate. They are fond of dance and music. The important dances are Dhemesha Nach, Gotar Nach and Ghumura Nach. Their main occupation is agriculture. They practise both shifting cultivation and wet cultivation, but they depend mostly on shifting cultivation. Collection of forest products like edible roots, fruits is often resorted to. Fishing is practised. Hunting is made at times. They are mostly exploited for their illiteracy. Interests at a very high rate are realised from them by the moneylenders and businessmen at the time of recovery. They are duped by the traders of cloth and salt.

55. Paraja

The Paraja are otherwise called Paroja, Porja or Parja. The name Paraja appears to be derived from the Sanskrit term

Praja, a subject. Carmichael has stated that by far the greater number of these Parajas are akin to the Kandhas of the Ganjam malias. Russell and Hiralal, on the other hand, hold the view that Parajas are akin to the Gonda and not Kandhas. Their tradition traces their original home to Bastar. The term Paraja is so broad a term that it includes in a very loose sense of the term, a number of other communities. At times the Bondas and Gadabas also refer themselves to be Bonda Parojas and Gadaba Parojas respectively.

Marriage is strictly prohibited by the members of the same clan. Cross-cousin marriage is the general rule. Marriage is performed after the boy attains 18 years of age and the girl is above 15 years. Marriage by arrangement is the common form of marriage but a few cases of marriages other than arranged marriages like love marriage, marriage by capture, marriage of the widows and the divorced women are seen. The Parajas are primarily cultivators, but the poorer sections are mostly landless labourers. They are not considered to be impure and some Paraja boys allow their hair to grow long and to form a bunch on the head. Educationally, the Parojas fall far behind like many other tribes. They have remained socio-economically backward as compared to the general population.

56. Pentia

The Pentias of Orissa identify themselves as Haluva Paiks or simply Haluva. Their language is Haluva as reported in the Gazetteers but they speak Oriya. They adopt adult marriage though the occurrence of child marriage is not rare. Cross-cousin marriage is preferred to. The widows can marry again. The younger brother may keep the wife of the deceased elder brother. Polygamy is permitted. The Pentia villages are mixed ones. They live on plains. Agricultural lands and forests surround their villages. Their main occupation is settled agriculture and they do not practise shifting cultivation. As major crops, they harvest paddy, ragi, niger, pulses and different kinds of gram. They grow vegetables. Fishing is often practised. Hunting is resorted to as leisure time activity. Collection of edible roots and other forest products play important role in their food quest. They live upon rice. In the months of scarcity they take ragi, mango kernel, sweet potato to supplement their diet. They do not eat beef, pork, but they take meat and mutton, etc. Fowl is their favourite food. However, they occupy a high social position.

57. Rajuar

The Rajuar or Rajwar is a minor tribe of Orissa. Most of the authorities have the opinion that the tribe is probably an offshoot of the Bhuiyans. They are mainly found in the district of Koraput. They practise both adult and infant marriage. Polygamy is allowed. Widow remarriage in the Sarga form is prevalent. Divorce is allowed on reasonable grounds such as adultery, incompatibility of temper, etc. Agriculture is their main occupation. But their economic condition is like those of the landless labourer. They do not eat beef, pork, and other unclean food. They take fowl and alcoholic drinks and the leavings of the higher castes.

58. Santal

The Santal tribal people inhabit in the districts of Mayurbhanj, Keonjhar and Balasore. They are one of the largest tribes of Orissa. Their population is 530,776. About 756.01 per cent of the total Santal population inhabit in the district of Mayurbhanj. The districts of Balasore and Keonjhar claim 11.20 per cent and 7.76 per cent respectively. They speak a language known as Santali. Apart from this most of the Santali tribal people speak and understand Oriya. In the past the Santals were nomadic. They wandered in search of agricultural land. Now they have permanent settlements. The Santal village consisting of a number of households is surrounded by agricultural fields. An average Santal village has 50 to 100 households. Consequent upon their interaction with the non-tribal people, there has been a change in the dress habit of Santal people. The Santal women do not use the traditional ornaments like the brass bangles, anklets, armlets, coral beads, etc. But tattooing remains to be a common practice. In addition to agriculture, the Santal people go for fishing as a supplementary occupation. They rear goats, pigs and fowl which are butchered on festive occasions. Handia, on festive occasions. Handia, a kind of rice beer, is their favourite traditional drink. Not only do they treat their friends and relatives with Handia, but they also offer this to their ancestral spirits on ceremonial occasions. Malaria fever, influenza, scabies, itches, etc. are the common diseases found among them. But the Malaria Eradication Programme of the government has helped to eradicate Malaria to a great extent.

Of late, there has been horizontal mobility in their occupation. Traditionally they were engaged as small and marginal farmers and agricultural labourers. The scope for occupational mobility was provided with the emergence of mining and industrial units in and outside the districts. A good number of them have migrated to Jamshedpur in Bihar for industrial work and to the neighbouring Koraput and Keonjhar districts. They work as unskilled workers in the industries. With the spread of education among them, some Santal people have taken up government jobs. Both the men and women participate equally in their day-to-day economic activities.

They harvest a single crop from their land. Therefore, agriculture does not prove to be profitable for them. Nor does it provide them adequate livelihood. They are, therefore, forced to depend on the forest products and wage earning for a living. The weekly market called hat plays an important role in Santal economy. They mostly depend on their hat for buying their daily requirements and selling their agricultural and forest products. Of late, the LAMPS and TDCC centres were established in the Santal area to provide articles of daily consumption at reasonable rates.

59. Saura

The Savaras or Sauras constitute a major tribe in the state of Orissa. They are one of the oldest tribes of the world.[38] They live in the Eastern Ghat region of Ganjam and Koraput districts of Orissa. The great majority of Sauras have lost their own language and now speak Oriya. A Saura is an uncultivated language and has no recognised standard. It varies considerably not only between villages but also between individuals. Lanjia marriage is not an elaborate affair. The most common form of marriage among them is arranged marriage. They have also marriage by capture and by service.

The main source of livelihood for the Saora is shifting cultivation. Whenever any valley of the hills are available they practise wet cultivation in terraced fields where two crops of paddy can be grown in a year. The Saora terraces reveal their magnificent workmanship. They grow several varieties of millets, pulses, oilseeds, turmeric and ginger in the clearing (bagad) on the slopes of hills by axe cultivation. Paddy is mainly grown in wetland. Tamarind and Karanja plants are plenty in the area. During summer they collect and sell them. Sometimes oil is extracted from Karanja seeds for their use. They grow sago-palm and collect Mahua flower for wine. It is said that Saoras generally grow comparatively more than many of the neighbouring tribes. But they lead miserable life due to chronic indebtedness. A large chunk of their expenditure is to meet the expenses of innumerable feasts, festivals and treatment of diseases. The main item of Saora food consists of gruels of rice, millet or pulses added with edible leaves. The Saoras sell some of their products in the local weekly markets. The local Doms and Kumtis who are the agents of the big merchants from the plains buy their items. The transactions which take place between the Saora seller and the Dom and Kumti buyers are mere exploitation.[39]

60. Sabar

The Sabars or Saharas or Sa-A-ars are a section of the great tribe of Saora. The Sabars and the Saharas are separate branches of the same tribe, though sometimes a line of distinction is drawn between them. The Sabaras speak clean Oriya. Generally, the village or ward (Sahi) inhabited by the Saoras is located and situated at the outskirts of the clean-caste village or near forests. Marriage by arrangement is the regular type of marriage prevalent among the Saharas of Orissa. Love marriages are also not infrequent among them. A widow is at liberty to remarry. The chief means of Sahara economy is cutting and supplying fuel in the neighbouring villages. They collect herbal plants and roots from the forest to sell to the local Kaviraj (medicine man). The Saharas also cultivate paddy fields of the neighbouring villages and work as labourer in the nearby towns. These simple tribal-folk remain as a prey to the Sahukar (local merchant) for their continuous poverty. In Ganjam and Koraput, the Dombs (a Scheduled Caste) also take advantage of their simplicity. However, impact of industrialisation, development of science and technology have brought changes in the social, political and economic organisation of these people.

61. Sounti

The name Sounti is derived from the word 'Sounta' meaning 'gathered in'. The Sounties of Orissa reported to have a separate identity only in the 16th century. They are considered ritually clean having some functions connected with the ruler of the state in the past. In their ceremonial customs and manners, they follow the Brahminical system and employ Brahman, Barber and Washerman. Marriage amongst them is mostly adult and there is no bar for child marriage. Bride price is paid by the groom before marriage. Polygamy is permitted and widow remarriage is allowed. It is not easy, however, to find exclusive Sounti villages. They mostly live in the midst of Hindus and other tribes such as Bhumij, Gonds, Kharia, etc. In such villages they occupy a separate ward. As most of them are landless, they work mostly as contract labourers, day labourer and agricultural labourer for the local cultivators who require the extraneous labour. Those who have land do cultivation themselves.[40] But in most cases, amount of land is not sufficient to meet the cost of their living. So some of them work as labourers and some do petty business such as buying rice at a cheaper rate from one locality and selling at a higher price in another place. Hunting and collection of jungle products have been given up due to depletion of forests. Their staple food is rice, which is taken throughout the year in whatever quantity it may be available. From rice flour, cakes are prepared and taken especially on holidays. Non-vegetarian food is much more relished, but they are handicapped by their low income.

62. Tharua

Their population in the state is 1304. Their concentration is more in Bolangir district in comparison to other districts of the state.

Conclusion

The numerical classification of the 62 tribes is only illustrative and not exhaustive. There are primitive classes and some are less primitive and others have already been exposed to modernity. Some tribes are residing in hilltops, some are in forests and others are in mining and industrial areas. Besides, the classification has been made on the basis of the diversity of their culture and multiplicity of their languages.

Notes and References

1. A. C. Sahoo, "Bagata", in *Tribes of Orissa*, Government of Orissa, Bhubaneswar, p. 34.
2. S. S. Sashi, *Our Tribal Children*, Government of India, New Delhi,1990, p. 25.
3. *Tribes of Orissa, op. cit.*, p. 264.
4. B. Choudhury, *"Bathudi"*, *Tribes of Orissa,* p. 36.
5. G. N. Satapathy, *"Bhattada"*, in *Ibid.*, p. 40.
6. B. B. Mohanty, *"Bhuyan"*, in *Ibid.*, p. 45.
7. T. Patnaik, *"Bhuyan"*, in *Ibid.*, p. 61.
8. H. S. Mishra, *"Binjhals"*, in *Ibid.*, p. 74.
9. N. Prasad, *Land and People of Tribal Birhor*, Tribal Welfare Research Institute, Ranchi,1964; S. P. Malhotra, "Kinship Organisations of Birhors", *Bulletin of the Bihar Tribal Research Institute*, Vol. V, No. 2,1963.
10. B. Chakrabarty, *"Relationship Between Ecology and Economy– A Study of the Birhors"*, *Bulletin of the Cultural Research Institute*, Vol.12, No.1 and 2,1976; W. H. P. Driver, "Birhors", *Journal of Asiatic Society*, Vol. 57, 1988.
11. K. N. Sharma, *"How the Uthulu Birhors Make Their Living"*, Vol.16, No.4,1958; B. K. Sen, *"Notes on Birhors"*, *Man in India*, Vol.35, No.2,1955.
12. Sachidananda, *"Directed Change Among the Birhors"*, *The Eastern Anthropologist*, Vol.9, No.1,1965.

13. L. P. Vidyarthi, "The Birhors– A Study of Ecology, Economy and Wandering", in *Selected Papers of 5th International Congress*,1960; L. P. Vidyarthi, "Cultural Types of Tribal Birhors", *Journal of Social Research*, Vol.1,1958.
14. M. Haque, "*Height and Weight Among the Upper Bonda of Koraput*", *Vanyajati*, Vol. XXXIV, No.4, October1986, p.17.
15. P. K. Mohapatra, "*Dhanua*", in *Tribes of Orissa*, p.95.
16. *Ibid.*
17. J. P. Rout, "*Godaba*", in *Tribes of Orissa*, p.103.
18. Makhanjha, *Readings in Tribal Culture*, Inter India Publications, New Delhi,1982, pp.24-26.
19. S. S. Shashi, *Our Tribal Children*, *op. cit.*, p.6.
20. S. Routray, "*Holva*", in *Tribes of Orissa*, p.119.
21. Verrier Elwin, "Notes on the Juang", *Man in India*, Vol. XXVIII,1998.
22. S. Bose, "Carrying Capacity of Land Under Shifting Cultivation", Monograph Series, The Asiatic Society, Calcutta, Vol. XII, pp.88-102.
23. N. Patnaik, "Caste in Formation Among the Juang of Orissa", *Man in India*, Vol.44, No.1, January-March,1964.
24. *Tribes of Orissa*, *op. cit.*, p.134.
25. Harimohan, "Socio-Economic Organisation and Religion Among the Hill Kharia of Dalbhum", *Bulletin of the Bihar Tribal Research Institute*, Vol.3, No.1,1961, pp.180-212.
26. R. K. Nayak, *et. al.*, *The Khonds, Handbook for Development*, Indian Social Institute, New Delhi,1980.
27. B. C. Ray, *Tribes of Orissa, The Changing Socio-Economic Profile*, Gian Publishing House, New Delhi,1989, p. XII.
28. P. S. Das, "Kondha", in *Tribes of Orissa*, p.138.
29. N. Patnaik, *Tribes and Their Development: A Study of Two Tribal Development Blocks of Orissa*, NIRD, Hyderabad,1972, p.108.
30. F. G. Bailey, *Caste and Economic Frontier: A Village in Highland Orissa*,1957, p. 301.
31. U. C. Mohanty, "An Analysis of the Improved Economic Life of the Tribals of Orissa and the Way Towards Integration", in B. C. Ray, *Tribes of Orissa*, pp.125-126.
32. G. B. Sahoo, "Kora", in *Tribes of Orissa*, p.168.
33. S. C. Mohanty, "Lodha", in *Ibid.*, p.191.
34. *The Imperial Gazetteer of India*, Vol. X,1908, p.153.
35. M. V. Grigson, *The Maria Gonds of Bastar*, Bombay,1938, p. 42.

36. K. C. Mahali, "Mahali, The Aboriginal Tribe– An Introductory", *Vanyajati*, Vol. XXXIV, No.4, October1986, p. 4.
37. L. K. Mohapatro and N. C. Das, *Tribes: Problems of Today and Tomorrow*, p. 9.
38. N. P. Mohapatro, "A Study of the Social and Health Conditions of Saora Tribe in Orissa", in B. C. Ray (ed.), *Tribes of Orissa, op. cit.*, p. 84.
39. U. C. Mohanty, "An Analysis of the Improved Economic Life of the Tribals of Orissa and the Way Towards Integration", in B. C. Ray, *Ibid.*, pp.126-127.
40. B. B. Mohanty, "Sounti", in *Tribes of Orissa*, p. 263.

4

AN ANALYSIS OF THE PROGRAMMES AT WORK

This chapter gives focus on various approaches to tribal development and gives stress on the programmes. It is divided into three parts. Part one deals with the tribal development strategy and different approaches viz., tribal sub-plan approach and ITDA, Micro Projects for Primitive Tribes, modified area development approach and cluster approach outside sub-plan area and dispersed tribal development programme under OSCSTDFCC. In part two, selected policies and measures of the State Government towards tribal development have been examined and in part three different sectoral programmes implemented in tribal sub-plan areas have been dealt with.

I

Sub-Plan Approach and Integrated Tribal Development Projects

Tribals in India as elsewhere in the world are as much a part of the country as the remaining population. Every effort should be made to include them in development plans so that they may enter in the mainstream of national life. Tribal development will automatically ensure national development and serve as a distinct advantage to the national economy.[1] A majority of these scheduled tribes commonly known as "Adivasi" are concentrated in isolated and inaccessible area of the state but they live amidst rich resources (forest, minerals, rivers, etc.) and are not able to reap their fullest advantage; hence they are left economically backward.[2]

With the advent of independence the policy of isolating tribals was reversed and measures were initiated to bring them into the mainstream of the social and economic life.[3] At the same time care was taken to cause minimum disturbance to the balance achieved by tribals with nature and preserve the traditional value of tribal societies and allow full scope for the play of tribal genius and aptitudes.

Tribal Development (Programmes) During the Plan Periods

In the years that followed independence the normal community development programmes made some impact on the economic development of the tribal communities. It was found that the tribal areas required intensive treatment because of prolonged neglect in the past.[4]

The strategy for tribal development has undergone definite and gradual change in orientation and emphasis in successive Plan periods. While in the First Plan special efforts were made to narrow down the wide disparities that existed between the socio-economic condition of Scheduled Tribes and the rest of the population, in the Second Plan, concerted efforts were made to accelerate the pace of development through opening of four Special Multipurpose Tribal Development (SMPTD) Blocks for all-round development of Scheduled Tribes.[5] Since it was felt that the intensive approach of the nature of SMPTD Blocks was quite essential to tackle the socio-economic need of the tribals as well as the tribal areas, this led to the formation of tribal development blocks. Seventy-one tribal development blocks in addition to four SMPTD Blocks were opened during this period.

Of the 314 blocks in the state, 75 blocks covering 61 per cent tribal population were constituted as tribal development (TD) blocks. These blocks continued to function and additional financial assets were provided by the Government of India till the end of the Fourth Plan period.

The planned efforts of the first four Five Year Plans had gone into helping the members of Scheduled Tribe to raise their levels of living and take before long their rightful place along with others. However, in view of the magnitude of the problems, more intensive efforts were needed to bridge the gap between the levels of living of the Scheduled Tribes and the better off sections of the society.

The formation of tribal blocks did not lead to significant improvement. It was felt that these blocks were too small to act as viable units for planning integrated economic development. This resulted in the formulation of the sub-plan approach and constitution of Integrated Tribal development Projects comprising a group of community development blocks having more than 50 per cent of tribal population during the Fifth Five-Year period.

Up to the end of the Fourth Plan period, socio-economic development of Scheduled Tribes was accepted as a general goal to be achieved through the implementation of sectoral programmes.[6] No special appreciation was made in the formulation of schemes of the needs of these communities, who had their own social and cultural milieu distinct from the rest of the population.

A total and comprehensive view of the tribal population was taken on the eve of the Fifth Plan when the Tribal Sub-plan strategy was evolved. The emphasis here came to be not merely developmental but also protective, not merely area based but with focus on the Scheduled Tribe population.[7]

The strategy, which has been adopted since the Fifth Plan has yielded results and has proved beneficial for the development of tribals and tribal areas. The strategy has generally helped in focusing the attention of the planners and implementers on the special needs of the tribal society and tribal areas and on adopting a more integrated approach for their development.[8]

The idea of grounding Integrated Tribal Development Project (ITDPs ITDAs) was conceived during the Fifth Plan and these have been continued since then for implementation of the strategy. Towards the end of Fifth Plan, Modified Area Development Approach (MADA) was adopted to cover smaller areas of tribal concentration having 10,000 or more population of which 50 per cent or more were tribals beyond the Sub-plan areas.

While the sub-plan approach, as initially conceived, was continued during the Sixth Plan period, Increased emphasis was laid on poverty amelioration programmes amongst the Scheduled Tribes. The objective was to ensure a sustained and reasonable level of income for them. This was reinforced with adequate provision of infrastructure, spread of education and elimination of exploitation, etc.

Thirteen primitive tribal groups have been identified in Orissa on the basis of pre-agricultural level of technology and low level of literacy. Their all-round development and upliftment is ensured through Micro Projects.

During the Seventh Plan, the cluster approach was adopted for contiguous area having population of 5000 of which 50 per cent or more were tribals. Thirteen cluster pockets covering parts of 12 blocks have been functioning for 44,535 Scheduled Tribe population.

The Tribal Sub-plan strategy was further refined and extended to cover all the tribals in the state including the dispersed tribals under beneficiary-oriented schemes through implementation of dispersed tribal development programme (DTDP). The rest 13,84,456 tribal population of the state who are living outside the umbrella of special projects like ITDA/MADA/Cluster/Micro Projects are covered under special projects for tribal development through Dispersed Tribal Development Project. The implementation of the DTDP has been entrusted to the Orissa Scheduled Caste, Scheduled Tribe Development Finance Cooperative Corporation Ltd.

Tribal Sub-plan Approach

The progress of tribal development programmes was reviewed on the eve of Fifth Five Year Plan by a Taskforce set up by the Planning Commission. This followed the observation of the Shilu Ao Committee that the Tribal Development Blocks continued till the end of the Fourth Plan had not yielded fruitful result. The Taskforce recommended, among others, that the tribal development programmes should be given an integrated approach over larger areas than those covered by the T. D. Blocks. The concept of tribal sub-plan emerged out of the recommendations of the Taskforce and guidelines were issued by the Planning Commission and the Ministry of Home Affairs, Government of India for preparation of Sub-Plan for tribal regions.

Area Under Tribal Sub-Plan

About 68 per cent of Scheduled Tribes are concentrated in 118 Community Development Blocks spread over nine districts out of 314 Community Development Blocks of the State. Sub-plan area covers the three districts of Koraput, Mayurbhanj and Sundargarh, nine Tahasils, viz., G. Udayagiri, Balliguda and Khondmals in Phulbani district, Kanjipani, Barbil, Champua and Keonjhar in Keonjhar district, Kuchinda in Sambalpur district and R. Udayagiri in Ganjam district and 5 Blocks, viz., Gumma and Rayagada in Ganjam district, Thuamal-Rampur and Lanjigarh in Kalahandi district and Nilagiri in Balasore district.

About 44.12 per cent of the State's geographical area is covered under Tribal Sub-plan for taking up development works in tribal regions. Sub-plan area covers 118 Blocks (of these 118 blocks, 71 are erstwhile tribal development blocks) spread over 12 newly created districts[9] out of 314 blocks of the states, besides 17 NACs and 10 Municipalities.

The entire sub-plan areas have been declared as Scheduled areas under the provision of the Fifth Schedule of the Constitution.[10] The Scheduled Areas account for 44.70 per cent of the State's area.

Concept, Objectives and Strategy

Evaluation of tribal sub-plan strategy at the beginning of the Fifth Plan was a significant step in the history of tribal development. A special policy for the all-round development of tribals and tribal areas within the financial frame of state plan was coined as tribal sub-plan, a plan within the State Plan.

The sub-plan has, thus, been conceived as a miniature plan for the areas of tribal concentration within the framework of the State Plan. It is an area development plan with focus and emphasis on tribal development.

Resources for Tribal Sub-Plan

It was for the first time that the total investment for tribal development was brought under one frame, which provided a check on the effort of individual departments. This approach has resulted in substantial step-up in the financial investment and also made Central assistance as the permanent resource in the form of an additive fund.

It has been laid down in principle that funds should be earmarked by all Departments[11] for the development of Sub-plan area and the quantum of budgetary allocation to this area should not fall short of the proportionate population equivalent of Scheduled Tribes of the state. When the State's Five-Year Plan and Annual Plans are prepared, each Department is required to show the flow of funds to tribal sub-plan area in the prescribed format. The funds earmarked for tribal development are shown in a minor head in the Department's budget by the respective Department, which is non-divertible.

Objectives During the Fifth Plan Period

The tribal sub-plan was considered to be a panacea for the tribals. It was expected to narrow the gap between the levels of development of tribal and other areas, improve the quality of life of tribal communities, protect them from all forms of exploitation, build their inner strength to make them effective agents of production, improve their organisational capacity and speed up the process of their socio-economic development.[12]

The first tribal sub-plan for the State was prepared during 1975 and Orissa was the pioneer state in this regard. The broad objective of Tribal Sub-plan Strategy have basically remained twofold, i.e., (i) socio-economic development of the scheduled tribes; (ii) protection of tribals against exploitation.

Objectives and Strategy During Sixth Plan

An assessment of the progress made in the Fifth Plan indicated that on the whole the concept of tribal sub-plan embodying integrated and total approach to the problem of tribal development was accepted and programmes initiated accordingly. But there was noticeable gap between planning and implementation. There was inadequacy of efforts in family approach of planning and development as the contribution of the financial institutions was not significant and as desired in tribal areas.

Keeping these shortcomings in view, the broad approach of the tribal sub-plan strategy was slightly reoriented during the Sixth Plan period laying greater emphasis on specific objectives. They are, raising the productivity levels in different fields like agriculture, horticulture, animal husbandry, cottage and village industries, etc. of tribal economic activities with a view to enable a targeted number of families to cross the poverty line.

Objectives and Strategy During Seventh Plan

In spite of the fact that the Sixth Plan had made positive strides in the field of tribal development, there were some lapses and shortcomings. All possible efforts were made to avoid the weaknesses in policies and their implementation during the Seventh Plan period.

(a) Raising the levels of productivity in the fields of agriculture, horticulture, animal husbandry, forestry, cottage, village and small industries. This was affected through provision of capital, inputs, technology, education, marketing, training, etc.

(b) Considering that the basic objective of universalisation of education and removal of adult illiteracy was set to be achieved by 1990, education both formal and informal was accorded high priority.

(c) More vigorous enforcement of the various anti-exploitative measures was necessary. Due publicity of such measures was emphasised.

(d) Attempts were made to create adequate infrastructure for production, anti-poverty, education and anti-exploitative programmes.

While the family-benefit oriented programmes were continued in the Seventh Plan by raising the productivity levels and creating necessary infrastructure to help generate income of tribals, more emphasis was laid on formal and non-formal education and the bias for vocationalisation in education and training. In order to reduce the high rate of dropouts at primary level, it was decided to provide one low cost hostel in the primary schools for 50 boarders at the rate of one for each Gram Panchayat in the Sub-Plan area. Special attention was focussed for the welfare of primitive tribes, shifting cultivators, forest villagers, displaced tribals and tribal women.

More number of tribals were brought into the cooperative fold and their credit needs as well as marketing facilities for their surplus agricultural produce and minor forest produce were provided by the cooperative organisations. LAMPS were strengthened to provide credit, marketing and consumer services to the tribals more effectively. In short, the Seventh Plan turned to be a landmark in putting the Scheduled Tribes on the national development map with their participation and involvement.

Objectives and Strategy During Eighth Plan

There was no fundamental change in this strategy during Eighth Plan period and efforts were made to consolidate the gains under the strategy and to re-orient them for the benefit of the target group.

During the Eighth Plan period, the tribal sub-plan strategy continued covering 21 ITDAs, 17 Micro Projects, 46 MADA Pockets, 13 Clusters and a number of Dispersed Tribal Development Programmes. They were financed by the Government of India.

Steps were taken to (i) make the tribal development programmes more purposeful and result-oriented; (ii) quantify funds under TSP through pool system; (iii) develop supportive infrastructure and (iv) development of primitive tribals. It was intended that, besides ensuring adequate flow of funds, such investments would directly improve the socio-economic conditions of Scheduled Tribes. The area which are being tackled, relates to the quantification of funds under TSP. This was backed up by decentralised planning, envisaging preparation of ITDP-wise plan and adoption of suitable administrative structure at the ITDP level.

Objectives and Strategy During the Ninth Plan

Efforts have been made during the Ninth Plan to consolidate the gains and to reorient them for the benefit of the target group. The thrust areas have been identified with an eye on the changed circumstances like shrinking land and forests, degeneration of quality of life, degradation of environment, fierce economic competition as a result of globalisation and liberalisation. It has become absolutely necessary for provision of adequate protective measures and urgent steps for development of skill and competitive ability of the tribals.

Its mechanical routinised and expenditure-oriented features are to be got rid of and revitalised through democratisation of institutional mechanism, participation of tribals in formulation, implementation and monitoring and evaluation. The thrust areas during the Ninth Plan included many important aspects. A ten-year perspective plan was envisaged. This made adequate resource provision to bridge the literacy gap between the Scheduled Tribes and other categories of people. In order to achieve this, free and compulsory education to all Scheduled Tribe children was provided. Importance was laid on vocational training. The on going District Primary Education Programme (DPEP) was expounded during the Ninth Plan period to cover all the tribal districts and blocks. A different health strategy was envisaged to be adopted. Increased emphasis was laid on the efficient implementation of existing tribal development programmes. Attention was focussed on Panchayati Raj institutions. Five Year Action Plans for each primitive tribal group were prepared. Priority was given for better levels of nutrition and drinking water facility. Rehabilitation policy for the displaced tribals was evolved.

Shortcomings of the Sub-Plan Strategy

The main limitations of the sub-plan strategy are absence of proper organisation, faulty process of identification of target groups and above all lack of proper coordination between different departments. These programmes were unsuitable for environmental realities and failed to transmit their effects through functional linkages of a spatial hierarchical system. All these led to haphazard implementation of many programmes. An evaluation study made on the working of the Malkangiri ITDP indicates that programmes like soil conditioning, soil improvement and green manuring, farmer's training and publicity were not taken up. Haphazard implementation of other programmes could not benefit the tribals in raising their levels of living.[13] The draft Five Year Plan 1978-83 emphasised to continue the sub-plan strategy with suitable modifications to remove the present inadequacies in programme implementation.[14]

Due to historical reasons, the tribal people of Orissa, until recently, were generally in a state of educational and economic backwardness and socio-cultural distinctiveness. Sixty-two Scheduled Tribes in Orissa speak as many as 74 tribal dialects. Their cultural heritage, which is rich and varied, acts as a unifying force. The skills, aptitudes and inclinations of different tribes are different. On the one hand, they are nomadic food gatherers, hunters and shifting cultivators. On the other hand, they are also agriculturists and horticulturists. The tribal scenario of Orissa, therefore, presents an extremely complex socio-economic panorama. No scheme or programme can be uniformly prescribed in the whole state as far as development of STs is concerned. Only such schemes, which are in tune with the agro-climatic conditions of the region/area and socio-cultural ethos of particular tribal community, can be successful. Accordingly, local planning at the level of districts/ITDAs/MADAs/ Micro Projects/ Cluster Projects has to be given adequate emphasis.

Sub-Plan Approach and Integrated Tribal Development Projects/Integrated Tribal Development Agencies

The concept of sub-plan approach for tribal development is being formulated and implemented in the state since the beginning of the Fifth Plan. The first tribal sub-plan for Orissa was prepared in 1975. For the implementation of the sub-plan strategy, the Integrated Tribal Development Projects (ITDPs), subsequently known as Integrated Tribal Development Agencies (ITDAs), were grounded in the state and have been continued since then.

Table 4.1
ITDA-wise Population (1991 Census)

Sl. No.	*I.T.D.A.*	*Total population (including ST, SC and others)*	*Scheduled Tribe Population*	*Percentage of ST population to total population*	*No. of Blocks*	*No. of GPs*
1	*2*	*3*	*4*	*5*	*6*	*7*
1.	Nilgiri	106468	53080	49.85	1	22
2.	Baripada	857884	429281	50.03	10	145
3.	Katipada	287989	188223	65.35	4	49
4.	Karanjia	330226	209454	63.42	5	60
5.	Rairangpur	408481	263668	64.54	7	62
6.	Keonjhar	646857	354605	54.81	7	135
7.	Champua	328437	152986	46.58	3	50
8.	Kuchinda	225086	125741	55.86	3	51
9.	Bonai	243188	163142	67.08	4	35
10.	Panposh	712421	271056	38.04	4	51
11.	Sundargarh	618008	364283	58.94	9	84
12.	Parlakhemundi	287799	195497	67.92	5	74
13.	Th. Rampur	116751	60874	52.14	2	24
14.	Koraput	553187	294718	53.27	9	114
15.	Jeypore	476799	227131	47.63	5	84
16.	Rayagada	356453	204779	57.44	4	58
17.	Gunupur	357519	195318	54.63	7	82
18.	Malkangiri	421917	246214	58.35	7	77
19.	Nowrangpur	846659	467919	55.26	10	147
20.	Balliguda	386076	204799	53.04	9	101
21.	Phulbani	160205	76587	47.80	3	43
	Total:	8728410	4749355	54.41	118	1548

Source: Welfare Department, "Tribal Sub-Plan for Annual Plan, 1995-96, Orissa", May 1995.

In order to give operational effect to the tribal sub-plan approach, areas of concentration of tribal population have been identified and separate administrative units in the form of ITDPs/ ITDAs were established for integrated development. The Blocks having 50 per cent tribal concentration were brought under the umbrella of tribal sub-plan. Under the sub-plan approach, 21 ITDAs have been constituted. In most cases, a Revenue Subdivision is taken as the operating area of an ITDA. Table 4.1 indicates the coverage of the ITDAs.

Objectives and Functions of ITDAs

The work of ITDA is multi-dimensional in nature. It functions not only as a nodal agency in terms of plan formulation, implementation of programmes and monitoring of progress but implements specific programmes.

The objectives of tribal sub-plan is to develop the areas constituted as ITDPs (Integrated Tribal Development Projects) subsequently known as ITDAs (Integrated Tribal Development Agencies) with focus on tribals. The focus on tribals is significant because development of tribal areas by itself does not contribute to welfare of tribals. Development of industrial and mining complexes have often resulted in major dislocation of tribal economy with little benefit to tribals. The strategy under Integrated Tribal Development Area and sub-plan is to harness the process of planned economic development to provide maximum benefit to tribals.

At the state level the outlays under various sectors meant for the areas included in the ITDAs are quantified and shown under a separate head in sub-plan. Apart from the state plan outlays, the sub-plan also indicates the resources flowing into ITDAs from central sector scheme, centrally sponsored schemes and credit expected to be obtained for various schemes. The sub-plan gives not only the total picture for the state but also the break-up for individual ITDAs presenting the totality of development effort taken up in the ITDAs sub-plan has facilitated planning for integrated development of the area. Two significant developments have followed since the commencement of the preparation of the sub-plan. By focussing the inadequate flow of resources compared to the requirement for narrowing the gap between the levels of development in sub-plan area and other areas, a trend has been set for providing larger allocation of resources from state plan to the sub-plan area. Secondly, the more significant development is the extension of planning from state level to ITDAs. Instead of preparing plans at state level the process of preparing plans at ITDAs level and formulating the state plan out of the plans of ITDAs has been initiated. This has made the entire planning exercise more realistic.

Schemes Implemented by ITDAs

Each ITDP/ITDA is given special allocation for the purpose of development of agriculture, irrigation, cooperation, etc. that have a direct bearing on the economic progress of the tribals. While certain infrastructural facilities like irrigation, cooperatives, etc. will benefit all people; some special schemes like horticultural development, special agricultural crops, and animal husbandry are to be introduced with marked thrust to enable the tribals to absorb direct economic benefit. In the intensive economic growth plan of the tribals, utmost emphasis has been given to development of agriculture, which at present is the primary means of livelihood of the vast tribal population of Orissa.

Modified Area Development Approach (MADA)

The coverage of tribal population in the sub-plan area constitutes about 68 per cent of the total tribal population of the state. Outside the sub-plan area there still remains about 32 per cent of dispersed tribal population.

The MADA concept, therefore, was evolved with a view to bring more tribal people under the fold of integrated approach outside the tribal sub-plan area. For the development of dispersed tribal population outside the tribal sub-plan areas, MADA was adopted as a special strategy towards later part of the Fifth Plan.[15] In pursuance of the guidelines issued by the Government of India, a group of contiguous villages with a minimum of 10,000 population of which not less than 50 per cent belonging to tribal were grouped under one MADA pocket. Although a development block has been taken as the smaller unit for inclusion in the tribal sub-plan area, this norm may cross block boundaries or a single block may have two MADA pockets. The areas of two adjacent blocks as in case of Daspalla-Gania, Banpur-Ranpur and several other MADA pockets have crossed block boundaries while Sukinda block in Cuttack district and Anandapur block in Keonjhar district have two pockets each.

The State Government in the first phase identified 30 pockets of tribal concentration under MADA. They cover 133 Gram Panchayats in full and 4 Gram Panchayats in part which include 1955 villages constituting 56.62 per cent of the total population.

During the Seventh Plan, the earlier norm has been relaxed by the Government of India. According to the revised norm, in a total population of 5,000 (instead of 10,000 fixed earlier), if there are not less than 50 per cent tribals, a MADA pocket could be justified. As per this norm, smaller pockets of tribal concentration were located and grounded in the state. A total of 46 MADA pockets are functioning in the state comprising parts of 47 blocks covering 5.67 lakh tribal population. The list of these 46 MADA pockets is shown in Appendix V.

While formulating plans for MADA pocket more weightage is given for family-oriented programmes like housing, agricultural, horticultural, animal husbandry, cottage industries, etc. A few habitation-based programmes for primary education, training centre for cottage industries, drinking water supply and roads have been included.

Most of the family-oriented programmes are implemented in the MADA pocket on loan-cum-subsidy basis. The rate of subsidy in bank loans is 50 per cent for tribal households owning land up to 10 acres and 331/3 per cent for households having more than 10 acres of land.

Both individual benefit-oriented scheme and community oriented benefit programmes for the welfare of tribals are under implementation in these pockets on 75 per cent and 25 per cent basis respectively out of special central assistance.

Financial support for the execution of programmes are obtained from the outlays under erstwhile ERRP, IRDP, Backward Welfare Sector and Special Central Assistance from the Ministry of Home Affairs as grant-in-aid and institutional finance from banks.

However, a substantial amount of special central assistance is sanctioned for implementing different development programmes for the socio-economic benefit of Scheduled Tribes residing in these pockets of tribal concentration. The MADA funds are released to the concerned Block Development Officers.

Cluster Approach

Beyond the MADA pockets, there are small areas of tribal concentration. These are called clusters. The norms for inclusion of an area under MADA have been relaxed by Government of India and cluster approach has been introduced during the middle of the Seventh Plan period. Contiguous areas having a population of 5,000 or more with at least 50 per cent tribal concentration are identified as clusters. These clusters are smaller pockets of tribal concentration. Thirteen such clusters covering parts of twelve blocks have been functioning. For the all-round development of tribals in these clusters, S.C.A. is provided for implementation of individual and community benefit-oriented programmes. The Block Development Officers of the concerned blocks are executing the cluster programmes.

In order that the limited resources are put to best use, the state government is implementing composite land based irrigation schemes in MADA cluster pockets. Besides these schemes, other income generating schemes like beekeeping, mulberry cultivation, etc. are also being implemented with a view to provide additional income to tribals. This is supplemented by development of community benefit infrastructural facilities under education, communication and creation of durable community assets.

Primitive Tribes of Orissa and their Development Through Micro Projects

Hunting and food gathering as food seeking activities constitute the pre-agricultural economy. Similarly, shifting cultivation is a prior stage of economic development. The communities who carry on pre-agricultural economic activities may be called primitive groups. Besides, the criteria of hunting, food gathering and shifting cultivation, low level of literacy, declining or stagnant growth rate of population may be taken as the characteristics to identify the primitive groups.

The first step towards the development of primitive tribes is their precise identification. In this context primitiveness should not be confused with backwardness. The former referring distinctly to the earlier stages of economic evolution like hunting, food gathering and shifting cultivation and the later referring to the lower levels of economic structure like subsistence economy and living condition. A primitive tribe may have developed several wants, but may not necessarily be poor in the modern context. Following this premise the primitive tribal communities are not same as the backward tribal communities.

In defining primitive groups some more distinguishing features have to be identified. Literacy may be one such feature, which may indicate the level of social development of the community. A tribal community, which has below five per cent literacy level, may be taken as primitive. Similarly, seclusion of the community may be taken as the important criterion to identify a tribal community as primitive. Many tribal communities inhabit remote and inaccessible areas. Location of the habitat of a tribal community at a distance of at least 10 km. from the main arteries of travel appears to be a good enough server for this purpose. However, the exercise covering identification of primitive tribal communities should take into account their wants and aspirations, their exposure and posture to external factors of change so that the degree of primitiveness of the community can precisely be ascertained.

The question of tackling the problems of the more backward tribal communities has received the attention of various communities and study teams. The Dhebar Commission (1961) identified four different layers.[16] At the base, they identified a class of tribals in an extremely underdeveloped stage. The study team on tribal development programmes (1969) known as Shilu Ao team discerned marked development imbalance among the tribal communities.[17] They reiterated the view of the Dhebar Commission that the 'lowest layer' needed the utmost consideration and should be made the special concern of the state governments. The study team included in its report a list of backward tribal communities.

At the time of review of tribal development programmes on the eve of the Fifth Plan, it was recognised that special programmes for the primitive groups should be taken up on the basis of proper identification on the lines suggested by the Shilu Ao Team.

As a preliminary step, a workshop on primitive tribal communities was held in the Ministry of Home Affairs in January 1975. Detailed guidelines were issued for identification of primitive tribal groups. Based on these guidelines, nine tribal communities of the state were identified as primitive tribes by the end of 1979-80. They were (i) Juang, (ii) Bonda, (iii) Kotia Kondh, (iv) Dongria Kondh, (v) Paudi Bhuyan, (vi) Soura, (vii) Lanjia Saura, (viii) Mankidia, (ix) Kharia. Besides these primitive groups, there were a few tribes who were subsequently identified as primitive tribes.

Micro Projects

Micro level planning was considered quite essential for the primitive tribes. The developmental projects meant for the primitive tribal communities are known as Micro Projects. Top ensure special attention for the development of the primitive tribes as well as to bring about their all-round upliftment, seventeen micro projects are now functioning in Orissa (Appendix-VII).

These micro projects were grounded to define and improve upon the traditional vocations of primitive tribes residing in the micro project areas while planning for their socio-economic development. Thirteen primitive tribal communities with as many as 61,240 Scheduled Tribe population are covered under these micro projects. Specific micro project has not been grounded for Birhor as their population is very small, but programmes for them are implemented through Bonai ITDA.

These Micro Projects aim at bringing about socio-economic development of a group of families in a compact area. They are made to refine and improve upon the traditional vocation of primitive tribes residing in the micro project areas while planning for their social and economic development. Emphasis is given on implementation of individual benefit-oriented schemes as well as development of critical infrastructure in the project area. Unlike the tribes of other areas the primitive tribes covered under micro project are allowed to avail 100 per cent subsidy under individual benefit schemes. The projects also aim at developing the core economic sectors like agriculture, horticulture, soil conservation and animal husbandry. Besides, facilities of drinking water, education and health are also provided under these projects.

The primitive tribes have some peculiar characteristic features. The schemes that are being introduced for the development of the other tribes will not be applicable to them. Based on their cultural specialities, ecosystem and aptitude, core programmes have been identified for different primitive groups.

Development of Primitive Tribal Groups during Plan Periods

During the Fifth Five-Year Plan, a decision was taken by the Government of India to the effect that the primitive tribal communities should be taken as a special category for whom specific programmes have to be initiated for their all-round development. Diagnostic research should be undertaken among them to evolve suitable strategies for their development and also for helping them in adjusting themselves to the new socio-economic forces of change. As a first step for ensuring this policy of the Government, the primitive tribes were identified on the criterion of pre-agricultural economy, low level of literacy and inhospitable and isolated habitat.[18] As a first step, nine tribal communities of Orissa were identified as primitive tribes with the approval of Government of India. Micro projects were started and family-oriented income generating schemes were taken up for their development.

On the basis of experience gained, the Working Group on Tribal Development during the Sixth Plan, recommended[19] that:

(i) High priority to the programme of primitive groups;

(ii) Identification of primitive tribal groups in accordance with the guidelines issued;

(iii) Completion of project reports for the tribal groups during 1980-81.

(iv) Incorporation of essential features like unique programme for each group, consideration of eco-system and conservation of traditional skills in the project reports.

Accordingly, THRTI of the state government conducted a survey on socio-economic and ethnographic aspects of the primitive tribes and suggested suitable action plans. Steps were taken for implementation of the programmes. For execution of the schemes/programmes, the schematic approach was discarded and an integration of programmes truly germane to the concerned primitive groups was executed. Since it is the human touch of the individual that will determine the quality of the programme and the future of the community, the administrative structure and the personal policies were paid the closest attention for the work.[20]

A holistic approach aiming at all-round development of the primitive groups living in the project areas was made during the Seventh Plan period. The principle was supplemented as is generally adopted for other tribal development programmes was emphasised. Instructions were issued to ensure larger investment of funds from different sectors for the development of primitive tribes residing in the Micro Project areas.

The Working Group on Tribal Development during the Seventh Plan recommended important strategy for development of primitive tribes.[21] They include family-wise economic development plans and programmes, spread of education, improvement of nutrition and immunisation programmes, restoration of resource base, ban on purchase of tribal land, etc.

In accordance with the recommendations of the Working Group, project reports for each of the ongoing micro projects were prepared. Steps were taken to develop road communication, marketing facilities, irrigation resources, drinking water facilities in the project area. Lack of minimum communication facilities has resulted in depriving the weakest section of the Scheduled Tribes the benefits of modern health facilities and access to the market. The state government had selectively took up development of certain essential roads in the primitive tribes project areas. They include ghat cutting, ghat widening and cross drainage works. The Government of India sanctioned special central assistance of Rs. 90.00 lakh, which helped to develop nine educational complexes (Table 4.2).

Table 4.2
Educational Complexes in Micro Projects

Sl. No.	*Name of the Micro Project where Educational Complexes were taken up*	*Total Amount (Rs. in lakh)*
1.	Lanjia Soura Development Agency, Puttasingi	13
2.	Bonda Development Agency, Mudulipada	13
3.	Dongria Kondha Development Agency, Kurli	13
4.	Soura Development Agency, Chandragiri	13
5.	Juang Development Agency, Gonasika	10
6.	Paudi Bhuyan Development Agency, Khuntagadh	10
7.	Kutia Kondha Development Agency, Belghar	6
8.	Kutia Kondh Development Agency, Lanjigarh	6
9.	Lodha Development Agency, Morada	6
	Total:	90 lakh

Source: Government of Orissa, Tribal Welfare Department, Nov. 1992, Tribal Sub-Plan for Annual Plan, 1993-94, Orissa (Draft).

However, the strategy adopted during the Seventh Plan period was to a considerable extent successful in highlighting the problems of the primitive tribal groups, creating an effective interface between tribal development agencies and the primitive tribes. The primitive tribes were covered by a number of schemes meant for their upliftment. In the process, the barrier between developmental agencies and the tribals became less formidable than before. This provided greater opportunities for more intensified efforts. The Eighth Plan accorded top priority for strengthening the economic base of the primitive tribes in the framework of their socio-economic and cultural context.[30] The aspects like crop production, marketing, skill development, healthcare, maternity and childcare received adequate attention.

Dispersed Tribal Development Programme (DTDP)

The Orissa Scheduled Castes, Scheduled Tribes Development Finance Cooperative Corporation Ltd. (OSCSTDFCC Ltd.) was constituted during August 1979. The programmes are implemented by utilising the allocations made available to the Corporation out of Special Central Assistance (SCA) under Tribal Sub-Plan (TSP) of the Government of India and funds under share capital out of State Plan funds. The funds are utilised by the Corporation for payment of subsidy under various income generating schemes, community irrigation projects under composite land-based schemes, training programmes, etc. while share capital is utilised for payment of margin money loan for income generating schemes under the Margin Money Loan Programme (MMLP).

Margin Money Loan Programme

Margin Money Loan Programme of Orissa Scheduled Caste and Scheduled Tribe Development Finance Cooperative Corporation (OSCSTDFCC) is a programme to assist and to improve the economic condition of Scheduled Caste and Scheduled Tribe people. The Corporation provides margin money up to 25 per cent of the unit cost to SC beneficiaries and up to 15 per cent of the unit cost to ST beneficiaries in respect of schemes having non-recurring cost at a concessional rate of interest. This programme was started for the SCs in the beginning. The state government at the instance of the Ministry of Home Affairs of the Central Government decided to assist Scheduled Tribe families in 1984. Previously, the Corporation was called OSCFCC Ltd. and after implementation of income generating schemes for development of ST population of the State, the nomenclature of the Corporation has been changed to OSCSTDFCC Ltd. Thus, this Corporation is providing margin money loan assistance at concessional rate of interest to the eligible Scheduled Tribe families on family oriented economically viable income generating schemes in addition to the subsidy. The subsidy was to be provided either by the ITDA/MADA/DRDA and various similar agencies or by the OSCSTDFCC. The margin money loan assistance is 15 per cent of the unit cost of the scheme for which institutional finance is being given. The Scheduled Tribe families having annual income of Rs.3500/- or less in rural areas and Rs.4300/- in urban areas are eligible for margin money loan from the Corporation.

The Corporation started financing from 28 March 1984. Thirty-six development schemes are financed by the Corporation. The Corporation promotes a few service-oriented schemes like retail shops, cycle repairing shops, auto-rickshaws, motorised rickshaws, vegetable shops, etc. in the urban and semi-urban areas with a view to opening up avenues of employment for the educated unemployed youths and diversifying occupations among SCs and STs.

However, non-availability of inputs like good quality raw materials, lack of improved technical know-how and upgradation of skills and unsatisfactory marketing outlets for the finished products are adversely affecting the traditional crafts. The OSCSTDFCC has, therefore, forged linkage with different agencies for removing these bottlenecks.

Dispersed Tribal Development Programme (DTDP)

The programme for the development of the dispersed tribal population remaining outside the coverage of Special Tribal Development Projects such as ITDA, MADA and Micro Projects, is being implemented through the Orissa Scheduled Caste and Scheduled Tribe Development Finance Cooperative Corporation since December1986. This programme is known as Dispersed Tribal Development Programme (DTDP). Implementation of DTDP has been extended to cover the entire dispersed tribal population in the state. The OSCSTDFCC Ltd. is provided with share capital out of State Plan funds and Special Central Assistance of Government of India, which is utilised by the

Corporation for implementation of various schemes under DTDP like (a) bankable income generating schemes under margin money loan programme and (b) wholly subsidised schemes.

(a) Margin Money Loan Programme under DTDP

The benefit of margin money loan at the rate of 15 per cent of the unit cost and subsidy at the usual rate of 50 per cent subject to a limit of Rs.5000/- per beneficiary in each case under various economically viable and bankable income-generating schemes is extended to the dispersed tribals under this programme.

Thus, under the Scheduled Tribe Sector, Margin Money Loan Programme is implemented by the Corporation for the benefit of the Dispersed Tribals. Under DTDP the Corporation provides 15 per cent of Margin Money Loan out of share capital and 50 per cent subsidy out of S.C.A. of T.S.P while under Scheduled Tribe (Normal) Programme, only 15 per cent Margin Money loans are provided, the subsidy being paid by the ITDA, DRDA and MADA authorities.

(b) Other Wholly Subsidised Schemes under DTDP

Apart from this, MMLP wholly subsidised schemes like small irrigation projects for the benefit of marginal farmers among the STs such as Tube Well Projects, River Lift Projects, Water Harvesting Structure under the composite land based scheme, employment oriented training programmes for providing avenues of self employment, wage employment and job opportunities to the STs, small infrastructure development works like repair and improvement of roads, school buildings, construction of hostel buildings are implemented by the Corporation for the benefit of the STs in the DTDP areas.

Funds out of S.C.A. are allotted to the Corporation for implementing these projects/schemes under the Dispersed Tribal Development Programme (DTDP).

II
Anti-Poverty Programmes

The composition of the State Plan outlays in the years prior to the Sixth Five Year Plan indicates that a major share of these allocation are tied up with programmes from which the tribals are not likely to derive economic benefits at the present level of their skill, expertise and knowledge.[23] This defect in the compositional character of the Plans was noticed by the Government of India and the working group on tribal development was directed to examine the problem and suggest remedial measures before the formulation of the Sixth Five Year Plan. Studies conducted by the working group revealed that 50 to 70 per cent of the State Plan budget was tied to capital intensive sectoral programmes leaving a balance pool to be shared among the non-tribal and tribal segments of the State's population and administrative costs. It was also calculated that only 0 to 5 per cent funds were earmarked for beneficiary oriented programmes. Therefore, the working group recommended to reorient the Planning process during the Sixth Five Year Plan to acquire a basis in favour of beneficiary oriented schemes.

In the State of Orissa two major programmes are in operation for generating income and for creating infrastructure for the poorest of the poor. These are Integrated Rural Development Programme (IRDP), which also covers Scheduled Tribe and Economic Rehabilitation of Rural Poor (ERRP). Since all these programmes meant for the rural poor and almost 90 per cent of the tribals come within this definition, all these programmes benefit the tribals. The 20-point programme lays special emphasis on the realisation of specific goals through the vigorous implementation of the aforesaid programmes.

IRD is a programme where development is the objective, integration is the method and rural poor the focus. It is intended to bring under one umbrella all the schemes and measures launched by different agencies to ameliorate the lot of the rural poor. It is a location specific planning in the rural areas. The objective of IRDP is to lift the target group consisting of small farmers, marginal farmers, agricultural labourers, share croppers, bonded labourers, rural artisans and persons belonging to Scheduled Castes and Scheduled Tribes above the poverty line through micro level block planning based on household survey. The basic objective of the new scheme of IRD is to provide full employment through productive programmes in a selected area. This objective was to be achieved by earmarking additional allocations for each one of the selected blocks for investment in such identified schemes as are suitable for the particular area. The schemes were designed to generate additional employment and raise the income level of identified target groups. The target is to cover an average 600 families per block per year. Under IRDP, it is the *Antyodaya* approach i.e., poorest of the poor is first identified and assisted. The integrated rural development is based on generation of employment through optimum utilisation of local resources in the district by an area centred integrated approach and assignment of task to the most appropriate agency. The Schemes which are being taken up under IRDP fall in four broad categories, namely, (a) individual beneficiary schemes, (b) medium and minor irrigation schemes, (c) schemes of infrastructure development and (d) support to credit institutions.

To the extent the Scheduled Tribes qualify as small and marginal farmers and agricultural labourers, they are eligible for assistance under this scheme. In view of the emphasis on the development of this category of persons, the agencies were requested to adopt a positive approach to extend benefits to them. While formulating the programmes, the Scheduled Tribes who quality as beneficiaries, were covered.

Economic Rehabilitation of Rural Poor (ERRP)

Economic Rehabilitation of the Rural Poor programme of the State Government was a programme to cover 5 lakh poorest families in the state over a period of 5 years starting from 1980-81.[24] On an average 10 poorest families per village out of which at least 30 per cent will belong to Scheduled Tribes and another 30 per cent Scheduled Castes are being considered. A poor family is being defined as one who has yearly income of less than Rs.1200/- but having no income earning assets at all. The selection of these families was made by associating the villagers themselves. The objective was to bring these people above an annual income level of Rs.1500/- per family. Out of the schemes implemented under ERRP only three schemes had got 25 per cent loan component and 75 per cent subsidy component. In the land based schemes and pisciculture, the entire expenditure was on subsidy and there was no loan component.[25]

Most of the families selected for assistance under this programme were likely to be landless, agricultural labourers and the best economic rehabilitation programme for them would be to allot them suitable cultivable lands or make available to them areas where plantations could be taken. Animal husbandry schemes, pisciculture schemes and schemes involving petty business and trade were encouraged. In the land based schemes and pisciculture, the entire expenditure was met by Government and there was no loan component. The ERRP Programme was closed in September 1991.[26]

Protective and Anti-Exploitative Measures

It is generally experienced that the conservation of the benefits accrued to the ST beneficiaries under various programmes of the tribal sub-plan largely depends upon the strict enforcement of the protective laws and regulations. The interests of the tribals on land, agriculture and forestry are to be safeguarded. In addition to general laws which are also applicable to the sub-plan area declared as Scheduled Areas, specific regulations have been framed and are in vogue to save the tribals from various forms of exploitation. Elimination of exploitation of the Scheduled Tribes has been accorded a high priority in the tribal sub-plan mechanism as development of a weak community without protection would only feed the exploiters. Thus, in order to arrest various forms of exploitations of Scheduled Tribes and safeguard their economic interests, various protective legislations have been enacted and being implemented in the state. Among others, the most important enactments are: (i) The Orissa (Scheduled Areas) Transfer of Immovable Property (by Scheduled Tribes) Regulation, 1956; (ii) The Orissa Land Reforms Act, 1960; (iii) The Orissa

Moneylender's Act, 1939; (iv) The Orissa (Scheduled Areas) Moneylenders Regulation, 1967; (v) The Bonded Labour System (Abolition) Act, 1976; (vi) The Orissa Protection of Scheduled Castes and Scheduled Tribes (Interest in Trees) Act, 1981; (vii) The Orissa Debt Relief Act, 1980; (viii) The Orissa Reservation of Vacancies in Posts and Services (for Scheduled Castes and Scheduled Tribes) Act, 1975 and (ix) The Protection of Civil Rights Act, 1955.

Some of these aforesaid acts and regulations have been amended from time to time to plug loopholes in the legislations.

Special Education Programmes

Article 46 of the Indian Constitution lays down the Directive Principles of State Policy. It provides that the State shall promote with special care, the educational and economic interests of the people and in particular of Scheduled Castes and Scheduled Tribes. Education of tribals is one of the cardinal basic inputs, the importance of which cannot be over emphasised. The role of education as an instrument of socio-economic transformation has been well established. This will also inculcate a sense of urgency and involvement of tribals for rapid economic development. This will also ensure bringing sizeable section of the population to the mainstream of national consciousness. The working group on tribal development recommended that education in the tribal areas should be given the highest priority for the reason that education holds the key to tribal development. Tribal economic development is closely related to their educational development. Programmes of economic development and the spread of education should go side by side if both are to succeed.

The Scheduled Tribe children are confined mostly to certain interior areas normally inaccessible for any kind of steady and ready implementation of development plan. These areas automatically become backward educationally or otherwise. The tribals thus, become educationally backward as compared to non-tribals. The gap between the tribals and non-tribals goes on widening in respect of higher educational attainment.

For a tribal family, to enrol the children in a school is essentially a matter of economics and entails dislocation in the traditional pattern of diversion of labour. Many parents cannot just afford to send their children to school. This is one of the main hindrances in promoting education among them.

Development of ST Education during Plan Periods

The country had in the past only traditional method of educational system imparted mostly by religious institutions. Formal education was introduced by the British. After independence, in the first two Five Year Plans not much emphasis was laid on education. The policy of government emphasised on providing the immediate basic necessities like food and shelter to people. It was only during the Third Five-Year Plan that the states allotted good amount of money towards education of SCs and STs. Accordingly, the State Governments were directed to implement all the schemes connected with education of SC and ST children.

Efforts to spread education in the tribal areas will have to be of special type and different from those made in non-tribal areas. *Ashram* Shalas, i.e., residential schools are more suited to tribal children. The Secondary Education Commission 1952-53 headed by Dr. A. L. Mudation recommended more residential schools in the rural areas. The Commission explained: "A number of Residential Schools should be established more particularly in certain rural areas to provide proper opportunities for the education and particularly to meet the needs of children whose education suffers at present owing to exigencies of service of their parents".[27] The Commission for the Scheduled Castes and Scheduled Tribes has analysed the problem of tribal education in its report of 1955 and has recommended opening of Ashram Schools. During the Second Five Year Plan, Ashram Schools were set up in different parts of the country. U. N. Dhebar Commission in 1960-61 examined the educational problems of the Scheduled Tribes. To overcome all these drawbacks, it suggested establishment of residential schools (to be called Ashram Schools) for tribal students in sparsely populated backward areas where educational institutions were not available. Table 4.3 indicates the level of literacy among the Scheduled Tribes.

Table 4.3
Tribal Literacy in Orissa

Sl. No.	*Census Years*	*State Average*			*Scheduled Tribes*		
		Male	*Female*	*Total*	*Male*	*Female*	*Total*
1	*2*	*3*	*4*	*5*	*6*	*7*	*8*
1.	1961	39.70	8.60	21.66	13.00	1.80	7.36
2.	1971	30.30	13.09	26.02	16.40	2.60	9.50
3.	1981	46.90	21.12	34.25	23.27	4.76	13.96
4.	1991	63.09	34.68	49.09	34.44	10.21	22.31

Source: (i) Government of Orissa, Tribal Welfare Department, November 1991, "Tribal Sub-Plan for Annual Plan, 1993-94".
(ii) Government of Orissa (Draft), H and T. W. Department, January 1994, "Tribal Sub-Plan for Annual Plan, 1994-95".

In order to promote education among them, Residential Sevashrams, Ashram Schools, high schools and hostels have been established in tribal areas. The students are provided with reading and writing materials, clothing and stipend to meet the expenses of food. Though such provisions have attracted a large number of tribal boys and girls, there has been large number of school dropouts. There are other difficulties like inadequacy of schools non-availability of right type of teachers and delay in payment of stipend and supply of other helps to the students. Keeping these in view, efforts were made during the Sixth Plan period to bridge the gap that existed between the levels of literacy of the Scheduled Tribes and the general population, but it was not possible to achieve the goal fully owing to constraints of adequate resources.

The Seventh Plan accorded priority to universalisation of elementary education for children in the age group of 6–11 years. In order to achieve this goal, a number of steps were taken. The local persons having knowledge of tribal language were given preference in the appointment of school teachers. The curriculum was redesigned keeping in view the requirement of the tribal people. Adequate number of high schools were proposed to be opened in the tribal districts. Suitable vocational subjects were introduced at the +2 level. Incentives for reducing dropouts and non-enrolment were provided. In order to cater to the higher educational requirement of the tribal people, colleges were proposed in those areas. Large number of residential schools were opened. Adult education programmes were expounded. Hostel facilities were expanded for the tribal students at the primary, middle and high school levels. And so on.

The Eighth Plan, 1992-97 and the Ninth Plan, 1997-2002 have been prepared keeping in view the basic objectives of the Planning Commission for development of tribal education and the recommendations of the Working Group on Tribal Development. For the spread of education in the Sub-Plan area, it has been programmed to invest funds out of the General Education Schemes of the Education Department and the special type education programmes for the Tribal Welfare Department.

Thus, efforts were made during different plan periods to provide various facilities for the educational development of ST students in Orissa. Special types of educational institutions were started in the backward areas in accordance with the recommendations of the Partially Excluded Area Enquiry Committee. Due to historical reasons, education in the tribal belt of Orissa has been looked after by both the Departments: Education and Tribal Welfare.

Educational Institutions

The Welfare Department has so far established 189 High Schools, 122 Ashram Schools, 112 residential sevashrams, 983 sevashrams, besides 1548 primary school hostels with capacity to accommodate 40 students each in every G.P of the sub-plan area. The educational institutions run by Welfare Department both in the sub-plan area and outside the sub-plan area of the state is indicated in Table 4.4.

Table 4.4
Educational Institutions by Welfare Department

Sl. No.	*Institutions*	*Sub-plan Area*	*Outside sub-plan area*	*Total Educational Institutions*
1	*2*	*3*	*4*	*5*
1.	Sevashrams	582	401	983
2.	Residential Sevashrams	72	40	112
3.	High Schools	139	50	189
4.	Ashram Schools	72	50	122

Source: Tribal Sub-Plan for Annual Plan, 1995-96, Government of Orissa.

Hostels, Stipend and Scholarships

Hostels are being constructed to give boarding facilities to post-Matriculate students, Matriculate students and to students in M. E. and L.P. Schools. In order to check the high rate of dropouts among ST students at primary school level, the H and T. W. Department decided to provide residential facilities at the primary level by opening one low cost hostel for 40 boarders in each G. P. of the Tribal Sub-plan Area in a phased manner by the end of 1989-90. As a result of consistent efforts for expansion of education in the sub-plan area during the past years, the percentage of literacy has also increased as will be seen from the literacy percentage table. Stipend and Boarding charges in H and T. W. Department schools are provided to ST/SC students residing in the hostels.

Pre-matric scholarships are awarded to students at pre-matric level. Post-matric scholarship is awarded to post-matric students. Graduate students in general courses, medical, engineering, agriculture, veterinary science students, etc. are provided scholarships. The value of Scholarship includes maintenance charge, fee and the expenses on approved study tours. It seems at present that this scheme is being operated with the limited objective of providing economic assistance for pursuing post-matric education. A career planning linked with the award of post-matric scholarships to Scheduled Tribe students may go a long way in this regard.

Educational Development Programmes out of Special Central Assistance

Some of the important programmes of Special Central Assistance of the Government of India are presented below:

Inspecting Organisations

The inspecting staffs of the School and Mass Education Department were inspecting the H and T. W. Department's Educational Institutions. The H and T. W. Department is spending considerable amount for maintenance of the educational institutions besides supply of other things. Effective inspection is, therefore, of prime necessity.

Health Measures in Educational Institutions

All the educational institutions in Sub-Plan areas are residential in nature and as such the doctors of the nearby hospital/PHC concerned have been appointed as part-time medical officers to check up the health of the boarders of these schools at regular intervals. Most of the schools in tribal areas have sufficient land around the school campus. Provision of a well not only helps in providing protected water for drinking but also helps in developing and irrigating school garden/orchards.

Cash Award for Increasing Enrolment and Checking Dropouts of Tribal Children at Primary Level

A scheme has been introduced for giving cash awards to the Head Sevaks at the rate of Rs. 500/- for the highest enrolment and lowest rate of dropouts taken together. The same primary school will get prize money of Rs. 300/-. It has been programmed to introduce 118 prizes in the sub-plan area.

Public Schools

Financial assistance is given to the SC/ST students reading in the English Medium Public Schools like Central School for

Tibetan Refugees at Chandragiri and other schools located at Berhampur, Sunabeda and Sainik Schools.

Tribal Development Through Cooperatives

The Cooperative sector plays a significant role in the socio-economic development of the tribals.[28] Their exploitation in the socio-economic spheres mostly in credit and marketing can be checked through the development of strong cooperatives dealing with various activities within the tribal areas. In the tribal areas of the state, the cooperatives are still the most familiar institutions as the commercial banks operate under several constraints providing only limited credit to more articulate schemes of productive nature and hence their role is limited in terms of coverage and amount. Cooperative institution has been playing a pivotal role in regard to extension of credit facility to the hill tribes.[29]

Large Sized Agricultural Multipurpose Societies (LAMPS)

The Primary Agricultural Cooperative Societies (PACS) functioning in the tribal areas have been restructured as LAMPS in accordance with the recommendations of the Bawa Committee.[30] A total of 222 LAMPS have been organised in the state during the Fifth Five-Year Plan, (Subsequently it became 223 when a LAMP was started in Malkangiri) with a view to render package of services[31] to the tribals at a single contact point in all the 118 TSP blocks of the state. They include, among other things, credit marketing and supply of consumer goods through fair price, etc. The LAMPS were expected to act 'as a more convenient and effective anti-exploitative device' to save the tribals from the credit cub-web of private moneylenders. LAMPS, besides providing financial assistance, embark on the culture of cooperative among the hill community. Through these efforts cooperative philosophy can be percolated among the community. The District-wise position of LAMPS is indicated in Table 4.5.

Table 4.5
District-wise Population of Lamps

Name of the District	*No. of Lamps*
Koraput	57
Sundargarh	47
Mayurbhanj	53
Phulbani	23
Keonjhar	19
Sambalpur	9
Ganjam	6
Kalahandi	6
Balasore	2
Total:	222

Source: Tribal Sub-Plan for Annual Plan, 1994-95, Orissa (Draft) Government of Orissa, Tribal Welfare Department, January 1994.

The Large Sized Agricultural Multipurpose Societies (LAMPS) were formed to establish an operational unit of command to serve tribals by providing an outlet for institutional credit, marketing of their agricultural and minor forest produce and ensuring full participation of tribals in the conduct of the business and management of the LAMPS. The LAMPS have been playing a significant role in distribution of consumer articles in the tribal areas and thus taking active part in the public distribution system in the state.

Since the inception of the LAMPS, concerted efforts are being made to strengthen the LAMPS in the sub-plan areas. Over the years, LAMPS have not been as effective as they were intended to be and the state governments are making efforts to strengthen them in order to provide better services to the tribals. The findings of a study on the activities of LAMPS in Orissa concluded that "LAMPS, as an outlet for products of tribals play a much subdued role than as distributing agency for meeting tribals' requirement of consumer goods and agricultural inputs. They also tend to be more effective in drawing out rather than pumping in resources to tribal members for generating surplus with them. Tribals are forced to sell a substantial part of their products outside the LAMPS to traders on account of the operational rigidities, lack of enterprise and corrupt practices of the officials".[32]

The increased volume of sales of consumer goods by LAMPS further indicates their negative impact on the tribal economy. By exposing the tribals to an assortment of consumer products, not so essential for them at their present level of economic existence, the LAMPS have positively contributed to the raising of their consumption propensities without a rise in their productive abilities. Thus, the transactions of the LAMPS have not only weakened the resource base of the tribals and caused adequate erosion in their repaying capacities, but also have pushed them to a status of 'modern deprivation' from a position of 'primitive affluence'.[33]

Tribal Development Cooperative Corporation (TDCC)

The Tribal Development Cooperative Corporation of Orissa Ltd. (TDCC) is functioning as an apex marketing organisation since 1972 for purchase and sale of surplus agricultural produce of the tribals. The consumer business of the corporation is being transacted through fair price shops functioning under the direct control of the TDCCOL.

The Corporation is functioning in 17 districts of the State with predominantly tribal population. It has 130 permanent procurement centres. The consumer business of the Corporation is being transacted through 67 fair price centres and is functioning under the direct control of the Corporation. The Corporation is one of the collecting agents of the Government for Sal seeds. The tribal collectors of Sal seeds get a fair price because of nationalisation of Sal seeds. The Corporation has also entered into an arrangement with NAFED for supply of Niger in 1985-86.

Procurement and Marketing by TDCC

A survey conducted in 1969 had revealed that a very little portion of farm produce is retained for future sale, consumption and investment. A major portion of marketed surplus is disposed off locally by the producers. This is due to inefficient marketing system and inefficient marketing structure, which leads to a colossal waste of limited resources. This is detrimental not only to the producers. The surplus agricultural produce and minor forest produce of tribals are procured and marketed by TDCC in tribal areas. For procurement of different minor forest produce and Surplus Agricultural Produce (SAP), the TDCC has been taking assistance of LAMPS situated within the area of its operation. The LAMPS have been working as primaries of TDCC. There has been a close link in the functioning of LAMPS with TDCC. Every year a joint programme is drawn up for procurement by the TDCC and the LAMPS after discussion at the field level.

The principal items of procurement of TDCCOL are oil seeds such as *niger*, mustard, ginger, food grains like *ragi, jowar*, maize, rice, pulses and turmeric. Among the forest produce, Tamarind, Sal seed, *myrabolan* nuts and *sal* and *siali* leaves, hill-broom, *mohua* flower, etc. constitute the bulk of the procurement. For procurement of SAP and MFP items the TDCC opens temporary procurement centres, besides fair price shops, which also function as procurement centres. About 800 temporary procurement centres were started to cover the remote areas for collection of SAP and MFP every year. LAMPS are too associated in the procurement of SAP and MFP. The TDCC has been endeavouring to pay higher procurement price on SAP/MFP. The Corporation arranges to sell its commodities both inside and outside the state with the assistance of all India organisations like NAFED and TRIFED, for marketing the commodities.

Revolving Fund

The LAMPS had not with some exceptions played the role envisaged for them. The main bottleneck of the functioning of the LAMPS, as per the original design, was the lack of working capital. It was considered necessary to create a revolving fund with the TDCC to make timely advance to the LAMPS in order to make procurement on behalf of the TDCC. The revolving fund has been constituted during the year 1984-85 with an initial capital of Rs. 6.00 lakh. It was augmented in course of the next three years with further financial assistance. Interest free advance is provided to the deserving LAMPS from this fund who are in a position to undertake procurement on behalf of the TDCC.

III
Tribal Development Through Sectoral Programmes

Agriculture

Land is our basic natural resource on which various human activities are dependent. The Indian economy as a whole is agro-based. It is little wonder than that the whole life of the tribals is centred round agriculture. Therefore, agriculture deserves and need to be accorded highest priority in the initial stages of a country's development. Later on, it should be developed at a rate necessary to support the development of the other sectors of the economy. The mainstay of tribal economy was and still is agriculture, which existed usually in a rudimentary form and provides a subsistence level of economy.

Agriculture is the means of livelihood for a majority of tribal population. About 52.38 per cent of the tribal workers are engaged in cultivation and 36.2 per cent are agricultural labourers. But the productivity of agriculture continues to be low and the main constraints of agricultural development in these areas are uncertain. Irregular monsoon rains, meagre irrigation facilities, traditional inefficient cultivation practices, inadequate input supply position, unsatisfactory marketing arrangements and extreme poverty of the tribal farmers are the factors which contribute low level of agricultural development.

From a stagnant agriculture, the planned approach to agricultural development has enabled us to achieve some positive results on the production front, especially on the production of food grains. Though some advance has been made in the field of agriculture, there is yet a large gap to be bridged up. The strategies in agriculture development during the Plan periods are as follows:

(a) To saturate all the irrigated areas with high yielding crops and adopt multiple cropping pattern.

(b) To gear up the credit institutions for providing adequate institutional finance to the farmers and to enable them to avail the subsidy component provided under various schemes.

(c) To take up oil seeds cultivation in an extensive scale.

(d) To adopt timely plant protection measures among the tribal cultivators.

(e) To organise demonstration over the lands of the tribal farmers to acquaint them with better agricultural practices.

(f) To adopt mixed cropping practices to ensure minimum substantive production under erratic weather conditions.

(g) To ensure adequate marketing facilities for the surplus agricultural produce of the tribals.

(h) To substitute less remunerative paddy crops by relatively more remunerative drought tolerant non-paddy crops like pulses, oil seeds and millets.

(i) To provide adequate irrigation facility through construction of more dug wells, energisation of dug wells and construction of irrigation projects.

(j) To popularise use of chemical fertilisers among tribals to increase crop productivity.

(k) To use quality certified seeds of improved variety.

Increase in the productivity of different crops has been envisaged through adoption of improved cultivation practices. Motivation of the farmers to adopt the technology for higher production is taken up.

In view of the agricultural character of tribal population it is necessary to observe their pattern of land ownership. Among the cultivating land owning Scheduled Tribe households, a large percentage of land owners own less than 2 hectares of land among the total cultivators.[34] There is an increasing trend of deterioration in the land ownership pattern among tribal households. Several studies made in the state revealed this trend.[35] Not only the pattern of land ownership is extremely unfavourable to vast majority of tribal households, but average per capita holding also shows a declining trend.

(i) For monitoring the agricultural programmes and motivating the farmers to adopt the improved technology for higher production, the extension system has been reorganised since 1975. As per the present set up, a village agricultural worker is in-charge of eight to ten villages, having 600 farming families. There are altogether 2084 VAW Circles in the tribal sub-plan area in which 1298 VAWs and 786 Agricultural Overseers are working for the economic growth of the tribal farmers.

(ii) The departmental seed sale centres have been increased from one at each block headquarters to two or more in the block area for easy availability of the seeds. Incentives have been provided to the Secretaries of the Primary Societies and VAWs to boost up the off-take of chemical fertilisers.

(iii) Agricultural education has been provided to the students in six high schools. Adaptive research stations located one in each district continues to evolve suitable varieties and agronomic practices for the area. Seed multiplication particularly of the varieties suitable to the area will continue in the department farms located in the sub-plan area.

(iv) For tribal culture whether it be agriculture, horticulture or silviculture, application of manure and fertiliser would be desirable to obtain higher yields. Hence, the farmers are educated for production of quality manure out of rural wastes and forest litters and their larger use for raising the productivity of their land.

(v) Soil testing is key for economic and efficient fertiliser use. Therefore, soil-testing laboratories have been established in each district except in the district of Keonjhar.

(vi) Incentives have been provided to farmers for free distribution of fertiliser for improved high yielding varieties.

(vii) Two Krushi Vigyan Kendras have been established in tribal sub-plan areas i.e., one at Keonjhar and the other at Similiguda in Koraput district. The principal goal of the scheme is to impart training in the latest technology relevant to a specific agro-ecological and socio-economic condition to practising farmers.

Over and above the general schemes which apply to tribal areas, special schemes have been designed to cater their needs under tribal sub-plan with an attempt to mitigate the disadvantages faced by tribal farmers and make them conscious about their role for agriculture production.

Large farmers have relatively greater access to the credit and subsidy for agriculture development than marginal and small farmers. This also corroborates the findings of many other studies conducted, which indicate that farm size and credit flow have a close but positive relationship.[36] However, funds have been provided for the purchase of debentures from Orissa State Cooperative Land Development Bank with a view to giving loans to the tribal agriculturists for land shaping, land development, horticultural and purchase of agricultural implements for agricultural purposes.

Tribals because of their tradition, orientation and closed group norms have not been able to introduce many new crops, new implements, new fertilisers and other new areas in agriculture. The experiments to introduce vegetable crops, cash crops, fruits and new fruit crops are likely to yield good results. Production of different major crops in the tribal sub-plan areas during the Sixth Five Year Plan and the Seventh Five Year Plan is indicated in table 4.6.

Table 4.6
Production of Different Crops During the Sixth and Seventh Plan Against the Target

Sl. No.	*Items*	*Unit*	*Sixth Plan (1980-85)*			*Seventh Plan (1985-90)*		
			Target	*Achieve-ment Cumula-tive*	*Per-cent-age*	*Target*	*Achieve-ment Cumula-tive*	*Per-cent-age*
1	*2*	*3*	*4*	*5*	*6*	*7*	*8*	*9*
1.	Production of food grains	'000 tons	2236.8	1780	79.5	2497	2244	90.0
2.	Pulse production	-do-	325. 0	250	77.0	2280	319	114.0
3.	Oil Seeds production	-do-	245. 0	196	80.0	260	248	95.0
4.	Sugarcane production	-do-	115. 0	100	87.0	105	73	69.0
5.	Mesta Production	'000 Bales	146. 0	100	68.0	147	91	62.0

Source: (i) Tribal Sub-Plan for Seventh Five Year Plan, 1985-90 and Annual Plan 1985-86, H and T. W. Department, Government of Orissa, 1985, p. 276.
(ii) Tribal Sub-Plan for Eighth Five Year Plan, 1992-97 and Annual Plan 1992-93 Orissa (Draft), H and T.W. Department, Government of Orissa, 1991, p. 24.

Horticulture

Horticulture constitutes an important component of the development strategy. It not only ensures better returns than traditional agriculture, it also generates more employment. The development of horticulture creates conditions for the growth of ancillary and tertiary sector industries. Horticulture is essentially a 'Podu' prevention programme in the context of tribal development. The tribals are probably the pioneer horticulturists and their love for and knowledge about fruit trees is indeed impressive. They have special attachment to fruit bearing trees and will not normally fell them. This attitude of tribals towards fruit trees is being taken advantage of and horticultural plantations are undertaken for discouraging the practice of shifting cultivation. Further, the agro-climatic condition of the tribal areas is suitable for horticultural development. The main thrust of horticultural development programmes in the tribal areas has been laid on creation of conditions favourable to extensive fruit tree plantations especially on deforested lands. The in situ method of fruit plantation was introduced during the Fifth Plan period in the tribal sub-plan areas. This method of plantation was found suitable for unirrigated high lands, undulating lands, hill slopes, podu ravaged lands and other lands, not suitable for annual cropping. By and large, this method has become popular among the tribals.

Soil Conservation

Water management, catchment area and wasteland management approaches are applicable to hill areas. Catchment area approach is to study the ecology, geo-physical property, etc. Watershed approach is mainly to study geo-hydrological position. Forest can catch and hold rainwater. Degree of conservation of rainwater is dependent upon soil. But in tribal areas, soil erosion is a serious problem owing to undulating topography, shifting cultivation, practised by the tribals besides, improper land use programmes. As such, to prevent soil erosion different approved soil conservation measures like land reclamation, land development including field bunding, contour bunding, terracing of agricultural land, construction of water harvesting structures, farm ponds, gully control measures, development of pasture lands, plantation of economic tree crops like fruit and fuel species, sisal, coffee, cashew, sabai and bamboo, etc. are taken up in the land of tribals in a government land in the sub-plan areas. In order to increase agricultural productivity, comprehensive and diversified land use programme on watershed basis was considered necessary. Therefore, during the Five Year Plans it was programmed to carry out different soil conservation measures in an intensive manner in the sub-plan area.

Forest

The tribal people have lived for hundreds of years in the forest areas and have an ineradicable conviction that forest is theirs. By tradition and necessity tribal people are forest dwellers, forests have shaped their life and economy. A study in Bihar reveals that while the forest dwelling tribes like the Bihor and the Maler depend on the forest to the extent of 90 per cent, the agricultural tribes like the Munda and the Oraon depend on it to the extent of 45 per cent. Forest caters to the basic needs of the tribals by providing food, fodder, fuel for domestic purpose and timber for construction of dwelling units, agricultural implements and other saleable minor forest products. Hence, forest management practices have an important bearing on the economy of tribal people. Development of forestry ensures agricultural progress while maintaining the ecological balance. As the forests are a part of the tribal economy, any forest policy with less stress on tribal development will be lopsided. On the contrary, any plan for tribal development should give priority to exploitation of forest for the benefit of the tribals. There must be interlinkage between tribal development and forest policy. The main objectives of the forestry planning have been to develop forests without destruction. This objective is set to be achieved by adopting the following strategy:

(i) Improving the environment by protecting forests meant for long-term vegetative cover and also undertaking massive afforestation on such land where the forest coverage is degraded.

(ii) Affording strict protection to wildlife and its habitat.

(iii) Undertaking a massive programme of social forestry, farm forestry and village fuel wood plantation to meet the over-growing rural fuel energy needs.

(iv) Linking forestry regeneration programme to individual tribal families to ensure regular income to them, consistent with ecological requirement.

(v) Increasing the productivity of forest products so as to achieve self-sufficiency in meeting economic, industrial and housing needs.

(vi) Generation of employment and rural development with the focus on the preservation of the existing forests through intensified protection measures and with the people's participation.

(vii) Increasing the forest cover through afforestation, wasteland development and restocking the degraded forests.

Fishery

In some tribal areas fishery development has great potential in existing reservoirs, tanks and ponds. Tribal fishermen are mostly agricultural labourers, who undertake fishing as an off-season occupation. Fishing provides them with a supplemented avocation. Stress was laid in the plans to improve the socio-economic conditions of the fishermen in tribal areas by enabling them to acquire country boats and nets at subsidised rates and fishing in inland waters and to take up pisciculture in the tank. Emphasis was given for production of quality spawn. To encourage the tribal people in pisciculture, subsidy in shape of inputs was given for water area. The main objectives of pisciculture development in tribal areas during the different Plans were to:

(i) Make tribals aware of the modern methods of pisciculture and its nutritive value.

(ii) To help them to supplement their earnings through self-employment.

(iii) Improve the nutrition standard of the tribals through intake of cheap animal protein like fish.

To achieve these objectives in the sub-plan area the following steps have been taken:

(a) Fishery extension officers have been posted in blocks of the tribal sub-plan area for dissemination of inland pisciculture technology.

(b) Institutional finance for operation of the fishery schemes has been made available.

(c) Training facilities in pisciculture are provided to tribal people.

(d) For supply of fry and fingerlings in tribal areas, the departmental fish farms are being remodelled to produce the required number of fry and fingerlings.

(e) Assistance is being provided to the traditional inland fishermen by way of subsidy for acquiring country boats and nets for fishing in rivers and reservoirs. Reclamation subsidy and input subsidy are given to tribals for development of pisciculture under FFDA.

(f) Fishermen cooperative societies, which are in moribund condition are being reactivated and new ones have been organised in the sub-plan areas for the improvement of the socio-economic condition of the tribal fishermen.

(g) The reservoirs in tribal areas are being developed by way of stocking fingerlings and giving them on long-term lease to fishermen cooperative societies of tribal areas for fishing.

In addition to normal state plan schemes, some schemes were implemented with special central assistance to help the tribal people to augment tank fisheries. Initially, much headway could not be made because most of the tribal people were landless. It was not possible to settle fishing right of the government on Panchayat tanks in their favour. Subsequently, the Gram Panchayat Act was amended. It allowed lease of G.P. tanks for 10 years with the beneficiaries. It is, therefore, felt that a lot of possibility is there to introduce tank fisheries amongst the tribal people.

Basing upon the status and need of the individual tribal in the sub-plan area, 100 per cent, 75 per cent and 50 per cent subsidy was provided in the first year to different categories of tribal beneficiaries to renovate a tank and take up pisciculture therein.

Animal Husbandry

Livestock rearing is one of the oldest occupations that man has adopted. This is practised as complementary to crop production and has traditionally been an important secondary source of livelihood in tribal sub-plan areas. Tribal economy is predominantly agriculture-based. Livestock occupies a position second to land in the tribal areas. Though the tribals practising shifting cultivation do not use animals in their farming operations, they rear animals and birds to meet their requirements of domestic consumption, community entertainments and for animal sacrifices resorted to propitiate Gods.[37] For many years to come, livestock will continue to be a source of supplementary income to all the tribals belonging to different occupational group.

Keeping in view, the inclination of the tribals for small animals like goat, sheep, pig and poultry, efforts have been made to implement programmes of development of small animals in the tribal areas. On the basis of the suggestions of the Planning Commission, the strategy under animal husbandry and dairy development sector were devised. Appropriate schemes were prepared for rehabilitation of a large number of poor families through animal husbandry programme and reciprocating mixed farming. Emphasis was land on multiplication and supply of small animals and on extensive programme for popularising artificial insemination to upgrade the breeds. In accordance with the recommendations of the Working Groups on tribal development, programmes for development of animal resource and dairy development were prepared during different Plan periods.

Health and Family Welfare

Poor health of the tribal people appears to be a major drag on their productive participation. The primary objective of the health policy of the national as well as the state governments is to provide healthcare consisting of preventive, promotive and curative aspects to all sections of the society, including the tribals living in remote areas. During the Plan periods attempts were made to provide health services.

During the Sixth and Seventh Five-Year Plan periods, attempts have been made to provide healthcare at the doorsteps of the tribals by means of establishing more number of Primary Health Centres (PHCs), Additional PHCs, Community Health

Centres (CHCs), Upgraded PHCs, Sub-Centres, Ayurvedic and Homeopathic Dispensaries in tribal areas. The main thrust of the Eighth Five Year Plan is to provide medical care to rural areas, especially in the tribal areas. As under the national norm, there should be one sub-centre for every 3000 population and one Primary Health Centre for every 20,000 population in tribal areas. The norm for opening of CMC is, however, common in both tribal and non-tribal areas i.e., one CHC for every 80,000 to 1.20 lakh population serving as a referral institution for four Primary Health Centres. In order to attain the goal, the 'Health for all by 2000 A. D.', several steps were taken in the tribal areas. Ayurvedic and Homeopathic dispensaries were constructed in some tribal areas. That is because these two methods provide cheap and effective means of treatment. The 'Health for all by 2000 A.D.' scheme envisaged establishment of two herbal gardens in the tribal districts of Mayurbhanj and Sundargarh. In addition to all this, health measures were taken in the Harijan and Tribal Department Schools.

Drinking Water Supply (Rural)

The problem of drinking water in tribal areas is acute. Tribals generally inhabit in hilly and forest areas. Tribal villages are scattered over high distance and consist of a number of hamlets. Because of these two reasons adequate drinking water for each of the hamlets is not available. The tribals have to go long distance for collecting daily minimum need of drinking water. Out of 19,204 inhabited villages existing in tribal sub-plan area, 17,148 villages have been identified as problem villages for provision of drinking water. Under minimum needs programme, provision of drinking water supply particularly in problem villages is considered a priority item.

Communication

To ensure that the benefits of the programme for economic, social and health development reach the tribals in remotest areas, it is necessary that there is a good system of road communication. Roads open up the tribal areas with the outside world. Villages in tribal areas are widely dispersed and do not have proper road communication system. Unless a proper network of roads in the tribal areas is developed, the tribal population and tribal areas will continue to be isolated from the mainstream of economic and social development. The Plan objectives for road development in the context of tribal development emphasised certain important aspects. It was envisaged to make the important administrative centres more accessible with all-weather roads. Further, it was planned to make the market centres, growth and the health centres accessible. It was to construct new bridges. Cluster villages with a population of 1000 were provided with linkage roads.

Irrigation

The development of agriculture depends upon, more than anything else, the availability of irrigation facilities. Water as an input contributes to agricultural productivity much more than fertilisers, seeds and pesticides. Since the beginning of the history of mankind, people have always tried to harness this natural resource for betterment of agriculture and for their own economic good. As a result of investment in irrigation and roads several countries were able to make substantial increase in their cultivated area.

The tribal areas of Orissa are rich in water resource and as such the potential for irrigation is very high. But development of irrigation facility in tribal areas has been very tardy. Irrigation in hill districts is apparently a misplaced priority in consideration to topographic peculiarities and lack of adequate wet paddy cultivation in areas of commendable size. Even the existing irrigation sources in tribal areas are becoming inefficient due to inadequate maintenance. Consequently, agricultural production in the tribal areas is far behind the national average and also of the state average. Expeditious exploitation of existing irrigation potential is, therefore, the felt need of the tribal sub-plan. It is, therefore, necessary to have a coordinated approach to irrigation development in the tribal areas, which should include major, medium and minor, lift irrigation and grouped water development.

During different plan periods, attempts were made to remove the imbalances and to provide adequate irrigation facilities in the sub-plan area through various measures. During the Fifth Plan period emphasis was given on construction of the irrigation projects in the drought-prone areas and in the backward tribal areas where the irrigation coverage is very low. Further, minor irrigation projects, dug wells were constructed and under lift irrigation programme, lift irrigation projects were energised in the sub-plan areas.

Rural Electrification

Electrification is an essential infrastructure in tribal areas for implementation of economic development programmes. The pace of village electrification in tribal areas was, therefore, stepped up. During the Sixth Five-Year Plan, 2338 villages were electrified and during the Seventh Five-Year Plan, 2240 villages have been electrified in the sub-plan area.

Industry and Technical Education

Agricultural development in areas where tribal population is largely concentrated is not always possible because of several factors. Therefore, the importance of development of industries in these areas, particularly in the small artisan and handloom sectors assume great importance in the context of economic development of tribal people. Even large and medium scale industries are likely to generate employment and occupational opportunities in the tertiary sector of tribal people. Fortunately, the national resources like rich mineral deposits and immense forest wealth abound in tribal areas. While exploiting these available resources through industrial development, large scale employment opportunities and opportunities of gainful engagement for tribal people can be ensured when various industrial projects are located in tribal areas.

Major and Medium Industries: A number of large and medium scale industrial projects have been taken up for implementation in tribal areas of Mayurbhanj, Keonjhar, Koraput, Phulbani and Sundargarh districts. Besides, greater number of similar projects have been identified in tribal areas.

Preliminary works for promoting these industries are well underway.

Infrastructure Development: The Orissa Infrastructure Development Corporation was set up in 1981 to provide industrial infrastructure facilities in an organised and systematic manner at different selected industrial growth centres. Out of 50 such growth centres selected for the purpose of providing infrastructure facilities for the development of various industries, 21 growth centres are in tribal belts extending over six districts. The Corporation provides built-in sheds and industrial plots for locating different industrial units in these centres. The Corporation has a programme to build industrial sheds and develop land for industrial purpose in the selected growth centres of tribal areas.

State Financial Corporation: The Orissa State Financial Corporation is in charge of providing term loans and other types of short-term loans mostly to small scale and artisan based industries up to an investment of Rs.1.0 crore. In five districts, in which there are concentrations of tribal population, the Corporation has disbursed funds to a number of industrial units. The integrated tribal development agencies in tribal sub-plan areas can identify prospective entrepreneurs in consultation with the concerned District Industries Centres and sponsor their cases to local branches of State Financial Corporation for financial assistance. The tribals who are trained in ITIs can avail themselves of the opportunity of starting artisan based industries and secure financial assistance from the State Financial Corporation with the recommendations of the concerned District Industries Centres.

Small-Scale and Cottage Industries: Small-scale and village industries provide large employment with small volume of investment. Development of semi-urban and rural areas can be achieved by establishment of suitable small and village industries by utilising the local resources. As a part of wider dispersal of industrial activities, a considerable number of small-scale industrial units have been taken up in tribal areas. The major thrust is on development of small industries in rural and semi-urban areas for generating employment opportunities. In the small-scale sector, tribals have not been able to set up many units because this requires a sizeable capital investment. But under these programmes the tribals can get opportunity for employment with proper training facilities in five ITIs set up in the tribal sub-plan areas. Under the scheme, large number of tribal beneficiaries are getting scope for availing loans for developing their own skill and technology in their own trades.

***Khadi* and Village Industries:** The tribal areas offer a good deal of scope for development of cottage, village and small industries. The programmes cover the entire spectrum from modern small industries, handloom, power loom, sericulture, handicrafts, coir, salt and village industries as identified by he Khadi and Village Industries Commission. Because of abundant natural resources in tribal areas a number of village industries based on these resources can be set up to provide gainful employment to tribal people. It is proposed to cover at least 3000 tribal artisans under the programme of gainful employment. Beekeeping, which is the traditional occupation of tribal people, occupies a predominant place in the village industries programme. Potteries, palm-gur, cane and bamboo products, products of natural fibre, soap and matchmaking, sabai rope-making, etc. are included in the village industries programme of Khadi and Village Industries Board.

Technical Education: Establishment of forest-based industries in the tribal areas will improve the economic condition of the tribals provided they are fully involved in these industries. The first requisite in this regard is to set up a network of vocational and technical training institutions. The need for providing adequate training facilities in technical trades and engineering disciplines for tribal people has been constantly kept in view while planning for necessary technical manpower in the context of the state's rapid industrialisation programme. Accordingly, most of the engineering schools and technical training institutions have been set up in tribal areas. With a view to provide special facilities for technical training diploma and higher engineering education to the tribal bys, 24 per cent of the total number of seats have been reserved for the students belonging to Scheduled Tribes. Out of 14 ITIs of the state, six

ITIs are located in tribal areas. Similarly, out of 9 Engineering Schools run by the state government,4 engineering schools are located in districts having largest concentration of tribal population.

Handlooms: Because of greater employment potential of the handlooms sector, steps are taken to develop handloom units in tribal areas. The programme consists mainly in bringing tribal weavers under organised sector by promoting cooperative societies. This is for the modernisation of looms, training of tribal weavers, supply of raw materials and provision of marketing assistance. Cooperative societies are bringing within their fold many tribal weavers and training facilities have been provided to such weavers.

Sericulture

Sericulture industry is an age-old predominant culture practised by almost all the tribal people of hill areas. Its historical perspective has been to satisfy man's quest for clothing with concurrent assurance of self-sustainment and self-dependence. Most of the schemes for the development of sericulture implemented in tribal areas provide employment to tribal people by way of rearing various types of silkworms, reeling and spinning yarn and cultivation of feeding plants. The state government provides technical and organisational support including training facilities, financial assistance, etc. mostly to tribal people for the development of sericulture. Orissa ranks the major non-mulberry silk producing states since tassar silkworms rearing is an important economic activity of nearly 40,000 Scheduled Tribe families in the state. Similarly, emphasis has been laid for expansion of mulberry sericulture in hilly areas where agro-climatic condition are quite conducive and tribals and other agriculturists have shown interest for such profession. ERI silkworm rearing, as a subsidiary income generation programme, has also been given importance. During the plan periods state government have, therefore, laid considerable emphasis on the sericulture industry.

Tassar: Tassar silkworm rearing is a traditional occupation of tribals in many districts. During the Plan periods cooperativisation of tribal tassar rearers, supply of disease-free Tassar silkworm eggs to the rearers, plantation of host plants for increasing tassar silkworm, rearing area, marketing of tassar cocoon as well as facilities for development of reeling and spinning of tassar cocoons were given due support. Attention was also given to the development of technological base under inter-state tassar development programmes (an Indo-Swiss bilateral project).

Mulberry: Mulberry sericulture has been taken up in the state having suitable agro-climatic condition from Seventh Plan period. Most of the tribal sub-plan areas provide congenial condition for such culture. In order to help the tribals in this culture, supply of mulberry cuttings, silkworm eggs and training the farmers are being planned. Seven mulberry demonstration farms and one seed supply station have been established in the tribal areas. Tribals are being assisted to take up mulberry cultivation in their own land and they are being assisted for plantation of mulberry, supply of rearing equipment, construction of rearing houses, etc. Mulberry rearers-cum-reelers cooperative societies are formed where the tribal growers are its members.

ERI: Under ERI silkworm rearing programme, tribal families have been assisted with supply of ERI silkworm eggs and training facilities providing them subsidiary income. The ERI seed cocoon production centre aims at popularising ERI silkworm rearing by tribals to supplement their income.

Land Reforms

Land reform measures were implemented to ensure personal cultivation and discourage tenancy and absentee-landlordism, which were detrimental to agricultural reorganisation. It is a prerequisite to give benefit to the tribals under the land reform laws. In the absence of land records, moneylenders and vested interests usurp land belonging to tribals. Civil courts also find it difficult to uphold the rights of tribals whenever settlement records are outdated or not available. Absence of land records makes it difficult for the tribals to avail of institutional credit. It is for these reasons that preparation of land records in tribal areas was considered urgent and was given priority.

Conclusion

Different programmes and policies for Scheduled Tribes have been classified and reclassified from different dimensions. On sectoral basis there are programmes like agriculture and allied sector, irrigation, cooperation, social services, like drinking water, electrification, health, education, etc. Programmes of the Government can also be classified on the basis of people and area. The people's development programmes are the IRDP, ERRP, DTDP, etc. and the Area Development Programmes are the MADA, ITDA and other infrastructure development programmes. Some programmes are intended to remove poverty and other programmes aim at generating mass employment. There are human resources development content like training and skill formation in some programmes like education and health.

The brief review of the tribal welfare programmes indicates that though efforts have been made during the last many years to improve the lot of the tribals, enough has not been done to bring them on par with the advanced sections of society. Both programme planning and implementation have remained stereotyped and devoid of tribal bias. Consequently, even the little that has been invested in tribal welfare could not percolate to the intended beneficiaries in its entirety. In spite of the recommendations of the expert committees and commissions, the programmes failed to give the desired results. The ultimate result of such defective planning and implementation is the emergence of an undulating socio-economic situation in which certain tribal groups and areas have progressed while others remained static. It is important to remember that, it is the human element that makes or mars the development of any region or group. Steps should, therefore, be taken to improve the quality of the development functionary working at various levels.

Notes and References

1. U. M. Deshpande, "*Gandhian Economy for Tribal Development*", in S. G. Deogaonkar (ed.), *Problems of Development of Tribal Areas*, p.77.
2. N. G. Somalwar, "*Strategy in Economic Development of Tribals*", in Ibid., p.71.
3. Tribal Welfare Department, Government of Orissa, *Tribal Sub-Plan for Annual Plan,1994-95*, Orissa (Draft),1994, p.1.
4. *Tribal and Rural Welfare Department*, *Revised Annual Sub-Plan,1979-80*, Orissa, April 1979, p. 1.
5. Government of Orissa, *Tribal Sub-Plan for7th Plan,1992-97, Orissa*, April 1979, p. 17.
6. Government of Orissa, *Tribal Sub-Plan for8th Plan,1992-97, Annual Plan*,1992-93 (Draft), p. 2.
7. Government of Orissa, *Annual Tribal Sub-Plan* (Draft),1986-87, p. 2.
8. Government of Orissa, *Tribal Sub-Plan for Annual Plan,* 1993-94 (Draft), November 1992, p.3.
9. Government of Orissa, *Tribal Sub-Plan for Annual Plan, 1995-96,* p. 1.
10. Government of Orissa, *Tribal Sub-Plan,* 1983-84, p.1.
11. Government of Orissa, *Revised Annual Sub-Plan,* 1979-80, p.1.
12. Government of India, "*Approach to Tribal Development in the Sixth Plan– A Preliminary Perspective*", New Delhi, 1977, p. 35.
13. B. Nighna and P. C. Mohapatra, "*Evaluation Report of Malkangiri ITDP, Koraput District, Orissa*", Utkal University,1980.
14. Government of India, Planning Commission, Draft Five-Year Plan, *1978-83*, p. 255.
15. Government of Orissa, *Tribal Sub-Plan for Eighth Plan,1992-97* and *Annual Plan,* 1992-93, Orissa (Draft), p. 95.
16. The Dhebar Commission was appointed by the Government of India in1961 to make an in-depth study on matters pertaining to tribes and their development. It recommended suitable measures for their development.
17. The Shilu Ao team appointed by the Government of India studied the problems concerning backward communities. It suggested policies and programmes for their development.
18. Government of India, "*Report of the Working Group on Development of Scheduled Tribes during7th Five Year Plan*", p. 87.

19. Government of India, "*Report of the Working Group on Development of Scheduled Tribes during Sixth Plan*, 1980-85", pp. 115-16.
20. Ibid.
21. Government of India, "*Report of the Working Group on Development of Scheduled Tribes During the Seventh Five Year Plan*", pp. 87-94.
22. This decision was communicated by the Commissioner-cum-Secretary, Government of Orissa to all the Collectors in the State vide Letter No.14869 dated15th May1984.
23. M. K. Mohanty, *Tribal Society, Programmes, Planning and Economic Change*, Chugh Publications, Allahabad,1990, pp. 89-90.
24. Government of Orissa, "Panchayati Raj Department, *Anti-Poverty Programme: Progress During the Decade,* 1980-90, p. 12.
25. Government of Orissa, Planning and Coordination Department, "*Evaluation Report on IRDP and ERRP Programme in Ganjam District–1987*", p. 2.
26. Government of Orissa, *Economic Survey*,1991-92.
27. E. V. Ramaiah, *Structural Constraints in Tribal Education: A Regional Study*, New Delhi,1977, p.174.
28. Government of Orissa, *Tribal Sub-Plan for Eighth Plan,* 1992-97 and *Annual Plan,* 1992-93, Orissa (Draft), p. 152.
29. Sujit Sikadar, *Economic Development of Tribal India*, Asish Publications, New Delhi,1990, p. 52.
30. The Bawa Committee was appointed during the 4th Plan period under the Chairmanship of K. S. Bawa to examine the working of cooperative organisations and to recommend measures for strengthening the cooperatives in tribal areas.
31. LAMPS not only provide credit to its members but also render certain non-credit services like supply of chemical fertilisers, improved seeds, implements, consumer goods, other essential commodities and purchase of surplus agricultural produce and minor forest produce.
32. M. K. Mohanty, op. cit., pp.108-109.
33. Ibid., p.111.
34. *Report on Agricultural Census of Orissa,1970-71.*
35. Government of Orissa, *Economic Survey of Orissa*, Vol. I, 1954-55, pp.130-131; Government of Orissa, *Living Condition of Scheduled Tribes, Scheduled Castes and Other Backward Classes in Orissa*,1963, pp.76-79.

36. C. H. Hanumantha Rao, "*Farm Size and Credit Policy*", *Economic and Political Weekly*, 28 December 1970; V. G. Rao and P. Vatam, *Agricultural Finance by Commercial Banks*, Asish, New Delhi,1980.
37. M. K. Mohanty, op. cit., p. 124.

5

FINANCIAL ASPECTS OF THE PROGRAMMES

Finance finally transfers policy into action by mobilising different forces. Finance plays a crucial role because it mobilises real force for achievement of goals. Therefore, its size and distribution of the total among various programmes are of critical importance for the tribal development process. This Chapter, therefore, deals with important aspects of resource flow and deployment.

Plan-wise allocation and sector-wise allocation for different tribal development programmes have been indicated in this chapter. Some programmes are centrally assisted with matching contribution by the state and central governments. Some programmes are fully funded by the central government or by the state government.

Sources and Pattern of Funding

The scheme of financing tribal development was revised in the Fifth Plan while working out the sub-plan strategy. The inherent weakness in the system of assistance provided by the central government in the form of central or centrally sponsored programmes was noted. It was accepted that unless the major thrust of tribal development was provided by the concerned sectoral authorities, the gulf between the tribal areas and other areas would continue to grow. It was envisaged that the investment under the new strategy for tribal development should be quantified systematically so that a clear picture may be available and conscious policy decision with regard to the size of investment, etc. may become possible.[1]

The tribal development programmes such as Tribal Sub-Plan, Modified Area Development Approach, Micro Projects and Primitive Tribes, Dispersed Tribal Development Programmes, etc. represent total development effort in the identified areas with the aid of resources pooled from various sources, viz. (i) outlays from the state plan, (ii) flow from central/centrally sponsored programmes of the central ministries, (iii) special central assistance and (iv) institutional finance. Various sources of investment for tribal development programmes are as detailed below:

State Plan Funds

As per the guidelines of the central government, adequate financial provisions should be made from the state's five-year plans for tribal areas keeping in view (a) the total population of the area, (b) the geographical area, (c) the comparative level of development and (d) the state of social services. The state plan outlays may be regarded as comprised of "divisible" and "non-divisible" components. Those investments whose benefits do not or cannot flow to any specific region or a particular target group may be called the 'non-divisible component'. From the 'Divisible Pool', apart from their due share weightage needs to be given to the tribal areas while from the 'non-divisible' portion, accrual of due share of benefits should be ensured to tribal region. On the whole, to compensate for the neglect and backwardness, the tribal areas should attract weightage in allocation of funds.

The process of quantification of funds having been accepted by the state government, one method is adopted for reflection of the quantified funds in the State's budget. Each sub-head of a minor-head in the budget of a sectoral administrative department is split up into two parts. One reflecting the share of the financial provision of the scheme for the tribal sub-plan areas and the other part reflecting the rest of the provision. This method is an improvement over the earlier nebulous position in as much as funds available for the tribal sub-plan area appear quantified under the respective departments. However, under the sub-plan approach, the quantification of funds in the state plan resources for utilisation in the tribal areas in reasonable proportion is almost mandatory. Further, by providing funds under separate minor head in the budget of concerned departments, diversion of state plan funds to the non-sub-plan area is prohibited. In the result flow of funds to the sub-plan area out of state plan resources and other resources increases.

Central/Centrally Sponsored Programmes

The centre having a special responsibility towards the Scheduled Tribes and Scheduled Areas, the role of central ministries assume significance. The Planning Commission has asked the central ministries and departments to have a clear idea of the problems of tribal area, prepare special programmes relating to their concerned sectors. They should adopt the ongoing programmes wherever necessary in consultation with the state governments keeping in view the requirements of the tribal areas. Hence, while making formulations commencing at the ITDP level and aggregating at the state level, fields where the central ministries can play a substantial role are identified. The estimated outlays are then projected. It is ensured that there is integration of such outlays with state plan investment at the local level.

While the state government have fallen in line with the concept of the tribal sub-plan as evolved by the Planning Commission, the Central Ministries are yet to play their full role. However, the Central Ministries assist those schemes, which they consider important for tribal areas and for which state resources are inadequate. The support is for programmes and not for staff, unless they are staff-based schemes like a research station or a cattle breeding farm. The Central Ministries not only quantify funds but also introduce budgetary mechanism adopted by the states. As a result of this, such funds are reflected in their respective budgets so that they are not diverted. If diversion of funds earmarked for tribal areas in the budget of the Central Ministries becomes necessary on any account, this will be done with the concurrence of the Planning Commission and the Ministry of Home Affairs. Some of the important items which are supplemented by the central ministries are shifting cultivation, minor irrigation, medium irrigation, horticulture, pastures and cattle development, tassar development, agricultural research, marketing and credit, elementary and adult education, qualitative improvement of education, distribution of health services, special health measures for declining tribes, drinking water, rural roads development, rural electrification, development of hinterland of industrial and mining complexes, etc.

Special Central Assistance

The Ministry of Home Affairs is the nodal ministry for tribal development. It operates the special central assistance. It has been recognised clearly that the basic investments in tribal areas and for tribal communities are to be made from the state plan and funds of the centrally sponsored and central plan schemes. The role of the special central assistance is that of a gap filler i.e., to make available resources for specially relevant schemes for which funds are otherwise not in sight. Hence, the special central assistance is supplementary in character. It is just an additive to the state plan resources and centrally sponsored schemes. It is to supplement the specially relevant schemes with particular focus and emphasis on the economic development of the tribals. The distribution of special central assistance among the state governments is being done on the basis of a three-factor formula. It takes into consideration the tribe population in the state, area occupied by the Scheduled Tribe population and the factor that represents the inverse proportion of net domestic product of the state. The three components determine the share in the proportion of 50:30:20. However, the performance of the state governments determines not only the share of the special central assistance but also the size of plan funds allocable by the Planning Commission. In fact, curtailment of resources on account of inadequate formulation or implementation of tribal development programmes is made in sensitive sectors so that it becomes result-oriented.

Institutional Finance

In view of the growing importance of individual economic programmes and schemes in the corporate sector, institutional finance has been accepted as an important constituent of the sub-plan outlay. Institutional finance has come to occupy an important position in the development process. It adds to the financial resources required for the development programmes. It is an important ingredient in the beneficiary-oriented programme for economic development. Subsidy element is available out of flow of funds under state plan, special central assistance and central plan schemes. The loan component has to flow from different financial institutions in the commercial and cooperative banking sectors.

In the formulation of programmes, specific problems of each area and the target group in terms of family need to be clearly defined and schemes directly benefiting the individual tribals are to be given the highest priority. In the field of agriculture, a tribal family is provided 50 per cent subsidy. Another 50 per cent is the loan component from the financial institution. Similar arrangements are made in the field of horticulture, sericulture, animal husbandry, small irrigation, forestry, cottage and small industries. In the field of credit-cum-marketing, the part to be played by institutional finance is vital. Consumption credit, no less than production credit, has come to occupy a crucial position in the gamut of measures for the promotion of tribal economy. The quantum of institutional finance is a derived figure. It is dependent on the loan component in the package of programmes with the improvement of infrastructure and effective implementation of programmes.

Non-Plan Resources

Besides these, there is an umbrella region in the financial picture. This is the non-plan budget of the state government programmes taken up in course of a plan period. It gets transferred to the non-plan side at the end of the plan period. The funds for maintaining the earlier plan programmes are taken to be committed to the non-plan budget for maintenance of services created as a part of the plan activity. It is provided by the award of the Finance Commission. The depressing aspect in respect of tribal areas is that the development effort in these areas having so far been scanty, the non-plan sector has remained exiguous. It is a matter of concern since some sectors are financed in the main from the non-plan side e.g. education, health, cooperation, agriculture. In the field of education the non-plan investment is many times of the plan outlay. A lion's share of the expenditure goes for meeting the salary of the teachers and building maintenance of the schools.

Flow of Funds

The financial arrangements for tribal development have been undergoing changes with the change in the administrative structure. The launching of tribal sub-plan since the Fifth Five-Year Plan witnessed significant growth in the share of public interest for tribal areas.[2] While in the First Plan only one per cent of the total National Plan outlay was earmarked for tribal development programmes, it increased to a little over five per cent during the Sixth Five-Year Plan.[3]

Flow of Funds from State Plan

Quantification of funds from different sectors and sources for tribal areas and fixation of targets to be achieved under different sectoral programmes are the characteristic features of the tribal development programmes in the state.[4] It has been laid down in principle that funds should be earmarked by all the Departments for the development of sub-plan areas and the quantum of budgetary allocation out of state plan to those areas must not fall short of the proportionate population equivalent to STs of the state. The funds earmarked for Tribal Sub-Plan areas are presented in a separate minor head in the budget estimate by the respective Departments. It cannot be diverted. Total State Plan outlay, flow to tribal sub-plan area and percentage flow from total outlay during different Five-Year Plans are indicted in Table 5.1.

Table 5.1 presents a grim picture of the financial diversion for tribal development. The allocation of funds for Tribal Sub-Plan Areas from First to Fourth Plan period was low. The lowest was during the Fourth Plan with 1.73 per cent. The percentage figures never exceeded 5.41 per cent during the first four Plan periods. It was only from the Fifth Plan onwards that the percentage figure increased with the highest of 35.55 per cent during the Sixth Plan period.

Table 5.1.
Plan-wise Flow of Funds to Tribal Sub-Plan Area under State Plan (Rs. in lakh)

Plan Periods	*Total State Plan Outlay*	*Flow for Tribal Development and to TSP Area*	*Percentage to total*
First Plan (1951-56)	2055. 49	111. 28	5.41
Second Plan (1956-61)	9998. 91	380. 00	3.80
Third Plan (1961-66)	16000. 00	463. 00	2.89
Fourth Plan (1969-74)	22260. 00	385. 00	1.73
Fifth Plan (1974-69)	88850. 00	12735. 00	14.33
Sixth Plan (1980-85)	150000. 00	53319. 00	35.55
Seventh Plan (1985-90)	508871. 10	178905. 05	35.16
Eighth Plan (1992-97)	1000000. 00	232801. 37	23.28
Ninth Plan (1997-2002)	1457801. 76	343153. 17	23.54

Source: Government documents.

Table 5.2

Outlay and Expenditure for tribal Development Programmes under Five Year Plans in Orissa (Rs. in lakh)

Sl. No.	Five Year Plans	State Sector		Central Sector		Special Central Assistance		Total	
		Outlay	Expenditure	Outlay	Expenditure	outlay	Expenditure	Outlay	Expenditure
1.	First Plan	111. 28	111.28	116.29	116.29	-	-	227. 57	227.57
2.	Second Plan	380. 00	332.00	336.73	328.58	-	-	716.73	660.58
3.	Third Plan	463. 00	371.43	378.67	373.94	-	-	841.67	745.37
4.	Fourth Plan	385. 00	384.38	488.50	558.00	-	-	973.50	942.38
5.	Fifth Plan	12,735. 00	14,167.07	2, 54.57	2,544.57	3,267.4	3,267.44	18,547.01	19,979.08
6.	Sixth Plan	53,319. 00	47,099.81	10, 67.00	11,743.02	5,659.00	5,844.55	69,745.00	64,727.38
7.	Seventh Plan	178,905	99,462.93	18,818.07	35,252.73	14,724.37	9,116.71	212,447.49	143,832.37
8.	Eighth Plan	232,801. 37	137,774.92	49,858.82	55,965.10	16,757.80	16,300.58	299,417.99	210,040.60
9.	Ninth Plan	343,153. 17	235,447.32	120,283.28	120,180.28	25,190.10	28,849.95	488,626.55	384,477.55

Source: Government documents.

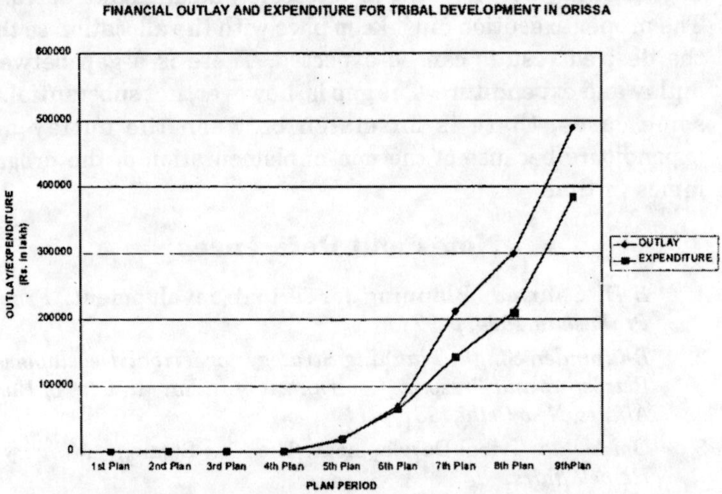

Outlay and Expenditure during Plan Periods

Besides State Plan, funds from different other sources and sectors were earmarked for tribal development programmes viz., Central Plan, Centrally Sponsored Plan and Special Central Assistance. The outlay and expenditure of all these sources during different plan periods of the State under tribal development programmes are indicated in Table 5.2 and Fig. 4.

Table 5.2 depicts the outlay and expenditure pattern and the various sources of finance for tribal development programmes. The total outlay weighs out total expenditure in all the Plans barring the Fifth Five Year Plan. Total expenditure falling short of total outlay is the redeeming feature of all the Plans. This picture, however, is not the same in case of individual sectors. There are exceptions in expenditure under state sector during the Fifth Plan period, central sector during Sixth to Eighth Plan, central assistance during Sixth and Ninth Plans. The expenditure remained above the outlay in those cases.

Conclusion

Allocation in itself does not guarantee in any way the attainment of lofty objectives proclaimed by the Constitution.[6]

Higher outlay does not always necessarily mean higher outcome. The proper execution must keep pace with the allocation so that the desired results can be expected. There is a gap between outlay and expenditure. The gap is, however, not substantial. In some cases, there is mismatch between the outlay and expenditure because of the non-implementation of the programmes in time.

Notes and References

1. *B.D. Sharma,* Planning for Tribal development, *Prachi Prakashan,1984, p. 92.*
2. *Bhupinder Singh, Planning Strategy for Tribal Development: Retrospect and Prospect, Government of India, Ministry of Home Affairs, New Delhi,1981, p.14.*
3. *Om Mehta,* Tribal Development: The New Strategy, *Ministry of Home Affairs.*
4. *Government of Orissa, Welfare Department,* Tribal Sub-Plan for Annual Plan,1995-96, Orissa, *May1995, p.12.*
5. *Government of Orissa, ST and SC Development Department,* Tribal Sub-Plan for Annual Plan,1999-2000, Orissa, *August1999, p. 3.*
6. *V. C. Kumaran, "Development of Tribal Areas", in S. G. Deogaonkar (Ed.),* Problems of Development of Tribal Areas, *p. 40.*

6

Process of Implementation

The desired result or the achievements of the goals vastly depend upon the process of implementation. If the desired result for the programme are not achieved, the fault may lie anywhere. There may be leakages, inefficiency, corruption, graft and time over run. Sometimes, the objectives are overstressed and at times it is taken very casually, which account for good or bad results of the programmes. Various administrative arrangements have been made, like different departments, autonomous bodies and corporations for implementation of different tribal development projects/programmes and schemes.

The administration of our tribal programmes has acquired a new significance after independence. The Republic of India has decided to do justice to the hitherto exploited Scheduled Tribes.[1] But until recently the issues related to strengthening the administrative capability for development work in tribal areas did not receive the attention they deserve.[2] During the last twenty-five years, the efforts are made to alter the fate of tribal people living in different parts of India. The desired results have not been achieved and our objectives have suffered. The lessons we have learnt from our failures are used to readjust the policy. The programme objectives are redefined, further allocations of funds are made and fresh targets are fixed again.

The tribal development programmes will not again speed up as long as complex formal structures of various departments are accorded prominence. The purpose of formulating plans in a rational manner is to facilitate their successful implementation. Possibly this, once again, brings us to the formulation stages of tribal development programmes. The Working Group on Tribal Development during medium term plan (1978-83) appointed by the Ministry of Home Affairs, in its report has categorically pointed out that, "with the level of financial investments moving up, administrative unpreparedness has appeared as an important constraint in purposive utilisation of resources. The establishment of a single line of command, organic integration of programmes in the field and effective delegation of powers to the project authorities have been agreed to in principle but remain to be fully implemented, in some states even first steps have not been taken."[3] While investments have been rising, a corresponding adequate matching administrative framework has not been brought into existence.[4] A working group, which studied problems and programmes of tribal development made this specific recommendation."The Government of India, in consultation with State Governments, may take up a review of level of administration of the tribal areas and suitable schemes may be prepared for upgrading it within a reasonable time frame."[5]

A new awareness has been created about the many problems that arise in implementing development programmes in tribal area. Goel and Goel pointed out that "among the three components required for developmental tasks– men, money and material (M^3), it is more the man (or the human element) than any other factor, which determines the quantity and the quality of the performance and output."[6]

However, implementation of these tribal development programmes is a joint responsibility of both the Central and State Governments and both the Governments, therefore, ensure the effective and smooth implementation of tribal development programmes in tribal areas.

Central Government

The Centre has a special constitutional responsibility towards the Scheduled Tribes. The role of the central ministries assumes paramount significance. The central ministries and departments after having a clear idea of the problems of tribal areas prepare special programmes relating to their respective sectors. They adopt the ongoing programmes in consultation with the State governments keeping in view the requirements of the tribal areas. The Central Ministries not only quantify funds but also introduce the budgetary mechanism adopted by the states. Funds are made available by the central ministries and departments for tribal development programmes in the form of centrally sponsored and central schemes. The Ministry of Home Affairs, the nodal Ministry for Tribal development, operates 'Special Central Assistance'. Under special Central assistance, resources are made available for specially relevant tribal development schemes. The Home Ministry and the Ministry of Welfare constantly monitor and review the implementation of tribal development programmes.

State Government

The State Government is not only charged with implementing massive programmes for all round development of the Scheduled Tribes, but it is responsible for adopting legislations for the good governance of the scheduled areas. All departments of the Government participate in the task of ensuring clean administration of the scheduled areas as well as implementing tribal development programmes. The Harijan and Tribal Welfare Development acts as a liaisoning and coordinating department so far as tribal development programmes and scheduled areas are concerned. Consequent upon the implementation of the tribal sub-plan and the declaration of the sub-plan areas as scheduled areas, the task of liaison and coordination has assumed paramount importance. In the state headquarters, the H and T. W. Department is in charge of implementation of multipronged development programmes of Scheduled Tribes through its field organisations.

Before dealing with the process of the implementation of tribal development programmes at different levels, let us deal with the administrative set up the H and T. W. Department of the state which is the sole policymaker and coordinating department of tribal development programmes.

Harijan and Tribal Welfare Department of State

The H and T. W. Department in the State headquarters now renamed as SC and ST Development Department is in charge of formulation, implementation, monitoring and evaluation of developmental programmes of Scheduled Tribes through its field organisations. The H and T. W. Department functions as a composite office of both secretariat and head of department. So far the headquarters set-up of the department is concerned, the department functions under the supervision of a Commissioner-cum-Secretary assisted by two Directors-cum-Additional Secretaries: one for tribal welfare and another for Harijan welfare. Besides, there are two Joint Directors-cum-Deputy Secretaries, one officer on Special Duty-cum-Deputy Secretary, one Financial Adviser-cum-Deputy Secretary, one Deputy Secretary of Establishment, an Under Secretary, two Special Officers-cum-Under Secretaries, one Welfare Officer, one Assistant Director (Headquarters), two Research Officers, three Special Officers, two Accounts Officers and Section Officers in different sections in the H and T. W. Department.

Committees and Councils

At the State level there is a State-level committee named "STATCOM" under the Chairmanship of the Chief Minister, which decides policy matters and reviews the progress of implementation of tribal development programmes from time to time. The State-level Committee was constituted in 1975. There is a standing committee of the H and T. W. Department where interdepartmental problems relating to implementation of tribal development programmes are reviewed. The Additional Development Commissioner is the Chairman of this Committee. The Secretary, Finance Department is the member and the Commissioner-cum-Secretary, H and T. W. Department is the Member-Secretary of this Committee. The Secretaries of the concerned departments are invited to participate in the discussions when their subject matters are discussed.

There is a 'Tribes Advisory Council' in the State where the progress of implementation of various programmes for development of tribals as a whole is discussed and suggestions of the members are taken into consideration in the matter of formulation of programmes and implementation thereof.

In pursuance of sub-paragraph 3 of paragraph 4 of the 5th Schedule of the Constitution of India, a Tribes' Advisory Council was formed in Orissa on 24th June 1950 to advise the Government on matters pertaining to the welfare and advancement of Scheduled Tribes in the State.[7] The business of the council is transacted according to provision contained in the Orissa Tribes' Advisory Council Rules, 1950. The Council consists of 20 members including the Chairman. The Chief Minister of Orissa and the Minister in charge of Tribal and Rural Welfare, Orissa are the Chairman and Deputy Chairman of the Council respectively.

Institutions and Academics

THRTI/SCSTRTI

A tribal research bureau was set up by the Government in 1952 to serve as a permanent research centre providing data and advisory service to Government on problems of SC and ST. An orientation and training institute was set up in 1967 to impart training to officers and workers posted in tribal areas. These two institutes were amalgamated into an integrated institute in 1972. This composite institute since then is known as 'Tribal and Harijan Research-cum-Training Institute' and now redesignated as 'Scheduled Castes and Scheduled Tribes Research-cum-Training Institute'. It is functioning under the supervision of the Director and assisted by the Deputy Directors, Asst. Directors, Research Personnel and ministerial staff for facilitating smooth conduct of research work. The tribal concentrated regions of the state have been divided into six research zones, each zone headed by a Research Officer assisted by some junior research officers and investigators.

Initially, the Bureau was meant for conducting scientific studies on life and problems of various tribal and non-tribal groups. This was meant to assess the usefulness of development programmes and to aid in providing a dependable database for the planned advancement of the Scheduled Castes and Scheduled Tribes.

After the tribal sub-plan came into operation during the Fifth Five Year Plan, there has been a shift in emphasis from socio-cultural aspects to socio-economic progress of change and development in tribal areas. As a result, the functioning of the Institute got widened beyond its staffing pattern and infrastructural facilities. The institute is now serving as:

1. A Centre for applied research and studies on demography, agricultural practices in hill areas, language, health and nutritional status, economic system, educational problems and such other subjects as are related to tribal societies.
2. A databank and a documentation centre to serve as a basis for formulating realistic plans directed towards the improvement of socio-economic conditions of tribal people.
3. A briefing and training centre for officers and workers among tribal communities (such as administrators, educators, forest, police and excise staff, extension workers and specialists in project formulation, monitoring and evaluation of development programmes).
4. A centre for carrying out evaluation of developmental programmes, which are implemented in tribal areas.
5. A bureau providing advisory services to Government on problems concerning implementation of educational, health and welfare services and improvement of communication, marketing facilities, agricultural practices and quality of life in tribal societies.

The institute plays a key role in the new strategy for tribal development to have close contact with various developmental activities. Six local or regional research zones have been created and attached to ITDAs. The major task of the zonal staff is to formulate the projects for the ITDAs to take up evaluation of developmental schemes and carry out socio-economic and benchmark surveys.

Academy of Tribal Dialects and Culture

The Academy of Tribal Dialects and Culture has been functioning since June1979. The salient objectives of the Academy are delineated below:

(i) To preserve and promote culture like dance, song, music, drama, arts and crafts by providing financial assistance to cultural institutions and tribal artists;

(ii) Organising tribal language training centres;

(iii) Conducting language study in tribal areas and promoting tribal dialects by preparation of multilingual dictionaries, grammar and primers;

(iv) Compilation and dissemination of tribal literature by holding seminars, workshops and exhibitions;

(v) Organising adult literacy centres; and

(vi) Providing audiovisual aids where required.

In pursuance of these objectives, the Academy has undertaken a study of five major tribal languages, namely, Kui, Santali, Saura, Kisan and Didayi. Multilingual dictionaries, grammar and primers have been compiled and are being published. The Academy has also taken up 18 tribal language training centres in 21 ITDAs for imparting training to Government employees of different categories working in the sub-plan area. This was to enable them to effectively communicate with the tribals and to win their confidence. The Academy has, by way of documentation, got recorded 182 Santali songs and music. Besides, song and music of Kondh, Koya and Gadaba tribes have been tape-recorded and preserved. A gramophone disc of 500 numbers in Santali, Kondh, Koya and Gadaba songs and music has been prepared by the INRECO, Calcutta. Some black and white and coloured photographs have been snapped and preserved showing cultural facts of Adivasis. Steps are being taken for recording songs and music of Saora, Paraja, Mundari and Juang. Seminar and cultural programmes on tribal drama, dance, songs and music have been organised both at the State and the district levels. Attempt is on for preparing films on tribal dances, lifestyles and developmental features.

Corporations

Tribal Development Cooperative Corporation of Orissa Ltd. (TDCCOL):

The TDCCOL started functioning in the state in 1972. This acts as an apex organisation for the purchase and sale of Minor Forest Produce (MFP) and Surplus Agricultural Produce (SAP) collected by the tribals. It is meant to protect the tribals from the exploitation of the middlemen and supply them essential commodities at a fair price. Its objective is to procure SAP and MFP from the tribals at a remunerative price. The procured commodities are then marketed by the TDCCOL. It too, supplies essential commodities and consumer goods to them. The Corporation functions with its head office at Bhubaneswar along with 3 divisional offices, 15 branches, 130 procurement-cum-collection centres, 69 fair price shops and 360 seasonal procurement centres in the sub-plan areas of the state.[9]

Orissa Scheduled Caste, Scheduled Tribe Development Finance Cooperative Corporation (OSCSTDFCC):

The OSCSTDFCC Ltd. was constituted in August 1979 to act as a catalyst to accelerate the pace of economic development of the Scheduled Castes and Scheduled Tribes. It plays a significant role in providing missing financial inputs required to improve the economic condition of Scheduled Tribes particularly the poorest segments by adopting suitable and viable family-oriented schemes through Dispersed Tribal Development Programme (DTDP).

The objectives of the Corporation are as follows:

(i) To plan, promote, undertake and assist programmes of agriculture development, animal husbandry, marketing, processing, supply and storage of agricultural produce, small scale industry, village industry, cottage industry, trade, business, etc. to enable the members of the Scheduled Castes and Scheduled Tribes to have a better living.

(ii) To undertake a programme for setting up employment oriented industries, cottage and small scale industries, village industries, etc. by itself or by providing technical know-how, managerial assistance, financial assistance or any other form of assistance which may be required in achieving the above objective including providing the necessary financial guarantees to institutions on behalf of the societies concerned.

(iii) To open its branches at district level and also at other places in lieu of district societies for transaction of its operation.

(iv) To provide working capital to the affiliated societies by advancing loans and cash credits.

(v) To coordinate, supervise and control the activities of the affiliated societies.

(vi) To act as the agent of the Government for procurement, supply and distribution of agricultural and other produce.

(vii) To provide facilities for survey and research of the problems relating to cottage and village industries. The intention is to assess potentialities in these areas.

(viii) To arrange publicity and marketing of the finished products manufactured by the members in the village industries if necessary by opening showrooms, emporiums, exhibitions, etc.

(ix) To invest or deposit surplus funds of the Corporation in Government securities or in cooperative banks.

(x) To issue bonds and debentures for raising resources for fulfilling any of the objectives of the Corporation.

(xi) Generally to purchase, take on lease or in exchange, hire or otherwise acquire, any real and personal property, any rights or privileges, which the corporation may think necessary or convenient for the purpose of its business.

(xii) To receive grants, gifts, donations, loans, advances or other money on deposit or otherwise from the governments of Orissa and India, cooperative or commercial banks, LIC, companies, trusts or individuals in order to fulfil its objectives.

(xiii) To provide for the welfare of the person in the employment of the Corporation and families including wives and widows of such persons, by establishing provident or other funds by grant of money, pensions or other payments towards educational and medical relief.

(xiv) To encourage self-help, thrift and cooperation among the affiliated societies and their members.

(xv) To own plants, machineries and other kinds of equipment necessary for implementation of small-scale cottage industries meant for providing a better living to scheduled castes and scheduled tribes.

The OSCSTDFCC has a Chairman-cum-Managing Director as its head. The General Manager, who is an OAS-I Officer, is in charge of its administration. The other officials who discharge responsibilities in the Corporation are the Credit Advisor, Development Officer, Assistant Development Officers, Officer in-charge of Programmes and so on.

Field Set-up

As mentioned earlier, different tribal development programmes are in operation in the state and they are implemented through various field organisations with necessary guidelines and directions from the State Government. The field organisation of the Department presents a four-tier system of administration at the divisional, district, sub-divisional and block levels. At the divisional level, the welfare schemes are administered under the supervision of the Revenue Divisional Commissioners. District Welfare Officers have been posted at the district level and they work under the supervision of the Collectors. Assistant District Welfare Officers have been posted at the Sub-Divisional Level and they work under the supervision of the sub-divisional officers. Block is the lowest level of welfare administration where Welfare Extension Officers have been posted to work under the control of the Block Development Officers. However, the process of implementation of the tribal development programmes at field level is discussed below:

Tribal Sub-Plan

The programmes under tribal sub-plan are implemented in the sub-plan areas. The Scheduled Areas of Orissa are coterminous with sub-plan areas of the State with the only exception that the Sorada Tahasil excluding Gazalbadi and Gochha Gram Panchayats of Ganjam District has not been included in the sub-plan area.

More than two-third of the total area of the state is covered with inaccessible hills and dense forests. They are inaccessible and underdeveloped in nature. About 44.59 per cent of the total area of the state has been declared as scheduled areas. The scheduled areas are largely inhabited by tribal communities. The following areas of Orissa were declared as scheduled areas according to the order issued by the Government of India in 1950 and subsequently revised in 1977.

1. Koraput district.
2. Sundargarh district.
3. Mayurbhanj district.
4. Champua, Kanjipani, Barbil and Keonjhar Tahasils in Keonjhar district.
5. G. Udayagiri, Balliguda, Kondhmal Tahasils in Phulbani district.
6. Kuchinda Tahasil in Sambalpur district.
7. R. Udayagiri Tahasil, Gumma and Rayagada blocks in Ganjam district.
8. Thuamul-Rampur and Lanjigarh blocks in Kalahandi district.
9. Nilgiri block in Balasore district.

Besides, the Surada Tahasil excluding Gazalbadi and Gochha Gram Panchayats of Ganjam district is included in the scheduled areas, but excluded from tribal sub-plan areas. In order to give operational effect to the tribal sub-plan approach in the sub-plan areas, 19 ITDPs were constituted during the period from 1974-75 to 1978-79 in a phased manner. In addition to these 19 ITDPs, 4 TDAs were functioning in the sub-plan areas. After abolition of the TDAs in 1979, two of them were merged in adjoining ITDPs and the other two were redesignated as ITDPs.

The ITDAs are the main organisation in the field to implement the Tribal Sub-plan programmes. Now, 21 ITDAs are functioning in 12 districts covering 118 blocks. Project administrators in ITDAs and Block Development Officers at block levels are mainly in charge of implementing the tribal sub-plan programmes in the field. The project administrator supervises the work programmes executed by different bodies.

An ITDA is a unit of planning, and a development block is a unit of execution. Administrative linkages from bottom to top in the ITDAs is as follows:

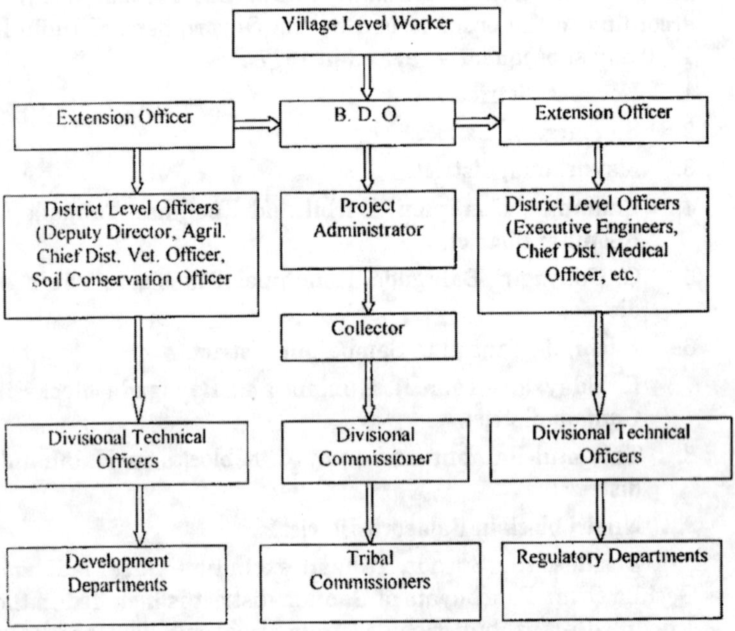

In this manner, a unified line of command has been sought to be set up. The administrative hierarchy for tribal development administration has been streamlined in a single line of command. The Tribal Development Commissioner at the State level operates through a whole time Director at the Secretariat level, the Collectors at the district level and the Project Administrators at the ITDA level. The BDOs are associated with all the tribal development programmes. The major chunk of the income generating schemes are implemented through the BDOs. They solely remain responsible for the execution of the ITDP programmes.

All the 21 ITDAs are now headed by project administrators. Previously, sub-divisional officers were functioning as ex-officio Project Directors. The work of ITDA is multidisciplinary in nature. It functions as a nodal agency in terms of plan formulation, implementation of programmes and monitoring of progress. Each Project Administrator is assisted by a Special Officer. In addition to all these, each ITDA has been provided with engineering staff for smooth execution of various works.

In order that the Project Administrators play their role effectively in the developmental administrative set up in the field and acts as a comprehensive coordinator, the State Government has vested them with powers of A.D.M. It has also been decided that the Project Administrators will give an annual report on the work of the BDOs under their respective jurisdiction to the Collector of the district. These administrative innovations may go a long way to enable the Project Administrators to play his role constructively and purposefully. It will also ensure discipline in the chain of command and coordination at District/ Project level.

For planning and overseeing activities at each ITDA, a Project-level Committee has been constituted. The Collector of the district is the Chairman of the Committee. The local MPs, MLAs, Chairman of the concerned Panchayat Samitis and district level officers in charge of development programmes are also members. The Project Administrator is the Member-Secretary and is fully responsible for formulation of plan programmes. Quarterly review of the progress of implementation of various programmes is undertaken in the project level committee.

Modified Area Development Approach

For all-round development of dispersed tribals living outside the tribal sub-plan area,46 MADA pockets in 17 districts covering 2553 villages are now functioning in the state.[10] These projects have been functioning since 1978-79 and a substantial amount of special central assistance sanctioned for implementing different development programmes for the socio-economic benefit of the Scheduled Tribes residing in the pockets of tribal concentration (Appendix– V).

Development block as the smallest unit for inclusion in the tribal sub-plan area has been relaxed while identifying MADA pockets. A MADA pocket may cross block boundaries and a single block may have two MADA pockets.

H and T.W. Department of the state is the policy formulating authority of the MADA programmes. The programmes are implemented in the districts under the overall supervision of Collectors. A special officer functions in the district for monitoring the implementation of MADA programmes. Block Development Officers implement the family-oriented programmes as well as the employment-oriented programmes under MADA with the help of Welfare Extension Officers and Junior Engineers.

For effective and expeditious implementation of various schemes in MADA pockets, Advisory Boards have been constituted for each MADA pocket under the Chairmanship of concerned sub-divisional officers. The local MPs and MLAs, Chairman of Panchayat Samities and Block Development Officers are its members. Apart from its role in formulating programmes, the Committee reviews the progress in implementation of the programmes.

Clusters

As said earlier, beyond the MADA pockets, there are small areas of tribal concentrations called clusters. Thirteen such clusters covering parts of 12 blocks in 263 villages have been functioning (Appendix– V). The administrative arrangement for the clusters is similar to that of MADA pockets except that no additional Welfare Extension Officer (WEO) has been provided.

The WEO of the concerned blocks under the supervision of the Block Development Officers are executing the cluster programmes. There is a cluster level advisory committee in the pattern of MADA pockets to plan, review and oversee the implementation of the programmes in cluster pockets.

Micro Projects for Primitive Tribes

For the total development of primitive tribal groups, 17 micro projects are operating in 12 districts of the state (Appendix-VIII). A Special Officer has been appointed for each micro project. Officers from agriculture department have been brought under deputation and appointed as special officers in some micro projects. This is the case where shifting cultivation measures are undertaken. In some other micro project agencies, officers who have worked for more than ten years as District Welfare Officers and have sufficient experience about tribal life have been appointed as special officers. Technical officers either from the Horticulture, Soil Conservation or Agriculture discipline have been posted to assist the special officers for implementation of the programmes. The programmes for the micro projects are implemented under the overall supervision of the District Collector at the district level and Special Officer at the project level. The H and T. W. Department of the State is the policy-formulating organisation of these projects at the top. A Governing Body operates for each micro project. The concerned Collector of the district is the Chairman of the Micro Project located outside the sub-plan area. The local MP, MLAs and Chairman of Panchayat Samities are members of the Governing Body. A special officer of the project is the Convener. The Governing Body is responsible for formulation of programmes. It monitors and reviews the progress in the implementation of the programmes.

Special Educational Programmes and Other Programmes For the Welfare of Scheduled Tribes

Special educational programmes and other programmes are implemented for the welfare of Scheduled Tribes. Education is imparted to Scheduled Tribe children at various stages in residential high schools, Ashram Schools, Residential Sevashrams and Sevashrams. Scholarships at pre-matric and post-matric stages are provided to them. Other programmes like legal aid to Scheduled Tribes and compensation to victims of atrocities are implemented for the welfare of the Scheduled Tribes. H and T. W. Department at the state headquarters is the policymaker and administrative department so far as implementation of special educational programmes and other programmes are concerned. The Revenue Divisional Commissioners at the revenue divisions and Collectors at the district level monitor the implementation of the programmes. District Welfare Officers in districts, Asst. District Welfare Officers in Subdivisions and Welfare Extension Officers in the blocks are in charge of implementing these programmes for the welfare of Scheduled Tribes. Welfare Extension Officers in the blocks function under the Block Development Officers.

Margin Money Loan Programme (MMLP) and Dispersed Tribal development Programme (DTDP)

Orissa Scheduled Caste and Scheduled Tribe Development Finance Cooperative Corporation (OSCSTDFCC) is operating the MML and DTD Programmes for the economic development of Scheduled Castes and Scheduled Tribes through implementation of economically viable schemes. Initially, the Corporation was looking after the schemes for development of Scheduled Castes only and the task of implementation of tribal development programmes was entrusted with the Corporation in1984.[11] The margin money loan programme is implemented by the Corporation at the state headquarters by the District Collectors and district managers at the district level, Sub-divisional Development Officers and Additional District Welfare Officers at the sub-divisional level and by the Block Development Officers and Welfare Extension Officers at the block level.

Taking into account the concentration of SC and ST population in different areas, district branches in the seven districts of Cuttack, Puri, Balasore, Dhenkanal, Ganjam, Koraput and Sambalpur were started. The Collector of each district is in overall charge of implementing the scheme of the

Corporation. He is assisted by a District Manager, OSCSTDFCC, Project Administrator of ITDA and District Welfare Officers for the smooth implementation of the schemes. The Collector, as the head of the district, plays crucial role in coordinating the activities of different departments associated with the implementation of the Schemes. The Collector issues instructions to the field level officers. However, instead of suggesting grandiose schemes, the model schemes prepared by the Corporation are adopted. The model schemes are tailored to the requirements of the SCs and STs particularly those who are below the poverty line. District Managers of the OSCSTDFCC in the district remain responsible for the execution of the programmes. Additional District Welfare Officers in the subdivisions and Welfare Extension Officers in the Blocks assist the District Managers for carrying out the programme. However, the Collectors take steps to ensure that the officers and the agencies involved in the implementation of the schemes go about the tasks assigned to them.

Protective and Anti-exploitative Measures

In order to safeguard the interest of the tribals pertaining to land, agriculture, allotment of ceiling surplus land and government wasteland, reservation in government jobs, etc. different kinds of measures are implemented. Further, to save the tribals from exploitation, various protective legislations have been enacted and enforced in the state.

(a) Programmes like land alienation, allotment of ceiling surplus land, allotment of government wasteland and distribution of house sites to Scheduled Tribes are implemented under the supervision of the Member of the Board of Revenue. The Revenue Department and the Member, Board of Revenue are the policymaking organisations in the state with regard to the implementation of these programmes. At the Divisional level, the RDC is the supervising and monitoring authority of these programmes. At the district level, these programmes are implemented under the direct supervision of the Collector. An

Additional District Magistrate in charge of land revenue and a Revenue Officer function under the Collector to monitor the implementation of these programmes. In the Tahasils, Tahasildars are responsible for implementing the land reforms programmes. He is assisted by the Additional Tahasildar. The Tahasildars and Additional Tahasildars through their revenue supervisors and revenue inspectors distribute ceiling surplus land and house sites and government wasteland to the Scheduled Tribes.

(b) The programme for abolition of the Bonded Labour system and their rehabilitation is implemented by the BDOs in the blocks. They identify the bonded labourers through their extension officers and provide them economic assistance under the programme of Economic Rehabilitation of Rural Poor. The SDOs in the sub-divisions, Project Officer, District Rural Development Agencies and Collectors in the district supervise and monitor the implementation of the programme. Revenue Divisional Commissioners at the divisional levels also monitor the implementation of this programme. The Panchayat Raj Department of the State is the policymaking organisation of this programme at the top.

(c) For reservation of STs and SCs in services, implementation of provisions of the Orissa Reservation of Vacancies in Posts and Services (for SCs and STs) Act, 1975 and the rules framed there under came into force with effect from 1.6.1976. A few amendments were made in the Act during 1982. It makes a provision of 23 per cent reservation for the tribals. Appointments made in contravention of the provisions of this Act shall be treated as violable. The percentage of reservation is monitored by the District Welfare Officers at the district level.

Anti-Poverty Programmes

Various family-oriented anti-poverty programmes like IRDP, ERRP, are implemented in the state to eradicate the poverty amongst the economically weaker sections of the society. The BDOs in the blocks are directly implementing the family-oriented poverty eradication programmes. They identify the beneficiaries. District Rural Development Agencies of the districts release the subsidy. They are distributed through BDOs in kind and banks provide the loans. The BDOs through their extension officers ensure proper utilisation of the assets by the beneficiaries. The SDOs in the subdivisions and the Project Officers of the DRDA monitor the implementation of these programmes. Project Officer of the DRDA is assisted by the Additional Project Officers and Assistant Project Officers. In case of employment-oriented infrastructure programmes, funds are released by the DRDAs to various departments executing the works operating in the districts. Funds are also released to Block Development Officers under these programmes to take up small projects and programmes. However, the Collector of a district as Chairman of DRDA is in overall charge of supervision of these programmes. Revenue Divisional Commissioners in the divisions too monitor the implementation of these programmes. The Panchayati Raj Department is the administrative department so far as the implementation of these programmes are concerned.

Monitoring and Evaluation

The sub-plan approach in tribal development was introduced during the Fifth Five Year Plan. In order to materialise the concept and to achieve the desired results, it is required to strengthen the monitoring and evaluation mechanism. The feedback from the field through regular monitoring and periodical evaluation is meant to take corrective measures and to provide necessary feedback for suitably reorienting policy approach and decisions. This aspect could not get adequate attention during the Fifth Plan period. Consequently, a lot of difficulties were faced to measure achievements.

This lacuna was removed to some extent in the Sixth Plan period. A monitoring cell was established in H and T. W. Department at the state level with a Joint Director, a Research Officer, a Junior Research Officer and other ministerial staff to monitor the tribal development programmes in sub-plan area. Similarly, at the project level, a statistical assistant was posted to maintain statistics on the progress of development schemes implemented in sub-plan area. Suitable formats to collect data on tribal development from the project-level were evolved and submission of regular progress reports was ensured on the basis of monthly progress reports. Regular reviews are made of the financial and physical achievements under individual benefit-oriented schemes and infrastructure development programmes. Copies of review notes are sent to RDCs, Collectors and Chairman of ITDAs, the Project Administrators, etc. The percentage of utilisation of the sanctioned amount is indicated in order to reflect the performance. The shortfalls in respect of overall performance and the coverage of beneficiaries are communicated in the review report for compliance by the officer concerned. Besides, Project-level Committees for ITDA, MADA and governing bodies for Micro Projects have been constituted to formulate and review developmental programmes. The decisions of the said Committees are reviewed in the Department and necessary instructions are issued to officers concerned.

A new feature introduced during the Sixth Plan period is to ensure concurrent monitoring-cum-evaluation through field officers to obtain data on the working of development schemes. A schedule has been prescribed for the purpose and the officers have been instructed to report number of the target cases regularly. The Commissioner reviews the findings of these reports and issues necessary instructions.

Family cards for all the beneficiaries of ITDA/Micro Project areas have been introduced since 1985-86 for ensuring proper check at the field level. Besides, evaluation of ITDAs has been entrusted to Tribal and Harijan Research-cum-Training Institute and other reputed consultancy organisations and Universities. The Joint Directors posted at the Divisional level assist the Divisional Commissioners in supervision, monitoring and evaluation of tribal development programmes.

In spite of all these arrangements, it is observed that the monitoring and evaluation of tribal development programmes are not done as expected due to several factors. The main difficulty is the lack of specialised manpower at ITDA level. As indicated earlier, there is only one Statistical Assistant at the ITDA-level for collection and compilation of statistics on tribal development. The flow of information is neither adequate nor uniform nor up-to-date. Therefore, it is necessary to develop and strengthen the monitoring and evaluation cell in each ITDA with specialised hands to tackle the problem at the root level. This is all the more important in view of decentralisation of planning and deolution of power at the grassroots level.

It is, therefore, imperative to streamline the entire system by suitably reinforcing staff at ITDA, division and state-levels for effective monitoring and evaluation of the tribal development programmes.

Voluntary Organisations

Till the emergence of tribal leadership, voluntary organisations need to play an important role alongside government machinery. The dedicated workers of the voluntary organisations can exercise healthy influence on the bureaucratic set-up. The government machinery and voluntary agencies should work hand-in-hand. Voluntary agencies could be used to plan the programmes on the basis of real local needs and resources at the village and block levels. They can be with the execution of programmes urgently required for tribal development. The gaps existing in different programmes can be filled up by the voluntary agencies to some extent.

A study of the history of tribal development indicates that the tribal community is a mere passive spectator of the development process. Development cannot be achieved unless beneficiaries themselves become conscious of their own rights and conditions, which make them socially and economically disadvantageous. They should have an urge to alter the situation with proper understanding of the correlations of social and economic forces. The voluntary agencies or civil societies, as we designate them, can make them active participants in the change process. They can play an active role in the process. It has many advantages, the plans are conceived and formulated on the basis of the needs of people, there is sizeable saving in expenditure, implementation becomes easier and finally people's aspirations are largely met. Dhebar has rightly said that they can also become the training ground for social service workers on a mass scale.[12]

In Orissa, there are 5817 voluntary organisations working in different areas of the state.[13] Many of these organisations work for the development of STs, SCs and other weaker sections of the community. Awareness raising campaign, infrastructure development works and individual benefit oriented schemes are the types of programmes undertaken by these voluntary agencies for the upliftment of the tribal people and tribal areas. The district-wise distribution of voluntary agencies in the state is indicated in Table 6.1.

New Areas of Intervention

There is no doubt about the fact that the voluntary organisations are doing appreciable work for the development of Scheduled Tribes. Yet, there are certain areas where greater involvement of these is needed. They are as follows:

(a) Wrong recording in survey by settlement authorities resulting in transfer of title of their land gives rise to tribal discontentment and unrest. Voluntary agencies should intervene in this area.

(b) Identification of tribal bonded labour is far from satisfactory. The voluntary organisations can come forward to solve this human problem.

(c) Various forms and forces of tribal exploitation can be prevented through 'Sanskar Kendras' on the pattern organised in the state of Gujarat.

(d) Apart from continued misery of some primitive tribal groups, risk of extinction of some of them is not far off. The voluntary organisations should come forward to accept the challenge in this regard.

Table 6.1
District-Wise Number of Voluntary Organisations/ NGOs in Orissa

Sl. No.	*District*	*No. of voluntary agencies/NGOs*
1.	Balasore	440
2.	Bhadrak	45
3.	Balangir	401
4.	Sonepur	130
5.	Cuttack	598
6.	Kendrapara	316
7.	Jagatsinghpur	289
8.	Jajpur	269
9.	Dhenkanal	107
10.	Angul	44
11.	Ganjam	38
12.	Gajapati	12
13.	Koraput	38
14.	Nowrangpur	34
15.	Rayagada	24
16.	Malkangiri	8
17.	Kalahandi	75
18.	Nawpara	12
19.	Keonjhar	586
20.	Mayurbhanj	1124
21.	Puri	576
22.	Khurda	317
23.	Nayagarh	12
24.	Phulbani	28
25.	Boudh	12
26.	Sambalpur	86
27.	Jharsuguda	54
28.	Deogarh	28
29.	Bargarh	65
30.	Sundargarh	49
	Total:	5, 817

Source: Planning and Coordination Department, Government of Orissa, *Directory of Non-Government Organisations in Orissa–1994.*

(e) The problem of shifting cultivation could be tackled easily if the voluntary agencies adopt a programme of educating the shifting cultivators on the advantages of settled cultivation.

(f) Various studies have revealed that development efforts have not reached tribal women. The tribal women should be encouraged to set up 'Mahila Mandals' and 'Mahila Samities'. Such organisations should be taken into confidence during planning and implementation of their welfare and development programmes.

However, there are lot of controversies about the performance and role of voluntary agencies. There are two diametrically opposed views about them. For example, Mohit Sen views, "It is wrong and even harmful to rely on voluntary agencies even partially for the implementation of plan projects, especially directed at poor millions".[14] K. N. Kabra opines, "Like so many false alternatives being propagated to so many genuine issues, the officially recognised, financed and co-opted voluntary agencies will provide another anachronism and false alternative".[15] On the other hand, we have a lot list of politicians, academics and social workers who have landed their role for development of the weaker sections. For example, the Prime Minister's directive to Chief Ministers in October1982 to involve voluntary organisations in development by forming consultative groups, and to move by the Government to set up a National Council of Rural Voluntary Agencies, are all signs of change for better in the official attitude towards voluntary organisations.[16] Planning Commission Members, C. H. Hanumantha Rao[17] and Raj Krishna[18] and social workers like Mahasweta Devi[19], B. K. Roy Burman[20] and many others have made some praise in favour of voluntary agencies. No doubt, there are good and bad voluntary agencies, but the government machinery alone cannot be effective enough to take up this gigantic task successfully. Hence, the decision has to be taken about the type of programmes to be entrusted to such organisations so that there may be a clear-cut demarcation of areas of operation between the programmes undertaken by the State Governments and those entrusted to the voluntary organisations to avoid duplication.

Conclusion

The entire backward tribal areas of the country can neither be covered by the voluntary agencies entirely nor Government organisations could reach these areas completely. There is, thus, no other alternative to the Government-Voluntary Agency partnership for solving the problems of tribal people. In the process of implementation of different tribal development programmes, top-down approach and bottom-up approach is followed, but there is not good fusion between the two approaches. The former only complies the latter.

Notes and References

1. Nirman Kumar Bose, *"India's Eastern Tribes"*, in *Tribe, Caste and Religion*, Macmillan,1977, p. 57.
2. Harimohan Mathur, *"Strengthening Administrative Capability for Development of Tribal Regions"*, in L. P. Vidyarthi (ed.), *Tribal Development and its Administration*, Concept Publishing Company, New Delhi, p.161.
3. Government of India, *"Report of the Working Group on Tribal Development During Medium Term Plan,1978-83"*, New Delhi, July 1978, p. ii.
4. Government of India, *"Report of the Group on Administrative Arrangements and Personnel Policies in Tribal Areas"*, New Delhi, 1979, p.1.
5. Government of India, *"Report of the Working Group on Tribal Development During Medium Term Plan,1978-83"*, New Delhi, 1978, p. 40.
6. S. L. Goel and B. B. Goel, *Administration of Personnel in Cooperatives*, Sterling Publishers, New Delhi, 1979, p. 1.
7. Government of Orissa, *"Report on the Annual Administration of Scheduled Areas in Orissa*, 1978-79", p. 12.
8. Government of Orissa, *Tribal Sub-Plan for Eighth Plan,1992-97* and *Annual* Plan1992-93, Orissa (Draft), p.160.
9. Government of Orissa, *"Report on the Activities of the Welfare Department* (for the year1995-96)", p. 6.
10. Government of Orissa, *Tribal Sub-Plan for Annual Plan,1995-96, Orissa*, May 1995.
11. Government of Orissa, *Tribal Sub-Plan for Seventh Plan and Annual Plan,* 1985-86, p. 128.

12. Devendra Thakur and D. N. Dhakur, *Role of Voluntary Organisations in Tribal Development*, Deep and Deep, New Delhi,1995, p. 97.
13. Government of Orissa, *Directory of Non-Government Organisations in Orissa*,1994.
14. Mohit Sen, "*No, No, Nothing With Them*", *Yojana*, Vol.28, Nos. 20 and 21, November 1984, p. 23.
15. K.N. Kabra, "Why Go for a False Alternative", *Yojana*, Vol. 28, Nos. 20 and 21, p. 30.
16. J. B., "*Let's First Understand Them*", *Yojana*, Vol. 28, Nos. 20 and 21, p. 45.
17. C. H. Hanumantha Rao, "*As Planning Commission Views the Concept*", *Yojana*, Vol. 28, Nos. 20 and 21, pp. 5-6.
18. Raj Krishna, "*It Would Just be a Futile Exercise*", *Yojana*, Vol. 28, Nos. 20 and 21, p. 7.
19. Mahasweta Devi, "*You Just Cannot do Without Them*", *Yojana*, Vol. 28, Nos. 20 and 21, pp. 52-54.
20. B.K. Roy Burman, "*Strategy for Tribal Development: An Anthropological Approach*", in L. P. Vidyarthi (ed.), *Tribal Development and its Administration*, Concept Publishing Company, New Delhi,1981, pp.141-142.

7

IMPACT OF THE PROGRAMMES

Impact study of the tribal development programme is split up into two parts. The first part deals with physical achievements, the assessment of which is based on secondary data. In the second part, impact of programmes is assessed on the basis of situational studies in a particular block.

I
Physical Achievements

The strategy of tribal sub-plan initiated during the Fifth Plan period led to one marked result i.e. spectacular rise of financial investment in tribal areas of the country.[1] The Working Group in Tribal Development during the Sixth Plan examined the relation between the growth in investment in tribal areas and the consequent accrual of benefits to the tribals. It observed that a good part of the investments under the State Plan budgets are committed to schemes in the capital-intensive sectors which do not benefit any specific region or any specific tribal group.[2] An examination of the 6th plan outlay for the tribal sub-plan areas of Orissa also reveals that 65.43 per cent of it is not of any immediate relevance to the tribals. In most cases, such investments are tied up with capital-intensive sectoral programmes like Power, flood control, large and medium industries, mining and transportation. The present level of skill, expertise and knowledge of the tribals do not bring them within the productive interaction of such schems.[3] The level of economic organization, skill and resources of the non-tribal population residing in tribal areas are of a higher order than the tribal segments of the population. The remaining 34.57 per cent of the expenditure tends to benefit the former more than the later. This shows that the tribal sub-plan has significantly triggered up public investment in the tribal areas of the state. But its compositional character makes it less accessible to the tribals.[4]

Sixth Plan Achievements

It was during the Sixth Five Year Plan period, an attempt was made in the state to rationalize financial and administrative procedure to focus special attention on implementation of tribal sub-plan programme. An important step in this direction was the quantification of funds for utilization in sub-plan areas. A reasonable portions of the plan outlay in each sector was made almost obligatory.[5] With the funds made available, a number of programmes were taken up and executed in tribal areas. Under each scheme specific targets were fixed and sought to be achieved within a stipulated time period. Under the programmes like oil seed development, fruits plantation, lift irrigation and tube-wells, distribution of milch animals, enrolment in Ashram Schools and hostels, the achievement was within 30 per cent of the target. In schemes like Pine apple plantation, irrigation through river position, improvement of lands, plantations under forestry, collection of milk, short term and long term loans through co-operatives, coverage of families under credit for consumption and social needs, technical education, primary health centers, identifications and release of bonded labourers etc. the achievement was more than 100 per cent against the targets. However, in most of the schemes the achievements were quite satisfactory.

Seventh Plan Achievements

Quantification of funds from different sectors and sources for tribal sub-plan area and fixation of physical targets to be achieved under different sectoral programme for speedier development of tribal areas become the characteristic feature of the tribal sub-plan approach.[6] Some programmes made resounding success. Achievements were more than the targets in schemes like pulse development, consumption of nitrogenous fertilizers, extension of area under mango and other fruits, vegetable processing and post harvest management, etc. But the performances were dismal pertaining to schemes of rural and urban sanitation, LIGH schemes, interest subsidy to handicraft co-operatives, lift irrigation, major and medium irrigation, etc.

Eight Five-Year Plan

Physical targets under various schemes of different sectors during the Eighth Five-Year Plan displayed a mixed result. In schemes like food grains, pulse, oilseeds and sugarcane, etc. achievement was more than the targets. But during the same period, schemes such as consolidation of holdings, creation of irrigation potential under major and medium irrigation, installation of lift irrigation points, construction of sanitary wells, housing, tree plantation, pasture development, etc. exhibited a very poor performance. Achievement was just or slightly over fifty percent in construction of rural roads, establishment of public health centers, economic plantation, etc.

Ninth Five-Year Plan

Setting up of physical milestones and their attainment was closely monitored during the Ninth plan period. Some schemes emerged very successful whereas a discouraging performance was noticed in many programme. For example, coverage of areas and production of food grains, minor irrigation, establishment of biogas plants, rural roads, sanitary wells, Indira Awas Yojana, Slum Development Programme showed satisfactory achievement. Schemes like completion of bridges, enrolment of students in primary schools, water area development for fisheries, etc. managed to achieve fifty per cent of their targets. But attainments were abysmally low in animal husbandry and dairy development schemes.

Thus, some sectoral activities have lagged behind, many have kept pace with and a few have forged ahead of the general targets fixed. Specific sectoral activities need strengthening for improving their performance in the development scale.

II

This section makes an effort to assess the impact of the programmes with the help of anecdotes. The cases have been chosen from Thuamul Rampur Block in Kalahandi district.

Thuamul Rampur is a tribal dominated backward block in Bhawanipatna sub-division of Kalahandi district. It is an ITDA block. Long ago, it was a part of Kashipur Block in Koraput district. In 1962, it was declared as a separate block and was annexed to Kalahandi district. It is now in the southern part of Kalahandi district. It is bounded by Kashipur Block on the south, Jaipatna block in the west and Lanjigarh block on the east. It is situated in the hilly tract region of Kalahandi district. It forms part of the drainage basin of Indravati river. The area can be divided into hills, pediments and valleys. The climate of the area is sub-tropical monsoon in type. The rainfall pattern in the block is erratic in nature. The average rainy days are 88 days in a year.

The Block stretches over an area of 1072 sq. kms. It has a large forest area. There are twelve Gram Panchayats and 293 villages in the block. The demographic features of the block shows the tribal character of the block. According to the 1991 census, the total population of the block is 55,777. The sex-ratio shows a tilt in favour of women with a total of 28,255 females and 27,522 males. The ST population is 31,042 which is 55.6 percent of the total population. There is, therefore, no difficulty in drawing the inference that it is a tribal dominated block. The density of population is 164 persons per sq. km.

Against this backdrops, the cases were selected to present the field reality of the impact of different programme and beneficiary oriented income generating schemes. A total of 27 beneficiaries assisted under the ITDA schemes of Thuamul Rampur ITDA were selected purposively from different villages under Gunupur, Nakrundi, Kerpai, Kaniguma, Gutrukhal, Dumerpadar, Gopalpur and Badchhatrang Gram Panchayats. A schedule as shown in Appendix–I was canvassed among the beneficiaries. Similarly, under the Area Development and infrastructure development programmes, a total of 18 projects executed under ITDA schemes were studied. The assessment was based on spot observation. It was supported by collection of relevant information and data from Thuamul Rampur ITDA office, concerned block office and informal discussion with people and knowledgeable persons connected with the project. Finally, it was found that 10 projects were successful out of the 18 projects executed. There were 4 completely failed 4 partly failed cases. Now, all these total successful, totally failed and partly failed cases will be briefly presented to make the study more sharp.

Cases Studied on People's Development Programmes of Thuamul Rampur Block of Kalahandi District (Assisted by Thuamul Rampur ITDA)

Failure Cases

Case No. 1 (Moti Dei): Moti Dei is a woman beneficiary of the Schedule Tribe community. She hails from Balisara village of Gunupur Gram Panchayat in Thuamul Rampur block. She was assisted under the ITDA for Brick making. The total cost of the scheme was Rs.1500/-. It contained a loan component of Rs.750/- and a subsidy amount of Rs.750/-. The Thuamul Rampur ITDA had sanctioned the subsidy component of the scheme amount to the beneficiary through Kalahandi Anchalika Gramya Bank of Gunupur Branch. The time lapse between disbursement of the loan and release of subsidy was two and half months. It also took one month for implementing the scheme after release of the loan amount. Regarding the mode of disbursement of the loan, Rs.1010/- was released in cash and Rs. 490/- in shape of implements necessary for the scheme.

The beneficiary was selected by the Welfare Extension Officer of Thuamul Rampur block on behalf of the BDO. The Brick making scheme was selected according to her choice. It was not thrust upon her. The suggestions of her family and friends helped her to select this scheme. She had past experience in brick-making. However, she lacks sufficient knowledge of the art of brick-making. The beneficiary implemented the scheme and did brick making for a few months, then she discontinued it despite the fact that the loan amount was enough to run her business. As she discontinued, it did not help to generate income nor could she create any tangible asset. Taking into consideration all the aspects it can be said that it is a failure case. The following reasons can be attributed to the failure of the scheme.

First, not the entire amount was utilized for running the scheme. After purchasing some articles like hand hoe, trench hoe (Rafa, Cainti, Sawal) etc. with the loan amount, a substantial portion of the amount was utilized for meeting the consumption requirement of herself and her family. Secondly, after some time the beneficiary.lost interest in the scheme. She lost initiative to run the scheme permanently. Thirdly, the Bank officials like the Field Officer/Branch Manager etc. or Block officials like BDO/WEO etc. and other Govt. officials did not motivate the beneficiary. Fourthly, the beneficiary did not get remunerative price for his product i.e., bricks. Hence, she did not get sufficient income from the scheme. During rainy season, she had to stop the operation of the scheme. But she did not have sufficient income to run the unit after rainy season.

Case No. 2 (Mal Dei): Mal Dei is an women of Schedule Tribe beneficiary, Kandh by caste. She belongs to Balisara village of Gunupur Gram Panchayat under Thuamul Rampur Block. She had been assisted for brick-making Scheme under ITDA. The total cost of the Scheme was Rs.1500 of which Rs.750 was the subsidy amount and Rs.750 was the loan component. The time gap between disbursement of loan and release of subsidy was around two and half months. The beneficiary took almost one month to implement the scheme after getting the loan and subsidy for the Scheme. Out of the total loan component of Rs.1500, Rs.1010 was distributed in favour of the beneficiary in shape of cash and Rs. 490 was released in kind.

The beneficiary herself had opted for the scheme on the suggestions of his friends and relatives. The scheme was not imposed on her not she was forced to take up the scheme. The scheme was neither her family occupation nor she had any previous experience on the scheme.

The beneficiary undertook the scheme, but it was shattered in torrential rain. Therefore, she never tried to run the scheme again. Regarding the loan amount disbursed to her, she told that it was not at al sufficient. The loan amount should be more. The scheme neither generated any additional gainful employment for the beneficiary nor accrued any additional income to her.

Reasons which can be attributed for the failure of this scheme are many:

1. Inability to maintain the scheme due to lack of funds with the beneficiary.
2. Substantial amount of the loan was utilized to meet the consumption requirement of the family.
3. The beneficiary had not previous knowledge on the scheme. She had not also received proper training or technical guidance to run and maintain the scheme.
4. Low rate of investment on the scheme was also a cause for failure of the scheme. The loan amount was inadequate.
5. Failure of the scheme in this case is also because of destruction of the scheme in the natural calamity of heavy rain. Destruction of the units due to this sort of accident also contributed for failure of the scheme.
6. The failure of the Scheme in this case like the preceding one is partly due to lack of motivation, supervision and monitoring of the scheme by the Bank and block officials.

Case No. 3 (Baidehi Dei): Baidehi Dei is a Scheduled Tribe woman beneficiary. She is Paraja by caste. She belongs to Gunupur village of Gunupur Grampanchayat. Assistance was given to her for 'Rice Vendor' Scheme under ITDA. The subsidy for the scheme was sanctioned to the beneficiary by Thuamul Rampur I. T. D. A. The total cost of the Scheme including loan and subsidy was Rs.1000. It includes Rs.500 as the loan component and Rs.500 as subsidy. There was a time gap of two and half months between disbursement of the loan and release of subsidy. It took about a month for the implementation of the scheme after release of the loan amount.

The beneficiary had discontinued the scheme after a few months because of low demand, low income and low profit. It is, therefore, a failure one.

The following factors seem to be responsible for the failure of the scheme.

First, the scheme was wrongly selected for the beneficiary without assessing the feasibility and viability. Secondly, the scheme was not up to the choice of the beneficiary. From the beginning she developed anathema for the Scheme. The beneficiary, in course of interaction, expressed that from the beginning, she was very much sceptical about the success of the scheme. Thirdly, some days after operating the scheme, the beneficiary sold away the articles and diverted the sale proceeds for meeting the consumption requirements of her family. Fourthly, this is a peculiar case where the beneficiary was not able to work in the unit. Since, she is a woman beneficiary, she did not prefer to work in the rice-vending unit. Fifthly, lack of proper motivation to the beneficiary from any outside agency is also responsible for this. Sixthly, the beneficiary stated that she fell ill after operating the scheme. She was not be able to revive the scheme after she recovered. Illness of the beneficiary was also partly responsible.

Case No. 4 (Ghasi Majhi): Ghasi Majhi is a Scheduled Tribe man beneficiary. He belongs to Chulbadi Village under Nakrundi Grama Panchayat of Thuamul Rampur Block. He had been assisted under "Fruit Vending" Scheme of ITDA. The subsidy for the scheme was sanctioned to the beneficiary by the Thuamul Rampur ITDA through Gunupur Branch of KAGB. The total cost of the Scheme was Rs. 450 of which Rs. 225 was the loan component and Rs. 225 was the subsidy amount.

Regarding choice of the scheme, the beneficiary took up the scheme on persuation by others. It was neither his family occupation nor had he any previous experience on that. Some days after operating the business, the beneficiary abandoned the scheme as he could not generate sufficient income to maintain his family. As regards, the amount of the loan and subsidy, he told that this should have been more.

The Scheme neither generated additional gainful employment for the beneficiary nor also accrued any additional income for him and his family. As a result, he was forced to abandon the scheme and took up other jobs. The scheme failed for the following reasons:

First, from the beginning the beneficiary developed a sort of disinterest. He had neither any aptitude nor any interest to run the scheme. Secondly, the factor responsible for the failure of the scheme was low level of investment. Thirdly, the beneficiary fell ill. Due to his prolonged illness, he could not continue the scheme. Lastly, there was absolutely no motivation by the bank or Block or ITDA staff who were in charge of monitoring the Scheme.

Case No. 5 (Dasaru Majhi): Dasaru Majhi is a Scheduled Tribe beneficiary. He belongs to Serkapai Village of Kerpai Gram Panchayat. He had been assisted under Grocery shop Scheme of ITDA. The total cost of the scheme was Rs. 3150 of which Rs.1575 was the loan amount and Rs.1575 was the subsidy component. The beneficiary started the scheme four months after getting the loan and subsidy for the scheme. Out of the total cost, Rs. 2775 was disbursed in cash and Rs. 375 was disbursed in kind. As regards the selection of the scheme, the beneficiary opted for the scheme. He did not have past experience or expertise on the scheme. The beneficiary could not operate and run the scheme for a long period. He continued the scheme for around six months. For meeting the consumption requirements of his family in a festival, he sold away all the articles and abandoned the scheme altogether. Regarding the amount of the loan and subsidy of the scheme, the beneficiary replied that the amount was sufficient for operating the Grocery shop in a village. It was due to his own fault, he got rid of the scheme and disposed off all the articles. The scheme proved to be a failure for the beneficiary.

The factors like misutilisation of the sanctioned fund, lack of adequate involvement and lack of supervision by anybody were responsible for the failure of the scheme.

Case No. 6 (Smt. Nua Dei): Smt. Nua Dei is a Scheduled Tribe woman beneficiary. She belongs to Kaniguma village under Kaniguma Gram-panchayat. She had been assisted under Rice Vending Scheme of ITDA. The subsidy of the scheme was sanctioned to the beneficiary by the Th. Rampur ITDA. The total cost of the project was Rs. 2500/- of which Rs.1250/- was the subsidy component. The beneficiary abandoned the scheme some days after operating it. She did not get sufficient profit out of that. The beneficiary was satisfied with the loan and subsidy amount. The beneficiary did not create any additional asset after adopting the scheme. She was neither able to derive additional income nor generate any gainful employment after taking up the scheme. This was a failure scheme for the beneficiary.

In this case, the scheme failed because identification of beneficiary was not properly done. There were already some units operating in the nearby areas. Consequently, the beneficiary did not get adequate profit from the unit. Secondly, the scheme failed due to inadequate personal interest by the beneficiary. She did not involve herself in the scheme. Thirdly, the beneficiary did not have any knowledge about the scheme, i.e., rice vending. Due to lack of adequate knowledge and expertise, she could not run the scheme for a long period. Fourthly, the beneficiary was not pursued to continue the scheme. Lack of adequate and proper supervision by the sponsoring officials also account for failure of the scheme. Lastly, the scheme was not up to the choice of the beneficiary. She felt that it was imposed on her to be taken up. Had it been the scheme of her own choice, she could have taken more interest to run and sustain the scheme.

Case No. 7 (Smt. Laxmi Dei): Smt. Laxmi Dei is a woman Scheduled Tribe beneficiary. She belongs to Polingpadar village. She had been assisted under Leaf-plate making scheme of ITDA. The total cost of the project was Rs. 570/- It contained Rs. 285/- as the subsidy amount and Rs. 285/- as the loan component. The beneficiary started operating the unit as soon as she received the loan and subsidy for the scheme. Regarding selection of the scheme, the beneficiary herself opted for the scheme. She expressed her willingness to take up the scheme after which the scheme was sanctioned. As regards the amount of loan and subsidy for the scheme, the beneficiary opined that the amount was not quite sufficient for adopting the scheme. The beneficiary operated the scheme for a few months and then abandoned the scheme because of the falling demand, low income and low profit. The Scheme could not generate any additional income and gainful employment for the beneficiary. Factors responsible for the failure of the Scheme are presented below:

The use of traditional practice and non-acquaintance with modern practice of use of sophisticated device by the beneficiary is a major factor responsible for failure of this Scheme. A modern device for pressing the leafs for making plates are used by well-to-do businessmen. Leaf plates made through modern techniques are attractive and there was a good demand for such plates. There was low demand for the leaf plates made through traditional methods.

Case No. 8 (Smt. Alang Dei): Smt Alang Dei is a Scheduled Tribe beneficiary of Krung village under Kaniguma Gram Panchayat. She had been assisted under Broom-making scheme of ITDA. The total cost of the project was Rs.500/-. The beneficiary took up the scheme immediately after receiving loan for the scheme. The scheme was sanctioned on her own choice. According to the beneficiary, the amount was not adequate to operate the scheme. The beneficiary continued the Scheme for about one year and then abandoned because of non-availability of raw materials. It was a failure scheme for the beneficiary as it could not generate additional income or employment. The scheme did not help her to create any permanent household asset.

The scheme failed because of non-availability of sufficient raw materials. Secondly, lack of proper involvement by the beneficiary caused failure of the scheme. She was neither involved adequately nor took any initiative to sustain and run the scheme. Lastly, the bank staff and various line departments did not properly supervise. They could not render advice and suggestions to the beneficiary for procuring raw materials and sustaining the scheme.

Case No. 9 (Sani Majhi): Sani Majhi is a Scheduled Tribe beneficiary. He is from Rampur village under Gunupur Gram Panchayat. He had been assisted under 'country tile-making' scheme of ITDA. The total cost of the project was Rs.1500/-. This had loan and subsidy amount of 50 per cent each. Out of the total unit cost of Rs.1500, Rs.1010 was disbursed in cash and Rs. 490 in terms of kind. It was on his own choice that he took up the scheme. According to the beneficiary, the loan and subsidy amounts were quite insufficient. The beneficiary continued the scheme for about six months. He diverted the sale proceeds entirely in meeting his consumption requirements. The purpose of the scheme did not fructify because:

First, lack of establishment of forward linkages like supply of tools, procurement of raw materials, requisite training, repair facilities for the equipment, etc. and backward linkages like transport and marketing of products, etc. account for failure of the Scheme. Secondly, selling the units and disposing of the assets after a few months and diverting the sale proceeds for meeting the family consumption needs by the beneficiary is a factor responsible for the failure of the Scheme. Lastly, he had no previous experience. He did not take any initiative to work with the unit after some days.

Case No. 10 (Smt. Hita Dei): Smt. Hita Dei is a women. She is a Scheduled Tribe beneficiary. She belongs to Tunapani village under Gopalpur G. P. She had been assisted under broom-making scheme of ITDA. The total cost of the project was Rs.500. A total of Rs.400 was disbursed in cash and Rs.100 in terms of kind. The Scheme was sanctioned on her own choice. The beneficiary continued the scheme for a short period. Then she discontinued the scheme. It was a failure for the beneficiary. Reasons responsible for the failure of the scheme are indicated below:

First, inadequate personal interest and lack of involvement by the beneficiary is the major reason. From the beginning she developed a sort of disinterest on the scheme and did not work in the broom-making activity. Secondly, she was selling the brooms at a very low price. Middlemen were exploiting her in purchasing the products. Lastly, she diverted the loan amount for consumption purposes. She did not utilise the entire loan and subsidy amount in the unit. Due to low rate of investment on the scheme, it failed after some days.

Successful Cases

Case No. 1 (Mani Majhi): Mani Majhi belongs to Palijore village under Gopalpur G. P. He was assisted under ITDA for Bamboo work. The total cost of the project was Rs. 500. It had Rs.250 as the loan component and Rs. 250 as subsidy. The scheme was financed in 1987. It took about a month to start the scheme after receiving the loan. Out of the total loan component of Rs. 500, Rs. 400 was disbursed in cash and Rs.100 in shape of kind. The Scheme was chosen by the beneficiary himself. It was his family occupation and hence, he had previous experience in it. The unit could generate additional employment for him and his family. The beneficiary created some assets. This is a success story. Several factors contributed to the success of the scheme. They are:

1. The beneficiary took initiative for successful operation of the Scheme. Involvement of the beneficiary on the scheme is really praiseworthy.
2. He had previous knowledge on the scheme because it was his family occupation. Before getting assistance the family members and the beneficiary himself were engaged in the work for earning their livelihood. The beneficiary was able to operate the scheme on a larger scale with government assistance. He did not face any operational problems nor did he require any training or technical guidance to operate the scheme.
3. There was adequate market for the product. He could get sufficient income for maintaining his family and running the scheme successfully.
4. The inputs, raw materials and infrastructural facilities did not pose any hindrance for the beneficiary to run the scheme successfully.
5. Proper beneficiary identification played a crucial role. His past experiences and family occupations are factors, responsible for the success.
6. After operating the scheme the economic condition of the beneficiary improved. The fund was not misutilised nor was it diverted for other purposes.

Case No. 2 (Handing Majhi): Handing Majhi is a Scheduled Tribe male beneficiary of Palijhore village under Gopalpur G.P. He was assisted for 'bamboo work' scheme under ITDA, Th. Rampur ITDA of Kalahandi District. The total cost of the project was Rs. 500. It included Rs. 250 as subsidy amount.

The KAGB Gunupur released the loan and subsidy component of the scheme in favour of the beneficiary. Around one month was passed to start the scheme and make it operational after receiving the loan from the Bank by the beneficiary. The beneficiary had himself opted for the scheme. He had already some experience on the scheme, which helped him to operate the scheme successfully. He and some members of the family were engaged in the unit. He created some home-stead articles after being assisted under the Scheme. Hence, this is a case of successful scheme for the beneficiary. There are a few factors, which helped him to run the unit successfully.

First, the scheme was sanctioned to him on his own choice. He had previous experience and sufficient knowledge about the scheme. Secondly, the beneficiary took proper initiative to run the scheme. He was adequately involved on the scheme from the beginning. This is a major factor responsible for success of the scheme. Thirdly, the raw materials for running the scheme and other inputs were available to the beneficiary. Lastly, there was a good market for his product. Demand for his product was also sufficient. Although there were a few units running nearby, they did not have any adverse impact on the scheme.

Case No. 3 (Gourang Bindhani): Gourang Bindhani belongs to Pollingpadar village. He had been assisted under carpentry unit of ITDA. The subsidy of the scheme was sanctioned to the beneficiary by Th. Rampur ITDA. The total cost of the project was Rs. 3000. The beneficiary had opted for taking up the scheme. Regarding the amount of loan and subsidy, the amount is quite sufficient to take up the scheme initially. The beneficiary is now working in the unit. He is getting additional income from the scheme. The Scheme has generated additional income and employment for the beneficiary and his family. This is a success story. Various reasons can be attributed for the success of the scheme in this case.

Carpentry was the family occupation of the beneficiary. He had all previous experiences about the scheme. He was already working as a Carpenter. After receiving the loan and subsidy for the scheme, he tried to strengthen the already existing carpentry unit.

Case No. 4 (Jayu Majhi): Jayu Majhi belongs to Pollingpadr village in Gunupur Gram Panchayat. He had been assisted under dealership of kerosene oil, rice and sugar scheme of ITDA. The total cost of the project was Rs. 6000. The beneficiary admitted that the amounts of loan and subsidy were sufficient for taking up the scheme. The unit operated by the beneficiary made profit. The beneficiary has been able to get desired level of income and employment from the scheme. He also regularly repaid the loan amount to the Bank. This is a case of successful scheme. Many factors contributed to the success of the scheme.

First, adequate and ample demand for the articles he was selling is a major factor responsible for the success of the scheme. He has engaged another member of his family besides, his own engagement in the unit. He is adequately involved in the unit and taking all interest and initiatives to get more and more income from the business activity. Secondly, the investment amount on the scheme is adequate. The loan and subsidy amounts were sufficient to make the unit fully operational. Lastly, the amounts of loan and subsidy sanctioned for the scheme were not misutilised.

Case No. 5 (Sukru Lohora): Sukru Lohora belongs to Raimal village in Nakrundi Gram Panchayat. He was assisted under black-smithy Scheme of ITDA. The total cost of the programme was Rs. 5000. The unit is now functioning and the beneficiary is himself working in the unit. Through the unit, the beneficiary has been able to derive income and employment for the family. He has engaged two other members of his family in the unit. He is also repaying the loan amount of the Bank regularly. The scheme was a successful one because black-smithy was the family occupation of the beneficiary. He had experience about the job he did. He manufactured qualitative items. Therefore, people demanded them. This has enabled to expand his unit and employed two more persons. Apart from this, proper identification of the scheme for the beneficiary is an important factor responsible for the success of the scheme.

Case No. 6 (Raising Parabhoi): Raising Parabhoi belongs to Karung village under Kaniguma Gram Panchayat. He had been assisted under black-smithy scheme of ITDA. The subsidy of the scheme was sanctioned to the beneficiary by Th. Rampur ITDA through KAGB, Gunupur. The total cost of the project was Rs. 5000/-. As regards the amount of loan and subsidy, the beneficiary expressed his satisfaction on the quantum of financial help given to him. The unit is now in operation. He is getting regular income from the unit. He has also engaged two of his family members in the unit. This is a case of successful scheme for the beneficiary. Factors responsible for the success of this scheme are as enumerated below:

It was on his own choice the beneficiary took up the scheme. He choose the black-smithy scheme because, it was his family occupation. Since, he had previous knowledge and experience in the activity, he was able to work in the unit effectively. Besides, the beneficiary did not face any difficulty of procuring raw materials. Raw materials, infrastructure facilities and market demand for the product did not pose any problem in making the scheme a success.

Case No. 7 (Darma Pujari): Darma Pujari belongs to Gunupur village. He had been assisted under tailoring unit of ITDA. The total cost of the project was Rs. 3000 out of which Rs.1500 was the subsidy amount. The unit is now functioning and the beneficiary is working in the unit. He has also engaged another member of his family in the unit. The scheme has improved his income level to a substantial level. He is repaying the bank loan regularly.

It was a successful one because tailoring units were not existing in nearby area. Secondly, he had adequate knowledge about tailoring.

Case No. 8 (Dian Majhi): Dian Majhi is a Scheduled Tribe beneficiary of Nichimaska village. He had been assisted under ITDA Scheme for Land Development and Supply of Bullock. The total unit cost of the Scheme was Rs.7900, which had Rs.3950 as the subsidy amount. The scheme enabled the beneficiary to develop his 3.95 acres of land. He was supplied with two bullocks for carrying out cultivation. Gram Vikas, a voluntary organisation, had borne the loan component of the scheme. The two bullocks, which were supplied to the beneficiary, are now in good condition and the beneficiary is using them for ploughing his land. This is a successful scheme. Factors responsible for the success of this scheme are enumerated below:

The one and the most important reason for the success of the scheme in this case is the proper supervision, monitoring, persuasion and motivation to the beneficiary by the Gram Vikas. Gram Vikas took all the responsibility to develop the land, always pursued and motivated the beneficiary to take up regular cultivation, regularly supervised and monitored the progress. It intervened immediately to solve the difficulties when there was a need.

Partially Successful and Partially Failure Cases

Case No. 1 (Sunasing Majhi): Sunasingh Majhi is a beneficiary of Ranidumer village. He had been assisted under country tile making scheme of ITDA. The subsidy of the scheme was sanctioned to the beneficiary by Thuamul Rampur ITDA. The total cost of the project was Rs.1500 of which Rs.750 was the subsidy amount. Regarding the amount of loan and subsidy, the beneficiary expressed that the amount was insufficient. He is not devoting his whole time in this activity. The unit is functioning in a moribund stage. Initially, when the beneficiary adopted the scheme, he had earned a good income and created some household assets. But after some days he abandoned the unit. After some days he again began to work in the unit. This is a case which is neither a failure scheme nor a successful scheme. This is a peculiar case of partial success.

The reasons which account for this are the low investment amount to start a tile-making unit. The beneficiary was not able to engage more labourers in the unit when there was good demand for the country tile due to lack of funds. He just managed to produce at a low scale. Again, he once sustained heavy loss when the tiles were destroyed due to cyclone and heavy rain. Then he abandoned the unit for some time. After arranging funds he tried to revive the unit. In this process, his interest and aptitudes for the scheme got dwindled.

Case No. 2 (Buthuli Dei): Buthuli Dei is a woman beneficiary of the ST community, who belongs to Amjhola village. She had been assisted under fruit-vending scheme of ITDA. The total cost of the project was Rs.450, of which Rs.225 was the subsidy component. The beneficiary started the scheme soon after receiving the loan and subsidy amounts. The beneficiary was not consulted regarding allotment of a scheme under anti-poverty programme. When the scheme was sanctioned, she did not refuse to take up. She took the scheme wit a hope that she would earn profit from the fruit vending activity. She expressed that the amount is not sufficient to start the scheme. It was her part-time job. Since she was dealing with perishable commodity, she sometimes sustained losses. This is an intermediary case of partly success and partly failure scheme. Factors responsible for such a position are like this:

She was not actually willing to work in the fruit vending activity. When this was allotted to her, she tried to work. But she was not able to put her mind and heart together in this business.

Case No. 3 (Mana Dei): Mana Dei from Hadkhursi village had been assisted under broom-making scheme of ITDA. The total cost of the project was Rs.500 of which Rs.250 was the loan amount. Out of the total unit cost of the project, Rs.400 was disbursed in cash and Rs.100 in shape of kind. The scheme was sanctioned to her after she exercised her choice. She opined that the sanctioned amount was insufficient to run the scheme. Broom-making was her part-time activity. Only when she did not have any wage work to do, she was engaged in this. As she told, she is not getting remunerative price for broom making. This is an intermediary case which is neither successful completely nor a failure one. Cases, which can be attributed to this peculiar situation are:

First, the raw materials i.e., hill brooms are not always available. Second most important reason is that she is not getting reasonable and remunerative prices for her products. She sells the brooms to a middleman who always pays a price lower than the market price. Thirdly, the beneficiary is not adequately involved in the activity. But she is not totally disinterested in the activity allotted to her. As a result, she has not discontinued the scheme.

Case No. 4 (Haiding Majhi): Haiding Majhi is a male Scheduled Tribe beneficiary of Sundergarh village. He had been assisted under Small Business scheme of ITDA. The total cost of the project was Rs.3150. As regards the amount of loan, the beneficiary opined that the amount is not at all sufficient for the scheme.

The beneficiary started the small business unit (a grocery) at a low scale. He is not getting sufficient income from it. At times he keeps it closed. In spite of low income and low profit margin, he has not abandoned the scheme. This is neither a successful nor a failure scheme. This is an intermediary case. Reasons for such a case can be due to many factors:

First, quantum of investment on the scheme is not adequate. The amount of loan should have been higher. Secondly, the beneficiary is diverting the sale proceeds for meeting the consumption requirements of his family.

Case No. 5 (Chaul Dei): Chaul Dei is a woman scheduled tribe beneficiary. She belongs to Dhuliguda village. She had been assisted under rice-vending scheme of ITDA. The total cost of the scheme was Rs.2500 out of which Rs.1250 was the loan amount. When she expressed her willingness to take up the scheme, it was sanctioned to her. Regarding the amount of loan, the beneficiary expressed her satisfaction on the quantum of assistance given to her. The beneficiary is not always working in the rice vending activity. But she has not abandoned the activity altogether. It is seasonal. This is an intermediary case, partly successful and partly failure scheme. Many factors are responsible for the partial success of the scheme:

Lack of adequate knowledge of the beneficiary on the scheme accounts for the partial failure of the scheme. Some rice-vending units are available in nearby areas. Hence, she is not having adequate demand for her item. Consequently, it gives her low income. She developed a sort of disinterest on the scheme resulting in partial failure of the scheme.

Case No. 6 (Sukru Majhi): Sukru Majhi belongs to Kanung village. He had been assisted under broom-making scheme of ITDA. The total cost of the scheme was Rs.570. The scheme was sanctioned to him not in accordance to his choice. It was thrust upon him. The amount of loan, as expressed by the beneficiary, was inadequate. It should have been slightly higher, he said. The beneficiary took up the scheme as a part-time activity. Apart from broom-making, he was engaged in other works. This is a partly successful and partly failure scheme. Reasons, which can be accounted for the partial failure of this scheme are that, he is not the only man engaged in broom-making activity. There is competition in this field. He is not getting adequate hill-brooms, which is the raw material. Inadequacy of raw materials account for the partial nature of success of the scheme in this case. To add to this inadequacy of raw materials, there is no market for his products. He, therefore, falls prey to the middlemen. The loan sanctioning and the funding agencies failed to monitor the scheme.

Case No. 7 (Kurunu Majhi): Kurunu Majhi belongs to Merkatora village. He was assisted under bamboo work scheme of ITDA. The total cost of the scheme was Rs. 500. The beneficiary had opted for the scheme. The amount of loan is not sufficient as stated by the beneficiary. The beneficiary is working in the bamboo work activity most of the times. He is getting raw materials adequately. But the price he is getting for his product is not adequate. This is not a fully successful scheme. This is an intermediary case of partly successful and partly failure one. There are a few factors responsible for the partial success.

Use of traditional method by the beneficiary is the only cause for low demand for his product. The beneficiary is not acquainted with the modern methods. Due to low demand for his products, the income he is getting is also low.

Results of Analysis

The foregoing analysis tends to reveal that the process of change of beneficiary-oriented anti-poverty programmes implemented in the rural areas have conferred differential impact on different cross-sections of the society. They have not been fully successful in changing the base, which breeds and perpetuates poverty. At times, they are detrimental to the interest of the rural poor. The above analysis and findings indicate that the reasons and factors, which can be attributed for the failure of the schemes to produce the desired results, are mainly: (a) non-involvement of the beneficiary due to imposition of unsuitable schemes generating personal disinterests, (b) lack of proper motivation by the financial institutions and administrative machinery, (c) inadequate monitoring and supervision by the implementing agencies, (d) non-availability of adequate raw materials, infrastructure support and marketing arrangement resulting in non-remunerative prices for the products, and(e) low level of investment consequent upon poor economic condition of the beneficiary.

Case Studies of Area Development Programme (i.e., Infrastructure Development Schemes) of Th. Rampur Block of Kalahandi District

Successful Projects:

Project No.1 (Diversion weir at Karanberi): The diversion weir is a minor irrigation project. It is meant to irrigate 20 acres to 100 acres of land. The weirs divert the water from streams, springs or 'nullas' for irrigating cultivable land. They are constructed in two phases. In the first phase, the construction of a weir checks the flowing water. Then the construction of canals helps the flow of water to lands for irrigation.

Construction of such a weir at Karanberi village in Gunupur gram panchayat was undertaken by the Thuamul Rampur ITDA. It was a infrastructure development scheme. The total cost of the project was Rs.1.5 lakh. The construction work began in 1991 and continued for six months. Consequent upon the construction of the weir, 44.70 acres of land was irrigated. Different kinds of crops were raised by the tribal people.

Project No. 2 (Diversion weir at Jhundingjhar): The diversion weir at Jhundingjhar is a small minor irrigation project situated in the village Jhundingjhar. The work is executed under infrastructure development schemes of Th. Rampur ITDA. The total cost of the project was Rs.1.40 lakh. Construction of the project was started in 1989 and it was completed after seven months. Of the 27.5 acres of land irrigated by the project, the benefit of 18 acres went to Scheduled Tribes. The total number of beneficiaries of the project was 17 which included five Scheduled Tribe beneficiaries. It can be construed to be a successful project because many people including ST people got the benefits of irrigation in their lands. This has enabled them to cultivate different types of crops.

Project No. 3 (Diversion weir near Dalguma on Phulrijharan Nallah): This diversion weir near Dalguma is a small irrigation project. It is situated near the village Dalguma under Karlapat Gram Panchayat. It was constructed on Phulrijharan Nallah. A total amount of Rs.1.08 lakh was spent for the project. It was undertaken in 1990 and took only five months for the completion of the work. As soon as it was completed, it began giving benefits of irrigation to 32 acres of land. The number of beneficiaries comes to 19. They cultivated different types of Kharif and rabi crops in their land. This has enabled them to earn more from their land.

Project No. 4 (Diversion weir at Kaniguma): The diversion weir at Kaniguma is a small minor irrigation project situated in the village Kaniguma under Th. Rampur block. The project cost was Rs. 88,868. It was completed in 1990. The ayacut area of the project is 25 acres during Rabi and 25 acres also during Khariff. The project is irrigating the lands of 13 beneficiaries. It is a successful project. Regarding the utility of the project, some beneficiaries, in course of interactions, stated emphatically, that the project is a boon to them. It improved their income substantially and their standard of living significantly.

Project No. 5 (Diversion weir at Kasalkupa): It is a small minor irrigation project situated near the village Kasalkupa. The cost of the project was Rs.1 lakh. The Ayacut area of the project is about 40 acres. The project is now yielding benefits. The beneficiaries are utilising the water of the project for irrigation of their lands and raising different crops. Their incomes have been increased.

Project No. 6 (Construction of Padipadar Primary School Hostel Building): The primary school hostel building was constructed at Padipadar village under Gutrukhal Gram Panchayat. This school hostel with 6 rooms was constructed in 1989. It accommodates 32 borders. It can be said to be a successful infrastructure project.

Project No. 7 (Primary School hostel building at Kathkura): The primary school hostel building was constructed at Kathkura village. The work was undertaken by the Th. Rampur ITDA. The cost of the project was Rs.25,450. The building was constructed in 1981. The construction of the building took long time, i.e., little more than one year. Six rooms were constructed for the primary school hostel building. The building is utilised for accommodating the school boarders.

Project No. 8 (Hostel building at Bisamgiri): It was constructed at Bisamgiri village of Dumerpadar Gram Panchayat for the students at primary level. The work was taken up under infrastructure development schemes of Th. Rampur ITDA. The project cost was Rs.37,250. It was constructed in 1984 during a span of 3½ months. It has 6 rooms. About 30 students are staying here.

Project No. 9 (Vented cause-way on Gopalpur to Jamuguda Road): The vented cause way on the road connecting the Jamuguda village from Gopalpur under Th. Rampur block was constructed during the year 1990. The project is serving the purpose of a low level bridge on the road. Its cost was Rs.60,000. The project work was completed in 1990 within a time of about 8 months. The vented cause-way on the road from Gopalpur to Jamuguda is now utilised by the villagers of Gopalpur and Jamuguda.

Project No. 10 (Community Development Work on Chasiguda to Champachua Road): Community development works on Chasiguda to Champachua road connecting the two villages was taken up during the year 1990 by Th. Rampur ITDA under the infrastructure development schemes. It was executed by the ITDA, not by any other agency. The cost of the project was Rs.1 lakh. Three culverts were constructed in the way during 1991 for use by the people. The culverts on the road from Chasiguda to Champachua are now in good condition.

Failure Projects

Project No. 1 (Perumanji minor irrigation project): Perumanji minor irrigation project is situated in the village Perumanji under Gunupur Gram Panchayat in Th. Rampur block. The total cost of the project was Rs.69,750. It was completed in 1984. Its construction took seven months. It enabled to provide irrigation facilities to 49 acres of agriculture land. Eleven ST farmers get irrigation facilities from this project. In 1986-87, the project was repaired with a total cost of Rs.20,000. However, it was totally shattered in 1991-92. As is said by the ITDA officials, it was due to heavy flood. Again in 1991-92, Rs.1.5 lakh was spent for renovating it.

Project No. 2 (Vented causeway on Saisurni to Hadkhursi Road): In 1990, a culvert was constructed on the Saisurni to Hadkhursi road by Th. Rampur ITDA. An amount of Rs.60,000 was spent for the work. The construction was started in 1989 and was completed in 1990, within a period of two months. It was damaged in 1991, after about a year of its construction. After it remained unused for sometime, the same ITDA spent Rs.45,000 for reconstructing and repairing it.

Project No.3 (Gully Control at Gokulam): Gully control is like a check dam constructed for storing the water of 'nallahs', which is utilised for irrigation purposes. The gully control at Gokulam was constructed near the village Gokulam under Gunupur Gram Panchayat. The project was constructed during the year 1989-90 by the Soil Conservation Department of Kalahandi District under 'podu preparation programme' of Th. Rampur ITDA. The total cost of the project was Rs.40,000. It was started during the year 1989-90 and was completed during the same year. For about a year the project worked well. Water was stored and utilised. In 1990-91, several leakages were found in the structure and the very purpose of storing water was defeated. The project is a failure one.

Project No. 4 (Bridge at Ranidumer): The bridge was constructed over river Indravati connecting the PWD road to Ranidumer village. It was constructed during the year 1990-91. The estimated cost of the project was Rs.1 lakh. It was constructed in 1991. After a few months of its construction, it was washed away by heavy rain. About 40 per cent of the bridge was completely damaged. It remained unused by the villagers. During the same year, an additional amount of Rs.1 lakh was earmarked to reconstruct it.

Intermediary Cases (Partially Success and Partially Failure Projects)

Project No.1 (Construction of diversion weir at Hadkhurshi): The diversion weir at Hadkhurshi is like a small minor irrigation project situated in the village Hadkhurshi. The construction work involved a total cost of Rs.1.40 lakh. It came into being in 1990. The diversion weir enabled to irrigate 26 acres of agricultural land. About 14 beneficiaries got the benefit of irrigation. Different kinds of crops were grown by the farmers. But the project did not last long. After a year of its completion, in 1991, leakage defects were noticed. Water could not be diverted for irrigation. In 1992-93, repair work was undertaken to make it operational and provide facilities of irrigation to the farmers.

Project No. 2 (Construction of Primary School Hostel building at Mardiguda): The primary school hostel building was constructed for providing hostel facilities to the students of the primary school at Mardiguda village of Kaniguma Gram Panchayat. The total cost of the building was Rs.45,000. The construction work began in 1983 and took one year and eight months for its completion. There were six rooms in the hostel. The building had tile roofs. As the building suffered from water leakage in rainy season, the tiles were replaced with asbestos sheets in 1986-87. The repair work involved Rs.22,243 and 14 months time period. There was further repair to the floors in 1990 with an expenditure of about Rs.12,000. All these tell many things about the failure of the hostel building project.

Project No. 3 (Construction of Primary School Hostel building at Perumanji): The primary school hostel building was constructed at Perumanji under Karlapat Gram Panchayat. The total cost of the building was Rs.60,000. The construction was started during 1984 and was completed in 1985. Six rooms were constructed with A.C. sheet roofing. Breakages in the flooring and plastering of the building were noticed during the year 1990. In 1990, flooring, plastering and other minor repairs of the building were undertaken with a cost of Rs. 8,600.

Project No. 4 (Construction of Primary School Hostel building at Chasiguda): The hostel building was constructed for the students of the primary school at Chasiguda under Badchhatrang Gram Panchayat. The work was executed by the Th. Rampur ITDA under its infrastructure development schemes. The total cost of the hostel building was Rs.52,199. It had six rooms. The work was taken up on 13.3.1985 and was completed on 31.8.1986. An unusually high time of seventeen and half months was taken for construction of the hostel building. Damages to the flooring and plastering of the building were noticed in the year 1990. It was then repaired with a cost of Rs. 4,740 in1991.

Result of Analysis

The above observations and findings indicate that the process of change was initiated in rural areas. Mere stepping up of investment without bringing out any structural change in the institutional framework causes utter failure of the programmes in many cases. The development impulses generated in small segments have failed to percolate to the catchment areas and consequently, failed to bridge the regional disparities and imbalances.

Conclusion

The forgoint analysis brings into focus that various development programmes have been implemented in the tribal areas for the welfare of the tribal people. The programmes are on family basis, community basis and on area basis. Further, they have been implemented without any regard to the people's propensity to adopt them. Many of them, therefore, failed bitterly on all fronts.

Area development approach has been adopted on the pretext that since the tribal areas have remained isolated for long due to inaccessibility, the tribal people living in such areas could benefit them.[7] They could not receive exposures of the developed societies. Hence, various State Governments, Central Government and voluntary organisations have undertaken the development programmes of time bound nature. For want of awareness, family programmes do not make headway and so are the community programmes for want of initiative and leadership.

Again, the functional system in which these people operate sustains and breeds poverty. The village artisans and traders encounter bleak marketing prospects in view of the low demand for their products. Flow of products from the urban manufacturing sector and the inaccessibility of these people to the doorsteps of modern manufacturing technology fails to extricate them from their limited economic horizon.[8] The tribal poor are most unfavourably affected by the deteriorating terms of their trade relationships. The inadequacy of infrastructural facilities compels them to fall easy prey to the middlemen. The inefficiency, corruption and operational rigidity in the Government agencies have been detrimental to the interests of the rural poor.

The production system, the economic and social framework in which the rural people work, insures them by and large, against a vertical rise in productivity asset accumulation.[9] The functional basis emanating from such a situation not only breeds poverty among them but also perpetually sustains them at that level. Therefore, unless the rural poor is freed from the quagmire of their narrow economic base and the various functional system, there is no possibility of a positive change in the poverty scenario of the tribal areas.

However, with all measures taken by the various governments to promote the quality of tribal life, much needs to be enquired into. It needs to be ensured whether the development programmes have made any impact on improving the quality of life of tribal beneficiaries. There is a strong feeling that selected few well-off tribals have been bagging subsidies from the programmes. Development programmes and people's development/income generating poverty eradication programmes have not fared well. The scenario is diluted as the author has seen. The overall picture is, however, neither gloomy nor encouraging.

Notes and References

1. Government of India, Ministry of Home Affairs, New Delhi, "Report of the Working Group on Development of Scheduled Tribes During Seventh Plan", p. 9.
2. Government of India, Ministry of Home Affairs, New Delhi,1980, "Report of the Working Group on Tribal Development During Sixth Plan", pp. 3-4.
3. *M. K. Mohanty,* Tribal Society, Programmes, Planning and Economic Change, *Chugh Publications, Allahabad,1990, p. 89.*
4. *Ibids.*
5. *Government of Orissa,* Tribal Sub-Plan for Seventh Plan,1985-90 and Annual Plan,1985-86, *p. 3.*
6. *Government of Orissa,* Tribal Sub-Plan for Eighth Plan,1992-97 and Annual Plan,1992-93, Orissa *(Draft), p. 8.*
7. M. L. Patel, "Direction of Tribal Development", Vanyajati, Vol. *XL, No.2, April1992, p. 33.*
8. *M. K. Mohanty,* op. cit., *pp. 81-82.*
9. *S. C. Patnaik,* Anatomy of Rural Poverty in Orissa and Strategy of Rural Development, *p. 11.*

8
Findings and Policy Prescription

This chapter has three parts. The hypotheses formulated in the first chapter are put to test in the first part. The second part presents the summary of findings of the work. The third part contains comprehensive policy recommendations for the future.

I
Testing of Hypotheses

Ever since the formulation of Indian Constitution, special emphasis has been laid on tribal development. The Constitution makers appreciated the need for special development strategy for tribal development. They incorporated specific provisions for the development and welfare of the tribes. As soon as the Five-Year Plans were launched, special provisions were made in the Plans for the tribals. The tribal areas received focussed attention. The tribal development blocks are examples of this. Not only funds were allotted for their development, emphasis was also laid for tuning the administration for their development. As it was realised that an integrated approach was necessary, concerted efforts were made and resources were allotted for their development in the areas of health, housing, communication, education, economic upliftment, etc. A number of protective and anti-exploitative policies and Acts viz. Forest Policy, Reservation Policy, Land Reform Act, Money lenders Regulation Act, etc. were also enacted. The purpose of all these was to improve their quality of life. The plethora of schemes and programmes implemented and a number of Policies and Acts promulgated for their betterment help us to surmise that the first hypothesis

(There is comprehensiveness in tribal development policy) is confirmed. As far as the resources flow for tribal development is concerned, colossal amount of financial provision has been made from the state exchequer. The total fund allocation of the state during the First Five-Year Plan was only Rs.111 lakh. It increased to about Rs.343153 lakh during the Ninth Plan period (3091 fold increase). Similarly, financial support has also been received in two ways from the Central Government, i.e., as Central Plan outlay and as Special Central Assistance for the tribal development programmes in Orissa. The Central Plan outlay has increased from Rs.116 lakh during the First Plan period to Rs.120180 lakh during the Ninth Plan period. Similarly, there has been manifold increase in the Special Central Assistance. All these lead us to say that not only funds have flown from various sources, there is no dearth of funds for the development of tribals in the State of Orissa. Notwithstanding this, tribals are wallowing in poverty, suffering from various diseases, their literacy level is at the very low level, their quality of life presents a dismal picture and so on. All these have happened because of prevailing corruption in the administration of tribal development programmes, apathetic and indifferent attitude of government officials. It was reported during the year 2000 that because of corruption and inefficiency of the government officials of tribal dominated Malkangiri district, eight students of different residential schools died. The stipend money of the tribal students is swindled away. The 78 residential schools of the tribal district are not properly managed because of corruption. The corrupt officials are not caught and adequately punished. Crores of rupees are spent annually for the schools. But the teachers and the students do not have chairs to sit on. Surprisingly, in the tribal districts of Koraput, Nabarangpur, Rayagada and Malkangiri, many general category students reside in the tribal residential schools in the fake name of tribal students. This goes on with the full knowledge of the headmaster and other officials. There are large number of cooperative organisations operating in the tribal districts and areas. They are meant to help in the procurement and marketing of agricultural and minor forest products. During the past years, it has been seen that the officials and employees of these organisations are indulged in myriad kind of corruption activities. Most of them have been closed down. The tribal people are exploited by the contractors and the middlemen for marketing their products. All these are enough to say that the second hypothesis (There is adequacy in flow of funds for tribal development. Corruption distorts people's and area development) is corroborated. Sufficient fund flow in the absence of adequate structural arrangement does not give the desired result. This has exactly happened in the implementation of tribal development programmes in the state. Financial investment for the purpose has always increased. But we are yet to get satisfactory result. During the Sixth Five-Year Plan, the Working Group on Tribal Development observed that a lion's share of the investment went for capital-intensive schemes. Perceptible benefit did not flow to specific region or any specific tribal group (Chapter VIII). Therefore, the immediate socio-economic condition of the tribals did not improve. During the Seventh Plan period, achievement under the programmes of education, health, horticulture, irrigation, etc. seldom crossed 30 per cent of the target. Similarly, the performance in the implementation of various schemes like IRDP, Village Housing Project, Interest subsidy, handicraft cooperatives, etc. were dismal. The result of the case studies undertaken by the author in Thuamul-Rampur block of Kalahandi district reveal that the lot of tribal people has remained unchanged. The success stories are seldom noticed. In the case of Area Development Programmes in the same block, a mixed result is noticed. The results are not in consonance with the amount of investment (Chapter-VIII). Therefore, the third hypothesis (Impact of development programmes on tribal people is less than satisfactory) is confirmed. Now, we come to test the fourth hypothesis (Implementation of programmes is tardy and faulty). After studying the implementation of the tribal development programmes in the state, it has been seen that the programmes fail because of inefficiency, corruption and leakages. Sometimes, appropriate emphasis is not laid on the programmes. We are not prepared to bring about changes after learning from the failures. It has been observed by the Working Group on Tribal

Development 1978-83 that the administration failed to cope up with the level of financial investment. It, therefore, posed constraints on utilisation of resources. Administrative reform was not brought about for effective implementation of programmes. The complex administrative structure hinders programme implementation. This hypothesis is also confirmed.

II
Findings

While evaluating the tribal development programmes and policies, the whole thing can be presented in terms of an input-output model. In order to lift the tribals out of poverty trap and stagnation, different types of resources have been pumped in. The resources may be in the form of money, human efforts and so on. Now it is to be seen how much of output has been obtained in the form of economic, social and political development of the tribes in Orissa. The economic output may be manifested in the form of level of living, poverty alleviation, employment, area development, income, etc. The development of the tribal areas can take place when industries are set up, power projects are commissioned, irrigation projects are undertaken in those areas. Social development of the tribals can take place when sufficient health provision is made for them, when literacy and education are accessible to the tribals and finally when they are modernised and assimilated in the main current of the Society. Political development of the tribals is vital for many things. Emergence of both formal and informal leadership among the tribals can accelerate their pace of development. When their level of national consciousness, political empowerment and decision-making power increases, not only do the tribals are benefited, the nation also stands to gain. In the light of these, we will now delve into finding the achievements in case of the Orissan tribes.

The different tribal development programmes have provided scope to some extent for their economic progress. But 90 per cent of the tribes in Orissa are living below the poverty line.[1] Most of them struggle for their subsistence living. There are a number of instances of starvation deaths. It has been reported that about 16 tribal people in Kashipur Block of Rayagada district have mortgaged their BPL cards with the moneylenders. This has prevented them from being able to avail the government rice at subsidised price. Some people have started consuming contaminated mango kernel powder in Kashipur Block. A huge amount of Rs.19.00 crore is spent every year for the development activities in the block.[2] But they give little result. The will power of Sari Pradhan, a 60-year-old tribal woman in Ora village of Raikia Block, is very high. Because of non-availability of employment opportunities, she is not able to get rice for consumption. She has started depending upon jungle roots, tubers and mango kernel. She says candidly, "There is no wage work, yet we will not die of hunger. As long as there are roots, tubers and mango kernel in the jungles we will continue to live".[3] This not only speaks of the plight of the old Kutia Kandha woman, but it reflects the efficiency of the tribal development programmes in generating economic output. The Juang and Bhuiyan tribal people in the Harichandanpur, Ghatgaon, Telkoi and Banspal Blocks of Keonjhar district do not have sufficient wage work. They do not get a square meal per day because of poverty. The economic condition of these people has not shown signs of improvement. They are always either half-fed or starved. A 20-year young man gives the appearance of 50-year old man. This is because of lack of nutritious food and poverty. Want of employment opportunities has led to the gradual decrease in their number.[4] The government's poverty eradication programmes are yet to have any impact on the Kutia Kondhs, a primitive tribe in Phulbani district. After so many years of independence, they still depend on the forests for their day-to-day living. They are either naked or poorly clad. The jungle roots constitute their main food item. Crores of rupees have been spent for their betterment through the Kutia Kandha Development Agency established in1982. After 22 years of its establishment, the KKDA has not been able to provide the minimum things to the Kutia Kandha tribal people. Huge amount of money is being spent by the State and Central Governments for the development of the primitive Juang tribal people in Banspal Block of Keonjhar district. Their socio-economic condition remains unchanged. They solely depend on the jungle for their living. But the jungles are gradually disappearing. They are, therefore, leading a miserable life. Often they are in the trap of the moneylenders. A survey has found that one thousand Juang families in 22 villages have borrowed Rs.1,44,280 from the moneylenders during the last two years. In addition to this, they have borrowed 2,850 kg. of food grains. Their woe is of high order during the months of July, August and September. During these three months, they borrow food grains from the traders and moneylenders. The repayment is made in terms of their labour.[5] The starvation deaths in the tribal dominated Kalahadi district of Orissa has caught the attention of the policymakers, academics and bureaucrats in the past. It is a recurring phenomenon. The tribals of this district continuously suffer from hunger and misery. In October 2001 alone, 24 tribals were the victims of starvation death. People suffer from malnutrition. Consumption of wild roots and mango kernel is an ordinary thing. All these deaths took place in Nakrundi and Kerpai Gram Panchayats in Thuamul-Rampur block. The people do not have any purchasing power to buy BPL rice, even if it is available in government ration shops once in every 3 to4 months. The people do not have any source of income other than minor forest product.[6] Poverty has kept the Juang tribes of Sukinda block half-naked. About 15,000 people have been registered as workers in the Lamatput block of Koraput district. Rarely do they get employment opportunities by the government. Therefore, 10,000 people from this block have left for Andhra Pradesh and Madhya Pradesh to earn their livelihood.[7] Similarly 15,000 tribals from 60 villages of Kashipur block have left for other States in search of employment.[8] The same thing is noticed in eight Gram Panchayats of Dasapalla Block in Nayagarh district. After starving for days, about 1000 people from these places have gone to Punjab and Haryana to work as Bonded Labourers.[9]

Education is the panacea for many social diseases. Realising its importance, large amount of money has been spent by the Central and State Governments for the development of education in the tribal districts of Orissa. There have been 15 High Schools, 2 M.E. Ashram Schools, 5 Kanyashrams, 13 Residential Sevashrams, 145 Primary Schools and 45 KBK hostels in the tribal district of Nabarangpur. About Rs.21 lakh is spent for managing all these schools by the Welfare Department of the Government of Orissa. During the last 40 years, the Government has spent Rs.150 crore for the TRW Schools. All these have yielded little result. The tribal literacy rate in this district is the lowest in the state.[10] School dropout figures are very high in the tribal areas of the state.

The Government's healthcare system has failed in the tribal districts. Tribals residing in the villages of Koraput district face tough time during the monsoon when diarrhoea cleans many lives. Over one-lakh tribals of Kandha, Saura, Paraja and Gadaba communities in the blocks of Laxmipur, Dasmantpur, Narayanpatna, Bandhugaon, etc. in the districts of Koraput are vulnerable to diarrhoea. The main reason behind the spread of this disease is the use of contaminated water. During 2001, a large number of cases of cerebral malaria have been reported from the tribal areas of Koraput, Malkangiri, Nuapada, Keonjhar, Mayurbhanj and Phulbani districts.[11] Cerebral malaria death rate is on the rise in Koraput, a tribal district. In 1998,31 people died of this disease, which went up to 34 in 1999 and 44 in 2000. Eight Primary Health Centres and 134 Health Sub-Centres do not have buildings of their own. The health workers in those centres do not distribute the medicines to the patients. In most of the times they are sold away in the markets. Some health centres only run in government files. Their physical existence is not known. Tuberculosis has been found to be a serious problem for the tribals in Phulbani district. About 2040 people died of this disease in the district during 2000. Similarly, this disease is taking away the lives of about 500 tribal people in Koraput and Rayagada districts every year. Over 20,000 people are now suffering from the disease in these two districts. Reports say that nearly 1000 tribal villages in these two districts are prone to tuberculosis.[12] After so many years of planning, the tribals still prefer lethal foods to treat fever instead of medicines. The infant mortality rate and the maternal mortality rate are very high among the tribal people. All these are a tip of the iceberg to show the distressing health scenario in the tribal areas.

There are number of factors which contribute to the aforesaid gloomy tribal picture. The most important among them are corruption, indifference, apathetic attitude and non-involvement of the Government officials who administer the tribal development programmes. In order to bring the primitive tribes into the mainstream, a total of 17 projects are in operation. But the utilisation of the resources shows a bleak chance of bringing the primitive tribes into the mainstream life in near future. It was seen during 2001-02 that only 23.09 per cent of the allotted money was utilised. About 30 per cent of this amount went towards the payment of staff salary. In the case of Micro Projects for Didayi, Kutia Kandh, Juang, Paudi Bhuinya, etc. the money utilisation was less than 15 per cent. The low rate of success of the welfare schemes is attributed to the lack of proper supervision and monitoring of the concerned department. There is a State level monitoring cell to ensure the proper management of the various tribal development programmes of the Government. However, its activity has now been minimised to the compilation work of the reports produced by the ITDAs and Micro Projects. Nevertheless, the top to bottom instruction oriented approach without touching the grassroots level adopted by the monitoring officials has not given sufficient result. The future of the programmes for the eight KBK districts, started during 1995, seems to be bleak. Sufficient coordination between the State and the Central Government is lacking. The tribal dominated KBK districts suffer form poverty, starvation death, disastrous health situation, low literacy level and lack of employment opportunities. Lack of administrative coordination may not help us to improve the condition of tribals in these districts. The tribal districts of Kandhmal show a similar problem. There is lack of proper coordination among the various departments of the district in implementing the tribal welfare schemes. One of the ITDAs is operating here for the development of the tribals in the Phulbani, Phiringia and Khajuripada blocks. It receives government grant of Rs.60 lakh annually. The ITDA undertakes different programmes like horticulture, irrigation, drinking water provision, land development, construction of school buildings, etc. But these programmes fail partly or wholly because of the lack of coordination of the departments.[13] The inefficiency in the implementation of the 17 Micro Projects has not provided the desired results. They are in operation in the State ever since 1978-79. Crores of Rupees have been spent for the development of 59,710 primitive tribal people in 537 villages. The 24.20 per cent literacy level among the 13 primitive tribes is a pointer to the success of the programmes. As against this, the Bonda primitive tribe has the lowest literacy rate of 4.79 per cent. The Bonda Development Agency functions for the total development of the most primitive Bonda tribe. Lot of resources have been used for their development during the past years. In spite of this, 500 Bonda people have died from various diseases during the last few years. There are five schools to impart education to the Bonda children. But the teachers occasionally go to school. The negative attitude of the Bonda people towards education combined with the low level of service rendered by the government people do not help to increase their literacy level.

Another prime cause of socio-economic backwardness in the tribal areas of Orissa is rampant exploitation and corruption. Local Adivasis are sitting ducks for unscrupulous traders, moneylenders, bootleggers, contractors and bureaucrats. Enormous sums have been poured into development programmes of all hues with no tangible results. In Bhawanipatna, one Contractor gave an account of the commissions that were 'due' to various officials for any development work at Panchayat level: three per cent for the BDO, 5 per cent for the Junior Engineers, 5 per cent for the Gram Panchayat Extension Officer, 5 per cent for the Block Chairman, 2 per cent for the Block Clerk, 2 per cent for the Block cashier. When asked about the honesty of the BDO, the Contractor confidently exclaimed that the BDO is honest because he always sticks to his 3 per cent.[14] Huge amount of funds in the name of poverty alleviation are swallowed by people in the administration. The Hrushikesh Panda Commission appointed by the Government to find out corruption in the tribal districts of Koraput, Bolangir and Kalahandi (KBK Districts) found out a little impact of the development programmes in ameliorating the condition of the tribal people. The Centrè had given nearly

Rs.60 crores got from the International Fund for Agriculture Development, exclusively for development of tribals over a period of 9 years from 1989 to1997. The objectives were to increase the income levels of the tribal people by developing the degraded farmland, forest, barren hills and other infrastructure like roads. As the project expired, it was found that the number of families living below poverty line in the Kashipur block has increased from 15,471 in 1992 to 24,582 by 1997. The project had created a large number of contractors and suppliers who made easy money without doing any work and had become a powerful group. No significant intervention in terms of increase in income and sustainable agricultural productivity was achieved, the report found out. There is no trace of a single plant claimed to have been planted under the programme. Payments were made against non-existent works. In many cases, works were executed without tender. The contractors, all non-tribals, were handpicked by the officials. The report further detected reckless revision of estimates of work done especially towards the fag end of the project. The worst corruption was between 1995-97 when nearly one-third of the project fund was taken away through fake bills. For example, on December 31,1997, the last day of the project, an amount of Rs.4.9 crore was adjusted. "It was impossible that this exercise could have been completed on a single day".[15] Corruption practice in the implementation of ITDA Project in Nabarangpur district is no less. The project has received funds under the Special Central Assistance from the Government of India for undertaking various programmes. Official files show that a road has been constructed from Baganaguda to Himaguda. Half of the funds in the construction work went to the pockets of the officials and contractors. Similarly, the boundary wall of the Patraput tribal school has not been constructed according to the estimated amount of Rs.2.0 lakh. Only Rs.20,000 has been spent for the repair of the tribal hostel of Dengaguda. The total sanctioned amount was Rs.70,000. The balance Rs.50,00 was enjoyed by the officials. The High School, M. E. School and78 Residential Schools under District Welfare Office of Malkangiri district are mismanaged. Because the officials are indulged in corruption activities.[16] When the Primitive Juang and Bhuinya tribal people in Keonjhar district are poverty-ridden and they do not have the basic necessities of life, the Government officials diverted money from their welfare fund and constructed a park in the town of Keonjhar.[17] Ward Member Bipin Bihari Majhi of Belghar Panchayat in Phulbani district narrates that the school teacher of their village does not turn up after15 days of reopening after the Dashara vacation.[18]

Sometimes faulty programmes are formulated without taking into account the actual requirements of the tribal people. In some areas of Koraput district, the plantation programmes were undertaken ignoring the interest of the tribal people. The forest land, where the tribals were cultivating, have been converted to plantation areas. They were worried about their livelihood and have threatened to take up agitation. The change in the procurement policy of Siali leaves of the Government of Orissa threatened the livelihood of tribals in Kantilo area. Because of the state government's pro-liquor lobby policy, lakhs of tribals in Western Orissa have been forced to sell Mahua flowers at throw away prices. At the time when reports of deaths are pouring from the tribal dominated pockets due to malnutrition and hunger, strong liquor lobby continuously exploit tribals with the support of the State Government. The State Government efforts relating to price fixation mechanism on minor forest produce empowering the district level committee handed by the District has got little hope for the tribals. Significantly, proper price fixation of minor forest products can influence the life of at least half crore tribals of the state who survive exclusively on these products. As per a resolution, the District Pricing Committee has to fix a minimum procurement price of each item. But the primary gatherer sells at a much lower price than the minimum fixed price due to lack of support price system by the government. It has been found out that the minor forest product market is highly unstructured and thus the power equation is biased towards the traders.[19] Lack of efforts by the Government to conserve the forest has led to the depletion of forest as an important resource to tribal living. About 1420 sq. km. jungles have been destroyed. The government has turned a blind eye to the destruction of forest by vested interest groups.

Four major Hydel Power Generation Projects of Machhkund, Upper Kolab, Balimela and Indravati have come up in the undivided tribal district of Koraput. However, about 65 per cent of the villages in Koraput region have no power supply. Out of the 6489 villages, only 35 per cent of them are electrified while the rest languish in dark. Padan Majhi, an evacuee of the project of Upper Kolab Project in Khaprapur village laments, "I have sacrificed 3 acres of fertile land for Upper Kolab Hydel Power Project. But I am yet to get electricity for a bulb in my house".[20] This is a glaring example of the policy of the government where a tribal area may develop, but the fate of the tribal people remain unchanged.

After half a century of planning, tribal people in the state suffer from hardship and deprivation. In many villages poor people survive on rice and salt, drink unsafe water and have virtually no access to healthcare. Real wages are incredibly low. On public works programme, labourers earn as little as Rs. 25/- a day. There are many signs of a crisis of a traditional livelihood especially in areas that use the practice of shifting cultivation. An elderly man while describing his woeful story says, "In the old age, even a single woman's work was enough to feed the family; now even if the whole family works, we go hungry".[21] Massive environmental degradation clearly contributed to this crisis. In many villages, the surrounding forests have been decimated and forest-based economic activities have virtually disappeared. In some areas this has been compensated by the expansion of other occupations, such as weaving and the production of cash crops. Elsewhere, labour migration is the overwhelming survival strategy. Many villages are almost absent of adult men. Everywhere the condition of local public services is abysmal. There are plenty of vacant posts in schools, health centres and administrative offices.

Government employees strive to avoid being posted in these challenging areas. The schooling system is at the Shambles. There are large number of villages where there are no primary schools. The public distribution system has flaws. Most people have ration cards and the official entitlements are far from negligible. The inadequate and unpredictable delivery of the BPL rice adds further woe to the tribal family. When food items reach the local ration shops, people have to rush there at short notice as the rice is distributed on a first-come-first-served basis. In many places, a BPL family has received 40 kg. of rice over the preceding 12 months instead of the official 120 kg. The Government officials blame the people for the low off-take of grain under the public distribution system. But the real problem lies in the defective supply arrangements. Behind all these failures is an over-reaching problem of political marginalisation. When complaints are made, they go unheeded. In some areas, the traditional livelihood have collapsed for various reasons, while alternative economic activities are yet to develop. All these, of late, have manifested in starvation deaths in different tribal areas of the state.

III
Policy Recommendations

This section presents policy recommendations for the speedy development of the tribals. Despite our stepping into the 21st century, development of tribals in the state remains a distant dream. The primitive tribes remain primitive. There are stray instances of child selling starvation death etc. mainly meant for their development are swindled away. Health services are in desarray. Literacy among the tribals is at a low ebb. Female literacy among them is negligible. In order to correct the pitfalls and mitigate the tribal problems, a few policy recommendations are presented here. They will go a long way in correcting the deficiencies in the tribal programmes and policies.

Adequate infrastructure under both overheads and services should be made available in the tribal areas because most of the tribal population of the state is found in the hill region, dense forest and inaccessible areas of the state. The tribal people who have specially suffered from relative isolation for centuries, suffer from backwardness, superstitions and many of the impediments. They need all types of encouragement and incentives for pursuing studies. Sometimes, when the government comes forward to provide adequate educational opportunities and incentives for the educational development of the tribal people, satisfactory results are not seen. All those incentives and facilities have failed to attract the girl children in particular. The tribal people are obviously newcomers in the race of literacy. Majority of them are yet to enjoy the benefits of modern education and assistance provided by the government. However, the efforts made by certain non-government organisations have proved beneficial. Keeping this in view, the government should encourage some committed voluntary organisations to undertake the task in the remote tribal areas. Besides this, appropriate policy should be developed to check drop out rates. More emphasis has to be given on elementary education. There is a need to open a good number of residential schools for tribal girls in particular. There is a need to upgrade the primary schools. Special vocational education is to be imparted to tribals in crafts like tailoring, typewriting, embroidery or other traditional skills. Besides, emphasis has to be laid on various types of incentives both for the teachers as well as the students. Undoubtedly, incentives play a major role in removing the educational backwardness among the tribals. The government's commitment to social justice is directly related with that of development of education among them. Considering the vastness in terms of geographical area and bulging population size and backwardness, policymakers cannot ignore the educational grievances of other sections of our society. In addition to all these, more resources, better utilisation and management of the incentives are needed to make tribal people equal partners of larger society. It has been studied that corruption and inefficiency siphons off a larger mount of resources. This keeps the tribal people where they were. In order to make efficient use of the resources, all steps need to be taken to remove corruption and inefficiency. The corrupt officials should be taken to task. And the committed officials should be rewarded amply. Necessary changes could be brought about in the existing laws to get rid of this social evil. The administrative structure needs to be simplified. Financial procedures warrant simplification. All necessary steps should be taken to involve the tribal people where it is possible while taking up major industries, power projects, etc. Guidelines should be prepared for giving them adequate rehabilitation and compensation. It should be monitored that the tribal people do not get exploited and harassed by the government officials for getting their compensation. There is a need for provisions for the development of the tribals along with the development of the areas. This will accelerate tribal development process. The tribal people are now being exploited in the process of procurement and price fixation of minor forest products. In most of the cases, the traders who are private people are hand in gloves with the government officials. The government people take extra interest to protect the interests of the traders than the interest of the tribal people. The policies of the government in this regard should be modified in order to safeguard the interest of the tribals. We have studied in the preceding section and chapters that minor forest products play a vital role in the day-today living of the tribals. Cooperatives have their merits and demerits. Rampant corruption in these organisations existing in tribal regions of Orissa has led to their closure. Consequently, the tribals have become victims of middle persons. If concerted efforts are made by the government to reorganise and revitalise these cooperatives, tribals would be benefited greatly. This is primarily because the cooperative philosophy envisages equitable distribution of benefits and eliminates the possibility of undue concentration of economic opportunities and power.

Notes and References

1. *"90 per cent of the tribals are below the Poverty Line in Orissa"* (in Oriya), *The Samaj*, 18 December 1999.
2. Arabinda Mishra, *"State Government Fails to Improve Plight of Starving Tribals"*, *The Times of India*, 21 October 2001.
3. *"As long as there are jungle tubers and mango kernel, we will not die"*, *Anupam Bharat* (in Oriya), 21 October 2001.
4. *"When the condition of the rare Juang and Bhuiyan tribe will improve?" Prajatantra*, 29 December 2000.
5. *"More than 1000 Juang families are indebted, victims of starvation"*, *Dharitri*, 5 September 2000.
6. *"More deaths in Kalahandi, Government remains blind"*, *The Times of India*, 11 November 2001.

7. *"Thousands of tribals leave their villages due to lack of employment opportunities"*, *The Samaj*, 27 December 2000.
8. *"15,000 villagers left their native place in search of employment"*, *Anupam Bharat*, 13 April 2001.
9. *The Samaj*, 24 December 2000.
10. *The Samaj*, 19 December 2001.
11. Imran Khan, *"Tribal Areas in the Grip of Cerebral Malaria"*, *The Times of India*, 14 October 2001.
12. A. K. Mishra, *"5000 tribals die of tuberculosis every year"*, *The Times of India*, 14 October 2001.
13. *Anupam Bharat*, 4 July 2001.
14. Jean Dreze, *"No More Lifelines: Political Economy of Hunger in Orissa"*, *The Times of India*, 18 September 2001.
15. *"How Officials Swallowed Tribal's Funds"*, *The Times of India*, 2 September 201.
16. *The Samaj*,25 December 2000.
17. *The Prajatantra*, 29 December 2000.
18. *The Sambad*, 6 November 2000.
19. Mihir Ray, *"Goverrnment's Price Fixation Bid on Forest Products Dampens Tribal Spirit"*, *The Times of India*, 27 November 2001.
20. A. K. Mishra, *"Despite Four Mega Power Projects in Orissa District 65 percent of villages have no Electricity"*, *The Times of India*, 28 June 2001.
21. Jean Dreze, *op. cit.*

Appendix– I

HOUSEHOLD BENEFICIARY SCHEDULE

1. Identification Particulars

1.1: District:

1.2: Block:

1.3: G. P.:

1.4: Name of the Village:

1.5: (a) Name of the beneficiary (Male/Female):

(b) Name of the father/husband of the beneficiary:

1.6: Age:

1.7: Name of the Sub-Caste and Community:

1.8: Educational Qualification:

1.9: Occupation of the Beneficiary:

(i) Before assistance:

(ii) After assistance (at present):

1.10: Traditional family occupation of the beneficiary:

Agriculture/Business/Labour/Service/Others (specify)

1.11: Whether the beneficiary has acquired skill for any work other than the traditional family occupation: YES/NO

1.12: If yes, please specify:

1.13: Whether the family has been listed as BPL family by the Block/DRDA authority? YES/NO

1.14: Category to which the beneficiary family belongs: Big farmer/Small farmer/Marginal farmer/Agricultural labourer/ Non-Agricultural Labourer/Others (specify).

2. Family particulars of the beneficiary

Age Group	*No. of family members at the time of assistance*			*No. of family members as on the date of survey*		
	M	F	T	M	F	T
1	2	3	4	5	6	7
(a) Below 14 years						
(b) 14 yrs – 60 yrs						
(c) Above 60 years						
TOTAL:						

M = Male; F= Female; T = Total.

3. Size of land holding by the beneficiary

Category of land	*Before assistance (in Acres)*	*At the time of Survey (in Acres)*
1	*2*	*3*
(a) Agricultural land owned		
(b) Agricultural land leased out		
(c) Agricultural land leased in		
(d) Agricultural land encroached		
(e) Operational land holding by the beneficiary [(a+c+d)-(b)]		

4. Annual family income at the time of identification as per Household Survey/Sanction of Scheme

5. Source of Motivation (Please tick mark the correct one)

(i) Motivated through Block Officials.

(ii) Motivated through DRDA Officials.

(iii) Motivated through VLC.

(iv) Motivated through Sarpanch/Ward Member.

(v) Motivated through MP/MLA.

(vi) Motivated through Voluntary Organisation.

(vii) Applied by self without any motivation.

(viii) Others (specify).

6. Scheme Particulars

6.1. (a) Name of the Programme:

(b) Name of the Scheme opted/applied for:

6.2. Reasons for opting the scheme:

6.3. Scheme provided and unit cost (as prescribed):

6.4. Reasons for accepting the Scheme (in case of difference between 6.1 and 6.3)

6.5. (a) Amount of loan sanctioned with date (in Rs.):

(b) Name of the Bank/Financing Institution:

(c) Distance of the Bank from the Unit:

6.6. Loan and Subsidy Disbursed: Amount (Rs.)

Date Loan Subsidy

(a) 1st Instalment:

(b) 2nd Instalment:

(c) 3rd Instalment:

Total:

6.7. Whether the total loan amount was sufficient for the Scheme: YES/NO

6.8. If 'NO', whether additional amount was invested: YES/NO

6.9. If "YES", indicate the amount invested:

6.10. Mode of Release of Loan with Subsidy:

(a) In Cash only: YES/NO

(b) In kind only: YES/NO

(c) Partly in cash and partly in kind: YES/NO

6.11. (a) Whether received any training for operating the Scheme: YES/NO

(b) If 'Yes", give nature, duration, place and name of training organising institute:

6.12. Please mention the time gap between disbursement of loan and implementation of major component of the scheme:

7. Quality of Assets Received

Sl. No.	*Name of Asset*	*Whether involved in selection process*	*Price (Rs.)*	*Quality of Assets*			*Reasons for accepting poor quality assets, if any*
				Good	*Average*	*Poor*	
1	*2*	*3*	*4*	*5*	*6*	*7*	*8*
1.							
2.							
3.							
4.							
5.							

8. Continuance of the Scheme

8.1. Whether the Scheme is operating as on date of Survey: YES/NO

8.2. If 'No', mention the date since when the scheme was discontinued:

8.3. Reasons for discontinuance of the Scheme:

(i)

(ii)

(iii)

9. Status of Assets

9.1. Whether intact on the date of survey: YES/NO

9.2. If 'No', give present status: Party existing/Not Existing

9.3. If partly available, whether the scheme is running? YES/NO.

9.4. Reasons for non-existence of assets either in part or in full:

9.5. If intact/partly available, whether it is generating any income? YES/NO

10. Availability of Linkages:

10.1. Backward linkages (specify): YES/NO/Partly available

(a)

(b)

(c)

10.2. Forward Linkages (specify): Yes/No/Partly available.

(a)

(b)

(c)

11. Problems faced by the beneficiary during implementation of the Schemes, if any

Type / Nature of Problem faced	*Steps taken by the beneficiary to solve the problem YES / NO*	*Whether problems solved YES / NO*	*If 'No', reasons thereof*
1	*2*	*3*	*4*
(a)			
(b)			
(c)			
(d)			
(e)			

12. Repayment of Loan

12.1. Amount of loan repaid by the beneficiary with date:

12.2. Amount of loan (including interest) outstanding on the beneficiary:

12.3. Whether repayment of loan was regular: YES/NO

12.4. If 'No', reasons thereof:

13. Total family net income of the beneficiary (excluding scheme income) during the year from different sources:

	Sources	Net Income (in Rs.)
	1	2
(i)	Agriculture	
(ii)	Services	
(iii)	Business/Trade	
(iv)	Other Misc. sources	
	TOTAL:	

14. (a) Income and Employment during the year from the Scheme:

Item	Unit	Quantification
(i) Income	(Rs. in '000')	
(ii) Employment		
(a) Self	(Nos.)	
(b) Salaried	(Nos.)	
(c) Wage	(Man-days) Nos.	

(b) Reasons for low generation of income and employment (if any):

(i)

(ii)

(iii)

(iv)

15. Impact of the Programme:

15.1. Whether the beneficiary family members were starving before assistance:
YES/NO

15.2. If 'yes', mention the frequency of starvation:
Occasionally/Very Often (Tick the appropriate one)

15.3. After assistance, whether the programme has played a successful role in alleviating hunger and improving health condition of the beneficiary family members? YES/NO

15.4. If 'No', reasons thereof:

15.5. Whether the beneficiary has been able to purchase any consumer's durable assets like watch, transistor, etc. after implementation of the programme? YES/NO

15.6. If 'yes', please furnish a list of durable assets purchased:

(i)

(ii)

(iii)

15.7. Whether the beneficiary has been able to provide nutritious foodstuff like egg, milk, meat, fruits, etc. for his family members after implementation of the programme? YES/NO

15.8. Whether the beneficiary family members have been able to visit certain places of tourist spots for entertainment after implementation of the programme?
YES/NO

15.9. Whether the beneficiary has been able to acquire certain social recognition after the implementation of the programme? YES/NO

15.10. Whether the beneficiary has been able to provide proper education to his children after implementation of the programme? YES/NO

15.11. Whether the hygienic and sanitation condition of the beneficiary's house has improved after implementation of the programme? YES/NO

15.12. Whether the beneficiary has been able to arrange necessary clothing for his family members after the implementation of the programme? YES/NO

16. Guidance and Monitoring:

16.1. Whether the beneficiary received the proper guidance from the executing agency (Block/DRDA/ITDA, etc.) as and when required? YES/NO

16.2. Whether Government Officials/Bank Officials have visited the unit? YES/NO

16.3. If 'yes', number of visits made during last 12 months:

(a) By the Block Staff/Other Government Officials:

(b) By the Bank Staff:

17. Views of the beneficiary on the present mode of implementation of the programme:

18. Suggestions of the Beneficiary for better implementation of the programme:

(i)

(ii)

(iii)

(iv)

(v)

(vi)

Appendix– II

State-wise Population of Scheduled Tribes in India (1991)

Sl. No.	*States/ Union Territories*	*Total Population*	*Scheduled Tribe population*	*per cent to total population*
1	*2*	*3*	*4*	*5*
1.	Andhra Pradesh	66, 508, 808	4, 199, 481	6. 31
2.	Arunachal Pradesh	864, 558	550, 351	63. 66
3.	Assam	22, 414, 322	2, 874, 441	12. 83
4.	Bihar	86, 374, 465	6, 616, 914	7. 66
5.	Goa	1, 169, 793	376	0. 03
6.	Gujarat	41, 309, 582	6, 161, 775	14. 92
7.	Haryana	16, 463, 648	-	-
8.	Himachal Pradesh	5, 170, 877	218, 349	4. 22
9.	Karnataka	44, 977, 201	1, 915, 691	4. 26
10.	Kerala	29, 098, 518	320, 967	1. 10
11.	Madhya Pradesh	66, 181, 170	15, 399, 034	23. 27
12.	Maharashtra	78, 937, 187	7, 318, 281	9. 27
13.	Manipur	1, 837, 149	632, 173	34. 41
14.	Meghalaya	1, 774, 778	1, 517, 927	85. 53
15.	Mizoram	689, 756	653, 565	94. 75
16.	Nagaland	1, 209, 546	1, 060, 822	87. 70
17.	Orissa	31, 659, 736	7, 032, 214	22. 21
18.	Punjab	20, 281, 969	-	-
19.	Rajasthan	44, 005, 990	5, 474, 881	12. 44
20.	Sikkim	406, 457	90, 901	22. 36

Contd.......

21.	Tamil Nadu	55, 858, 946	547, 194	1. 03
22.	Tripura	2, 757, 205	853, 345	30. 95
23.	Uttar Pradesh	139, 112, 287	287, 901	0. 21
24.	West Bengal	66, 077, 965	3, 808, 760	5. 60
UNION TERRITORIES				
1.	Andaman and Nicobar Islands	280, 661	26, 770	9. 54
2.	Chandigarh	642, 015	-	-
3.	Dadra and Nagar Haveli	138, 477	109, 380	78. 99
4.	Daman and Diu	101, 586	11, 724	11. 54
5.	Delhi	9, 420, 644	-	-
6.	Lakshadweep	51, 707	48, 163	93. 15
7.	Pondicherry	807, 785	-	-
	Total – India	838, 583, 988	67, 758, 380	8. 08
(Excluding) Jammu and Kashmir				
India (Excluding Assam and J and K)		816, 169, 666	64, 883, 939	7. 95

Source: Table No. 5 and 6.

Census of India, 1991, Series– I, Paper–2 of

Final Population Totals: Brief Analysis of 1992 of Primary Census Abstract.

Appendix–III

LITERACY RATE FOR SCHEDULED TRIBES POPULATION BY SEX (1991)

Sl. No.	*States/ Union Territories*	*Scheduled Tribes*		
		Persons	*Male*	*Female*
1	*2*	*3*	*4*	*5*
	INDIA*	29.60	40.65	18.19
1.	Andhra Pradesh	17.16	25.25	8.68
2.	Arunachal Pradesh	34.45	44.00	24.94
3.	Assam	49.16	58.93	38.98
4.	Bihar	26.78	38.40	14.75
5.	Delhi	-	-	-
6.	Goa	42.91	54.43	29.01
7.	Gujarat	36.45	48.25	24.20
8.	Haryana	-	-	-
9.	Himachal Pradesh	47.09	62.74	31.18
10.	Karnataka	36.01	47.95	23.57
11.	Kerala	57.22	63.38	51.07
12.	Madhya Pradesh	21.54	32.16	10.73
13.	Maharashtra	36.79	49.09	24.03
14.	Manipur	53.63	62.39	44.48
15.	Meghalaya	46.71	49.78	43.63
16.	Mizoram	82.73	86.67	78.74
17.	Nagaland	60.59	66.27	54.51
18.	Orissa	22.31	34.44	10.21
19.	Punjab	-	-	-
20.	Rajasthan	19.44	33.29	4.42

Contd.......

21.	Sikkim	59. 01	66. 80	50. 37
22.	Tamil Nadu	27. 89	35. 25	20. 23
23.	Tripura	40. 37	52. 88	27. 34
24.	Uttar Pradesh	35. 70	49. 95	19. 86
25.	West Bengal	27. 78	40. 07	14. 98
UNION TERRITORIES				
1.	Andaman and Nicobar Islands	56. 62	64. 16	48. 74
2.	Chandigarh	-	-	-
3.	Dadra and Nagar Haveli	28. 21	40. 75	15. 94
4.	Daman and Diu	52. 91	63. 58	41. 49
5.	Lakshadweep	80. 58	89. 50	71. 72
6.	Pondicherry	-	-	-

* Excludes Jammu and Kshmir

Source: Registrar General of India, Decennial Census, 1991 Series– I, Paper–1 of 1993, Primary Census Abstract for SC and ST.

Appendix– IV

DISTRICT-WISE DENSITY OF SCHEDULED TRIBE POPULATION OF ORISSA (1991)

Sl. No.	*Name of the District*	*Area in sq. km.*	*Density of Population*	*Density of Scheduled Tribe Population*
1	*2*	*3*	*4*	*5*
1.	Angul	6279. 1	153. 02	17. 87
2.	Balangir	6895. 2	178. 52	39. 38
3.	Balasore	3601. 5	471. 08	49. 78
4.	Bargarh	5830. 1	207. 06	40. 49
5.	Bhadrak	2709. 5	408. 13	6. 90
6.	Boudh	4289. 3	74. 05	9. 56
7.	Cuttack	3928. 2	502. 20	17. 53
8.	Deogarh	2781. 0	84. 23	28. 06
9.	Dhenkanal	4547. 9	208. 46	26. 45
10.	Gajapati	3460. 6	131. 34	62. 86
11.	Ganjam	9095. 4	297. 32	8. 72
12.	Jagatsinghpur	1765. 2	574. 58	3. 53
13.	Jajpur	2894. 5	478. 90	35. 43
14.	Jharsuguda	2202. 6	202. 82	64. 66
15.	Kalahandi	8315. 4	136. 00	39. 28
16.	Kendrapara	2554. 1	450. 06	1. 78
17.	Keonjhar	8303. 0	161. 03	71. 68
18.	Khurda	2970. 8	505. 59	26. 00
19.	Koraput	8406. 7	122. 52	62. 08
20.	Malkangiri	6024. 0	70. 04	40. 87

Contd.......

21.	Mayurbhanj	10418. 0	180. 90	101. 69
22.	Nawapara	3456. 6	135. 82	48. 83
23.	Nowrangpur	5058. 7	167. 37	92. 50
24.	Nayagarh	4068. 3	192. 38	11. 46
25.	Phulbani	6004. 7	90. 98	46. 88
26.	Puri	3142. 9	415. 34	1. 11
27.	Rayagada	7471. 6	95. 56	53. 55
28.	Sambalpur	6702. 3	120. 71	42. 34
29.	Sonepur	2017. 8	236. 31	22. 44
30.	Sundargarh	9712. 0	162. 03	82. 22
	ORISSA:	155707. 0	203. 33	4. 52

Source: Government of Orissa, State Planning Machinery, P and C Department, Block Profile of Orissa–1995.

Appendix– V

MADA Pockets in Different Districts (1991)

Sl. No.	*District*	*Name of MADA Pocket*	*No. of villages covered*	*Total population as per 1991 Census*	*S. T. population as per 1991 Census*	*percentage of ST to total population*
1	*2*	*3*	*4*	*5*	*6*	*7*
1.	Jajpur	1. Sukinda-I	33	23543	13352	57. 56
		2. Sukinda-II	12	14375	7339	51. 05
		3. Sukinda-III	24	19161	9931	51. 83
		4. Danagadi	23	24189	13268	54. 85
2.	Khurda	5. Banapur-Ranapur	82	17052	10330	60. 58
3.	Nayagarh	6. Nuagaon	107	11248	7863	69. 91
		7. Gania-Daspalla	196	28906	13155	45. 51
4.	Balasore	8. Jaleswar	31	24259	19633	80. 59
5.	Keonjhar	9. Anandapur-I	55	24362	19633	80. 59
		10. Anandapur-II	29	23623	13952	59. 06
		11. Hatadihi	28	20199	10673	52. 84
		12. Ghasipura	33	20978	13022	62. 07
6.	Angul	13. Pallahara	145	51034	24434	47. 88
		14. Athamallik	56	15933	7755	48. 67
7.	Dhenkanal	15. Kankadahada	52	36482	17614	48. 28

Contd......

8. Ganjam	16. Tamabudi	90	12611	5981	47. 43
9. Gajapati	17. Kashinagar	34	11290	6847	60. 65
10. Boudh	18. Boudh	149	17458	8179	46. 85
11. Bolangir	19.	56	26216	13118	50. 04
	Khaparakhole	22	13202	6818	51. 64
	20. Tureikela	38	15824	7863	49. 69
	21.	31	16137	8851	54. 85
	Tentulikhunti	47	20690	10728	51. 85
	22. Deogaon-Patnagarh				
	23. Saintala-Muribahal				
12. Sambalpur	24.	24	19430	11031	56. 77
	Dhanakauda	92	47947	25363	52. 90
	25. Jujumura				
13. Jharsuguda	26. Kolabira-	41	33958	19016	56. 00
	Rengali	19	14793	8042	54. 36
	27. Lakhanpur	35	21278	10394	48. 85
	28.	45	29688	19349	64. 16
	Jharsuguda-Lakhanpur				
	29. Laikera-Kirmira				
14. Bargarh	30. Paikamal	30	16779	8445	50. 33
	31. Paikamal-Jharbandha	45	34301	16721	48. 75
15. Deogarh	32. Barkote	44	18696	8004	42. 81
	33. Tileibani	162	35184	19301	54. 86
16. Kalahandi	34.	94	19781	11293	57. 09
	Bhawanipatna	17	13995	7727	55. 21
	35. Kesinga	41	14160	8234	58. 15
	36. Junagarh	157	24710	14218	57. 54
	37. Madanpur-	24	19064	11144	58. 46
	Rampur	23	11219	5504	49. 06
	38. Jayapatna				
	39. Narla				

Contd.......

17. Nawapara	40. Komna	73	48923	27465	56. 14
	41. Boden	50	38931	20881	53. 64
	42. Nawapara-	36	19531	9761	49. 98
	I	41	32316	16330	50. 53
	43. Nawapara-	16	12277	7208	58. 71
	II	27	14248	7618	53. 47
	44. Khariar-I	44	18607	9823	52. 79
	45. Khariar-II				
	46. Sinapali				
TOTAL:		2553	1048588	567966	54. 08

Source: Government of Orissa, '*Tribal Sub-Plan for Annual Plan, 1995-96*', Orissa, Welfare Department, May 1995.

Appendix– VI

No. S. 11011/40/79-IRD-III Government of India, Ministry of Rural Reconstruction

Krishi Bhavan,
New Delhi
Dated:3rd Feb.1981.

To

The Secretary, In-Charge of IRD Programme All State Governments/UTs.

Sub: Coverage of SC/ST families under IRD Programme– Revision of norms- regarding.

Sir,

According to existing instructions, at least 20 per cent of the families assisted under the IRD Programme should come from Scheduled Castes and Scheduled Tribes families. In areas where the percentage of SC/ST population is higher than this figure, the existing instructions are that Scheduled Castes/ Scheduled Tribes families should be assisted at least in the same proportion which they have in the total population of the block concerned.

2. The coverage of Scheduled Cates/Scheduled Tribes under the IRD Programme has been further considered and it has been decided to revise the guidelines. Since IRD programme is aimed at the poorest amongst the poor and since SC/ST families constitute a very large proportion of the target group to be covered by the IRD Programme, it has been decided that at least 30 per cent of the families selected for assistance under the IRD

programme should come from SC/ST groups. It is clarified that this is the minimum that is to be attempted. Wherever it is practicable, a larger percentage of families assisted under IRD programme may be selected from SC/ST categories.

3. From experience, it appears that in many instances, assistance provided to the SC/ST families is very meagre and it is in the nature of a gesture. What is expected is substantial assistance which should generate adequate incremental income from the SC/ST beneficiaries to enable them to go above the poverty line on a lasting basis. Consequently, it has been decided that at least 30 per cent of the resources invested under the IRD programme, in terms of subsidy of loans, should also go to SC/ST families. All implementing agencies are requested to monitor, both the number of SC/ST families assisted and the quantum of assistance provided to them, through subsidies and loans, separately.

4. These instructions may kindly be brought to the notice of all concerned for their guidance.

Yours faithfully,

Sd/- (3.2.81) (C. N. S. NAIR)

Deputy Secretary to the Government of India

Appendix– VII

THE MICRO PROJECTS FOR PRIMITIVE TRIBES

1. Paudi Bhuinya Development Agency, Khuntagaon, Bonai Subdivision.
2. Paudi Bhuinya Development Agency, Jamardihi, Pallahara.
3. Juang Development Agency, Gonasika.
4. Bonda Development Agency, Mundulipada.
5. Kutia Kondh Development Agency, Belghar.
6. Dongria Kondh Development Agency, Kurli-Chattikonda.
7. Lanjia Saora Development Agency, Thumba, Ganjam District.
8. Lanjia Saora Development Agency, Seranga.
9. Saora Development Agency, Chandragiri.
10. Lanjia Saora Development Agency, Puttasingi.
11. Lodha Development Agency, Murda.
12. Paudi Bhuinya Development Agency, Rugudakudar.
13. Chauktia Bhunjia Development Agency, Sunabeda.
14. Didayi Development Agency, Bayapada.
15. Dongria Kondha Development Agency, Parsali.
16. Kutia Kondha Development Agency, Lanjigarh.
17. Hill Kharia and Mankidia Development Agency, Gudugudia.

Index

C

D

H

I

J